SCOUTING FOR GIRLS

SCOUTING FOR GIRLS: A CENTURY OF GIRL GUIDES AND GIRL SCOUTS

Tammy M. Proctor

PRAEGER

An Imprint of ABC-CLIO, LLC

Santa Barbara, California • Denver, Colorado • Oxford, England

w

Library of Congress Cataloging-in-Publication Data

Proctor, Tammy M., 1968–
    Scouting for girls : a century of Girl Guides and Girl Scouts / Tammy M. Proctor.
        p. cm.
    Includes bibliographical references and index.
    ISBN 978–0–313–38114–0 (hard copy : alk. paper)—ISBN 978–0–313–38115–7 (ebook)
    1. Girl Guides—History. 2. Girl Scouts—History. I. Title.
HS3353.G35P76   2009
369.46309—dc22   2009020659

13 12 11 10 9   1 2 3 4 5

This book is also available on the World Wide Web as an eBook.
Visit www.abc-clio.com for details.

ABC-CLIO, LLC
130 Cremona Drive, P.O. Box 1911
Santa Barbara, California 93116-1911

This book is printed on acid-free paper ∞

Manufactured in the United States of America

For Sandra Nelson Modlin, who claims she never got to carry the flag

Contents

A photo essay follows page 100

Preface

As I type this preface, I cannot help but notice the tiny white scar that slashes diagonally across my left index finder, just below the knuckle. It is a Girl Scouting scar, the result of an ill-advised whittling project at camp with my official Scout knife. While few can point to such literal marks from their Guiding or Scouting days, most former members of the movement will admit to being marked in no less tangible ways by their time as Guides or Scouts. In the past century, millions of girls worldwide have been exposed to some version of Scouting for Girls. For some, the stay was a short one, but for many others, a lifetime commitment ensued.

This book examines the worldwide Guide and Girl Scout movement in its first 100 years, looking at successes and failures, transformations and traditions. While not meant to be an exhaustive history of the organization, *Scouting for Girls* will try to highlight some of the important people and events that gave Scouting and Guiding their popularity and longevity. While I no longer have my official Girl Scout knife (well, maybe I do have it tucked away in a treasure box), I hope to whittle away at the misconceptions about worldwide Guiding and Girl Scouting, while also building an accurate picture of the challenges that face such a large international movement for girls.

As I have researched and written the book, I have relied on the advice, wisdom, and help of many colleagues and friends. Academic researchers in the Scout and Guide community are a select and small group. I was fortunate to be able to interact with many of these excellent scholars over the last decade, and to see all of us come together in spring 2008 for a conference marking the Scout movement's centenary. In particular, my thanks go to Nelson Block for his enthusiasm and energy in initiating and organizing the conference. My gratitude as well goes to those who have commented on my work or discussed Guiding with me; my particular thanks to Kristine Alexander, Bodil Formark, John R. Gillis, Benjamin Lammers, Susan Miller, Timothy Parsons, and Sophie Wittemans. In addition to these researchers, I would like to thank the people who have shared their Guiding and Scouting experiences with me in oral histories.

I owe a lot to my supportive colleagues, who will cover classes, bring me materials, chat in the hallways, and ask how things are going. Special thanks to Darlene Brooks Hedstrom, Charles Chatfield, James Huffman, Amy Livingstone, Miguel Martinez-Saenz, Tanya Maus, Joseph O'Connor, Christian Raffensperger, Scott Rosenberg, Thomas Taylor, and Samuel Thomas, in particular. My writing groups offered good advice and good company throughout the process, including Molly Wood and Nancy McHugh at Wittenberg, and the fabulous VICKIs: Carol Engelhardt Herringer, Rick Incorvati, Barry Milligan, Christopher Oldstone-Moore, and Laura Vorachek.

Also instrumental in the project are the institutions that have sponsored and sustained my work. Without the financial support of Wittenberg University, I would have had difficulty traveling to all the necessary archives and libraries consulted for this project. Other important institutions and their dedicated archivists include Margaret Courtney and Karen Taylor at Girlguiding UK, Paul Moynihan and Patricia Styles at the UK Scout Association, Sophie Wittemans at the Guide Catholiques de Belgique, and Meghan Seki, Pamela Cruz, Kelly Chatman, and Yevgeniya Gribov at the Girl Scouts of the USA. This project also benefited from materials consulted at New York Public Library, Yale University Beinecke Rare Books Collection, the Library of Congress, the Herbert Hoover Presidential Library, the School of Oriental and African Studies, the British Library, the National Archives (formerly the Public Record Office), Bowling Green State University's Browne Popular Culture Library, Ohio-Link, and Wittenberg's Thomas Library. My thanks as well to Elizabeth Potenza at Praeger, and to Simon Mason for originally asking me to write this book. It has been a good exercise to try to understand how and why an organization grows.

My personal thanks to my large family for their support over the years and to my parents, Archie and Eleanor Proctor, for introducing me to

Scouting. While I only lasted as a Girl Scout until the age of twelve, like many others, I found the movement made a lasting impact on my life. Finally, my gratitude and love to Todd Shirley, who knows more about Girl Guides and Baden-Powells than he really ever wanted to know.

List of Figures

List of Photographs

Scout and Guide founder Robert Baden-Powell poses with his wife, Olave Baden-Powell, who served as Chief Guide of the World.

Juliette Low, founder of U.S. Girl Scouting, presenting a pin to a member.

An unofficial group of Girl Scouts from 1909 in Bristol with their leader, Miss Wise.

The 1st Weymouth Girl Guides (UK) collecting waste paper for the war effort during the First World War.

As Girl Guiding expanded internationally, diverse populations were drawn to the movement, as with this Belgian Girl Guide, Rosalie Pastijn, in 1919.

It was not uncommon for whole families to be involved in Guiding and Scouting; these siblings belong to the Deldoncker family in Belgium, 1919.

American Girl Scouts in the 1930s demonstrate the Scout law promoting "kindness to animals."

Brownies in Britain practice first aid in the 1920s.

Marguerite de Beaumont (third from left) with her Ranger Company at their "Daydream" camp at the British seaside in 1933.

A Brownie and Guide in Singapore, ca. 1930s.

A U.S. Girl Scout learning arts and crafts with her leader, ca. 1950s.

Introduction

In the summer of 2008, the Children's Commissioner of Great Britain told the media in an interview that the British Girl Guides had a waiting list of 50,000 girls, all clamoring for entrance into the movement. These girls, aged 5 to 25, had to cultivate patience as it became increasingly difficult to recruit enough adult leaders for Guiding, many of whom were disillusioned at having to endure long criminal background checks before working with girls. As Chief Guide Liz Burnley explained, "We're one of the country's largest organisations so it's not surprising that we need more leaders ... [plus] more women working full time is a major factor, both with changes in work and leisure patterns."[1] Almost 100 years after a few girls demanded entrance into Scouting at a rally in 1909, girls were still asking for admittance to a program of adventure and service.

Scouting for Girls examines why Girl Guiding developed and how it has remained relevant and attractive to girls in Great Britain and around the world a hundred years after its founding. Guiding, envisioned as a girls' version of Boy Scouting in Edwardian Britain, was initially led by Agnes Baden-Powell, the 51-year-old sister of Boy Scouting's founder, Robert Baden-Powell. Agnes and her committee of "ladies" had little formal experience working with girls or with setting up a large organization, but they had time, resources, and initiative. From Guiding's official founding in 1910 to the outbreak of the First World War, the fledgling organization expanded its leadership and structure, developed rudimentary training programs, held its first camps for girls, and grew its membership to almost 40,000 girls by 1916.[2] Out of these humble and somewhat disorganized beginnings, Guiding transformed itself from Scouting's protégé to the largest voluntary youth movement in Britain by the early 1930s, surpassing even the Boy Scout membership.

Despite its size and importance in British, and indeed world history, few scholars have made Guiding the subject of scrutiny. Those who have attempted histories have done so for one country and one period of its history.[3] Because of this scarcity of scholarly works, many of the published works on the Guide and Girl Scout movement are either "official" histories sponsored by Girlguiding UK and its counterparts in other countries, or biographies of Robert Baden-Powell and other leaders.[4] With the impending centenary celebrations for Guiding in 2010 and American Girl Scouting in 2012, a nonofficial global history of Girl Guiding and Girl Scouting from the creation of these youth movements to the present is overdue.[5] While much of the present book will focus on Britain and the United States as the two most influential movements in Guiding's early development, the study's scope is international and includes information on how the movements adapted to specific local conditions based on race, class, religion, political realities, and demographics.

In short, *Scouting for Girls* argues that Guides filled a need in pre-World War I Britain for a girls' service organization to parallel the Boy Scouts. By combining "fun" and "usefulness," the movement appealed to a broad range of girls and women throughout the world by the 1930s. After the initial programmatic success of Guiding, it faced a series of challenges in trying to maintain its mission and still appeal to girls in a variety of settings. In order for the Guides and Girl Scouts to survive such changing social, political, and economic conditions over the course of the twentieth century, they needed to prove flexible in dealing with changing educational and social realities for girls, while also remaining "modern." Their flexibility has kept the movements alive for a century, but this very willingness to transform their goals has undermined their original ideologies and fundamentally changed Guiding and Girl Scouting into movements that appeal mostly to younger girls. The changes have also meant quite varied national contexts for Guiding and Girl Scouting.

While roughly chronological, the chapters of *Scouting for Girls* focus around central questions that Guiding has faced in its 100-year history, providing a broad thematic approach to the movement's development. Chapter 1, which covers roughly the period from 1907 to the end of the First World War, provides an overview of the founding and growth of Girl Guiding in Britain and Girl Scouting in the United States, with particular emphasis on the personalities of the founders, the girls who were drawn to these organizations, and the main missions of the organizations. Chapter 2 builds on the earlier consolidation of the movement and focuses on the centrality of the First World War in launching and revising worldwide Guiding. The 1930s to the 1950s were years of controversy and challenge for Guiding, especially as it sought to combat the growth of nationalist youth organizations in Europe and elsewhere, and Chapter 3 follows Guiding's perilous path into the world scene. In particular, this chapter explores the early worldwide expansion of Girl Scouting and Guiding, the development of international institutions, and the earliest forms of adaptation and competition the organizations faced.

As with World War I, the Second World War and its aftermath also had a profound impact on Guide and Scout history. The war destroyed movements in some countries, reenergized them in others, and led to the development of relief schemes. The major impact of this period, however, was felt in the late 1940s and early 1950s, when the movements reinvented themselves through uniform, handbook, and personnel changes. Chapter 4 charts the developments within the movement and in the larger world that contributed to a new "look" for the global Guide association. With the death of the founder, Robert Baden-Powell in 1941, possibilities for major revision of the program could be discussed.

With shifting ideas by the late 1940s, Chapter 5 charts the transformations of some of the programmatic initiatives that have defined Guiding during its first 100 years. Many of these ideas grew from the demands of girls themselves, such as special initiatives for Lone Guides, physically and mentally disabled guides, and refugees. Other programs arose as Guiding developed its organizational capacity, especially fundraising schemes such as the U.S. Girl Scout Cookie, British Pantomimes, and other fund drives. Finally, Guiding has periodically had to alter its activities to meet new leisure needs and possibilities for girls.

A key focus of Guiding and Scouting has been international friendship from early in their histories, but this became a central emphasis in the post–World War II period, as pen pal schemes, world centers, and international conferences spawned even more connections among members worldwide. Yet the insistence on international friendship became especially charged and difficult as national liberation movements led to independence of many former British and French colonies with strong Guide movements, especially in Africa, Southeast Asia, and India. Chapter 6 outlines the triumphs and the tragedies of Guiding's international ambitions in the twentieth century.

Chapter 7 explores the development of competing activities for girls, particularly the rise in girls' organized sports, multiple clubs, and digital universes in an age of changing political realities for women. Competing leisure pursuits as well as shifts in women's roles in family, workplace, and society helped spur the Guide and Girl Scout movements to continually strive to innovate. This race to maintain Guiding's relevance in a brave new world of leisure by the 1960s and 1970s, combined with the opening of Boy Scouting to girls in some countries and with the decline of adult volunteers, has led to significant challenges for the organizations as they move past their first 100 years.

Finally, the book's short conclusion lays out a few of the continuing issues that Guiding faces as a twenty-first-century youth movement. To survive for another 100 years, Guide and Girl Scout officials will need to find more effective ways to recruit and train leaders, if they are to sustain their organizations. Also, with the movements' demographics shifting to younger and younger girls, they may need to reexamine their goals and mission in light of the move from adolescents and teens to predominantly preteen members.

Guiding has had an underrated impact on the modern world, touching millions of girls and women worldwide. While it is hard to quantify Guiding's success in shaping the futures of girls, a recent study in Britain suggests that its combination of character building, adventure, and practical training might bear fruit for girls' future lives. In a study of 250 "award-winning women" in business, politics, sport, and other public occupations in 2007, two-thirds of them had been in the Guides as girls. More than 70 percent of those who had been Guides credited the movement with helping them succeed later in life.[6] These results suggest that Agnes Baden-Powell was right, when in Guiding's first handbook in 1912 she told fellow adult leaders: "The girls of the nation are full of enthusiasm and spirit, and only want their heads to be turned the right way to become good, useful citizens . . . [Guiding] is a means of bringing out the noblest and most useful qualities in girls, and gives them interests which will brighten all their days . . . ."[7]

NOTES

1. Sophie Borland, "50,000 Queue to be Guides as Red Tape Deters Leaders," *Daily Mail* (June 18, 2008).

2. Girlguiding UK Census, Girlguiding UK Archives, London (GGL). The first official census took place in 1916.

3. Some examples of such national studies include, for the United States: Susan Miller, *Growing Girls: The Natural Origins of Girls' Organizations in America* (New Brunswick: Rutgers University Press, 2007); for Britain: Tammy Proctor, *On My Honour: Guides and Scouts in Interwar Britain* (Philadelphia: American Philosophical Society, 2002); for France: Marie-Thérèse Cheroutre, *Le scoutisme au féminin: Les guides de France, 1923–1998* (Paris: Les Éditions du Cerf, 2002); for Belgium: Thierry Scaillet, Sophie Wittemans, and Françoise Rosart, eds., *Guidisme, scoutisme, et coéducation: Pour une histoire de la mixité dans les mouvements de jeunesse* (Louvain-la-Neuve: Bruylant-Academia, 2007); for Malaya: Janice Brownfoot, "Sisters Under the Skin: Imperialism and the Emancipation of Women in Malaya, c. 1891–1941," in *Making Imperial Mentalities: Socialisation and British Imperialism*, ed. J. A. Mangan (Manchester: Manchester University Press, 1990), 46–73. Some studies of Scouting also contain substantial material on Guides, such as Timothy Parsons, *Race, Resistance and the Boy Scout Movement in British Colonial Africa* (Athens, Ohio: Ohio University Press, 2004).

4. Biographies of Robert Baden-Powell include at least a dozen volumes. Most important among these are E. E. Reynolds, *Baden-Powell: A Biography of Lord Baden-Powell of Gilwell* (London: Oxford University Press, 1943), William Hillcourt, *Baden-Powell: The Two Lives of A Hero* (New York: G. Putnam's Sons, 1964), and Tim Jeal, *The Boy-Man: The Life of Lord Baden-Powell* (New York: William Morrow and Company, 1990). As yet there is no biography of Agnes Baden-Powell, but there is an "official" autobiography for Olave Baden-Powell, [as told to Mary Drewery], *Window on my Heart* (London: Hodder & Stoughton, 1973). Several other leaders have been featured in official and nonofficial biographies, including Juliette Low (USA).

5. An edited volume in 2009 was one of the first global histories of Boy Scouting and Girl Guiding marking the centenary: Nelson R. Block and Tammy M. Proctor, eds., *Scouting Frontiers: Youth and the Scout Movement's First Century* (Newcastle upon Tyne: Cambridge Scholars Press, 2009).

6. "Two-thirds of high-flying women had a Guiding hand," *Daily Mail* (October 30, 2007).

7. Agnes Baden-Powell and Robert Baden-Powell, *The Handbook for Girl Guides, or How Girls Can Help Build the Empire* (London: Thomas Nelson & Sons, 1912), 447–448.

1. Origins

Calling herself only "A Returned South African," the author of a strident yet concise Letter to the Editor of *The Spectator* opined in early September 1909, "English girls are too much afraid of roughing it." By denouncing the frivolity and uselessness of English girls and their parents who pampered them, "A Returned South African" fired the opening shots in a battle that would rage for the next decade over the question of how to "train" girls in a modern world. According to the letter, colonial girls, in contrast to English girls, should be seen as role models because they learned early how to care for a home, make their own jam, bake, brew, and nurse the sick. In contrast, the boredom and uselessness of English middle-class girls' lives had led only to "votes for women" and "walking in processions through the streets of London." The author drove her point home by describing the colonies "full of young men who sorely need the civilising and restraining influence" of English women lest they give in to "the inevitable whisky or gin." Real "joy" for a woman or girl, the author concluded, came from managing your own house and being useful.[1]

This short letter appeared at an opportune time in *The Spectator*'s history, just a week before a flutter of correspondence regarding the new and popular Boy Scout movement. Started by a former military officer, Robert Baden-Powell, with an experimental camp in 1907, Scouting had established a firm foundation by September 1909, when it sponsored a large rally at the Crystal Palace in London. One of the side notes to this rally sparked additional debate in *The Spectator*'s pages, namely, the appearance of a group of girls at Crystal Palace. These self-styled "Girl Scouts," wearing makeshift uniforms and badges obtained through subterfuge, were attempting to claim for themselves a part in the Scout movement. As "A Returned South African" had hoped, these English girls were tired of frivolity and wanted a sense of purpose, service and adventure, much of it colonial in tone, that they saw in Scouting. The girls, like their male counterparts, were caught up in what *The Spectator* described as a "spare-time occupation which is something between an adventure and a military discipline . . . [that] appeals to that in the heart of all children which makes them say 'Let's pretend.'"[2] Scouting captured the imaginations of youth with its mix of service to community and country, its innovative small-group patrol system, its ostentatious Boss-of-the-Plains Stetson hats and its emphasis on adventure.

For boys and many girls, the movement was immediately attractive and accessible through its handbook, *Scouting for Boys* (1908). In its follow-up coverage of the September rally, *The Spectator* ran a review of the volume, calling it a "manual of sound citizenship." The review rhapsodized about the simple yet effective formula Scouting had discovered, namely:

> Boys dwelling in a dull suburb are given the training of pioneers, and feel themselves already living the life of their favourite romance. That is one main side of the appeal; another is that the training is not a mere thing for leisure moments, but a complete discipline of life. The Boy Scout is always playing the game . . . . In emphasizing this side General Baden-Powell shows himself a man of real genius. Boys are uncompromising idealists, and they want a game which they can play all the time and give their whole mind to.[3]

Scouting for Boys did indeed create an alternative world of frontier challenges such as tracking, camping, and woodcraft, while emphasizing health, morality, leadership, and discipline. All of this was packaged into a system with explicit patrol organization, uniforms, games and merit badges, and a law/promise to tie things together. Baden-Powell organized the book around "yarns" told around a campfire, and the whole book was chatty and colloquial, easily read by youngsters of 11 or 12. An illustrative case is Camp Fire Yarn No. 8 on stalking, in which Baden-Powell advised, "When you want to observe wild animals you have to stalk them, that is, to creep up to them without their seeing or smelling you." Using examples from Zulu and Native American cultures, Baden-Powell described a successful stalking expedition, but also provided little tips for the Scout—"At night, keep as much as possible in low ground, ditches, etc." or "walk quietly" and "be sure which way the wind is blowing." The lesson finished with a series of games and practices for Scouts to try out their newfound knowledge.[4] Badge work incorporating these skills could then follow.

With such a book as a guide, it was no wonder that youth flocked to buy or borrow a copy. As one early girl member noted, "It was a wonderful game, so full of something that was utterly lacking in any other."[5] Any enterprising youngster could start a troop of Boy Scouts unofficially using the guidelines in *Scouting for Boys*, and for the first couple of years the organization's leaders made little attempt to reign in this enthusiasm. Some of these early troops were quite unorthodox indeed, as with 10-year-old Robert Harrison's troop described to Baden-Powell in a letter asking for advice:

> My sister, Jenny aged 11 and I are running a troop of young boys and girls, the members are Magdalen Ogle, age 11, Jack McDougall, age 8, Martin Ogle, age 6, Kathleen Southey, age 11, Nancie McDougall, age 6 , Mary Holdgate, age 13, and Evelyn Holdgate, age 11 .... The girls are not allowed to go out with out a grownup with them, so can you think of any outdoore [sic] games we do not have to scatter much. We would love to be reviewed.[6]

Harrison's little group, formed in 1916, demonstrated the appeal of the movement to both boys and girls, but it also suggested the challenge Scout leaders faced in designing an organization that could meet the needs of various ages of boys and girls. In short, Scouting needed to allow for the enthusiastic spread of the movement, but also to provide the proper guidelines and regulations to control its growth and its message, especially in order to gain the respect and trust of parents. Eventually, its answer to this problem was a separation of boys and girls into discrete movements, with divisions by age within each of these organizations.

From the beginning, parents and many adults saw the appeal of Scouting and recognized it as a valuable activity for their boys. As someone interested in charitable and social work with youth, Violet Markham, writing in the September 25, 1909, issue of *The Spectator*, added her voice to the praise of the movement. Having observed a group of Boy Scouts camping on the grounds of her home, she was interested in proposing adult "protectors" (both male and female) to help facilitate Scout camps and activities. These helpers would be temporary volunteers, not formal Scoutmasters. Markham herself seemed drawn to the Scout activities despite being "a mere woman." She wrote in her account, "Personally, I shall never forget the acute delight of crawling along a hedge and capturing a enemy's brigade single-handed, my joy in this great victory being scarcely damped."[7]

Like Markham many adults became enthusiastic supporters of Scouting, with teachers, soldiers, civic leaders, and parents signing on to be leaders or patrons. Some of these adults were women like Markham, and for those with the time and the access to girls, Scouting provided an option for girls' training. One such woman was Agnes Maynard, a teacher at a school for "difficult" girls in Wimbledon. She began a Girl Scout troop after hearing of the success of Scouting with local village lads. Maynard, known affectionately as "The Carpenter," used the Scout method to change the attitudes of the girls at the school. Wearing home-made uniforms and developing activities from *Scouting for Boys*, Maynard's group became one of the first registered as a Guide company. For Maynard, the secret to Scouting and Guiding was the "co-operative pride in one's company" that created a sense of exclusiveness and belonging for girls. In addition to school companies, Girl Scout and Guide companies began in churches, synagogues, and girls' clubs. Gladys Thorndike incorporated *Scouting for Boys* into the girls' club she was running in Kent, while Ida Edwards started Guiding in a church company in Liverpool.[8]

Not just adult women, but teen girls also got copies of Scout literature and started their own companies. Elizabeth de Beaumont enlisted her governess's help in beginning a small Scout patrol composed of three— Elizabeth, her brother and her sister. Marguerite, Elizabeth's younger sister, described this unorthodox little troop: "We had Scout hats and poles and scarves and belts. We were the Seal Patrol, and were desperately in earnest about it all."[9] In another case, Dorothy "Cloughie" Clough, daughter of a well-off mill owner, got a copy of *Scouting for Boys* and absorbed it long before she became a member of the 1st Steeton [Yorkshire] Guide Company in 1912, at age 12. Her brand of Guiding included Scout challenges such as taking a loaded trek cart with her company "from Robin Hole over the moor to Ben Rhydding—taking stiles, walls, and hedges in our stride, over which the cart, complete with camp equipment had to be lifted."[10]

As girls showed interest in the movement and began their own patrols, the male community of Scouting faced a threat. Many Scout leaders felt that the presence of girls would make boys less willing to participate, while others felt that Scouting's activities were not appropriate for girls. Yet girls themselves saw Scouting as a great game, and they were not above using subterfuge to get what they wanted. Kathleen Davies-Cooke joined the Scouts at age 10 by registering under the alias "John Webb" in 1913.[11] In Sheffield, two sisters started a Scout troop of 16 girls, with copies of Baden-Powell's writings (his earlier book, *Aids to Scouting*, and other Scout materials) and Scout hats.[12] Alison Cargill and her friends at a private school in Glasgow began a Scout troop in 1908, meeting in a stable loft. The loft provided a good (if dangerous) way to test their knots, when they lowered each other from the loft to the stable floor on ropes. This group later became a Girl Guide Company, albeit reluctantly.[13] As another Girl Scout, Evelyn Goshawk, wrote with some disgust, changing from Scouts to Guides led to a "feeling of anti-climax, or being let-down, almost insulted. Who wanted to be womanly at our age?"[14]

Some of the girls who joined Girl Scout groups enlisted the help of Boy Scouts or Scoutmasters in starting their troops. In Camberwell (London) in mid-1909, several girls created their own troop with help from the local Scoutmaster at St. Mark's Church. Sybil Canadine, one of these early Girl Scouts and an attendee at the Crystal Palace rally in 1909, described this fledgling group in an interview:

> [The Scoutmaster] gave us a tiny room in a house near the church. It only measured eight feet by nine feet. He put a union jack in the corner and we learned to tie knots. We learned about the Law and the Promise, sang songs but every fine day we were out on Peckham Rye, lighting fires, and we were very careful. Ring tracking and stalking, administering to casualties, jumping streams and paths with a pole, flag raising on a home made flagstaff, learning about trees and wild flowers and birds.[15]

Canadine remembered walking the six miles to the Crystal Palace rally in blue school skirts with borrowed Boy Scout shirts and hats. When Baden-Powell saw them, he did not make them leave, so they marched with some other Girl Scouts in the official march past. As she recalled it, "We were laughed at, we were whistled at, there were catcalls but we didn't mind. We were there and we were part of the show."[16]

Another "Girl Scout" from Crystal Palace had been playing the Scout game since 1908. Nesta Maude Ashworth recalled her start as a Scout in an article for a Guiding magazine:

> From the moment [*Scouting for Boys*] had fallen into our hands we were determined to be Scouts. Instinct, I think, warned us that Scouting was a movement for boys and the only way we could get in was by hiding the fact that we were girls. This we did by applying to the Scout Headquarters for registration as a Troop of Scouts and by signing our application with only an initial instead of a given name . . . Scouting opened up a whole new vista of ideas: we learned to light fires out-of-doors and to clean and cook our own fish; we laid trails and took over the care of our own ponies instead of handing them over to a groom.[17]

Nesta Ashworth, like Sybil Canadine, warmed to the active outdoor life that Scouting promised her. As "A Returned South African" had predicted in her letter, there was appeal for girls in the colonial fantasy life of tracking, camping, outdoor cooking, and adventure that Scouting offered. It was especially appealing to middle-class girls who often felt confined by the societal expectations for females. Girls enjoyed the chance to be boyish.

As historian Sally Mitchell has noted, "girls' boyishness developed a publicly acceptable face ... [T]he boy dream had multiple resonances: girls wanted active games, a serious education and adult rights and responsibilities."[18] The early twentieth century also represented an expansion of sporting and physical education activities for girls of all classes, paralleling girls' desire for more "boyish" adventures and outdoor life. By the 1910s, girls across Britain could swim, cycle, skate, and play team sports such as hockey and engage in recreational hiking. Increasingly advocates began to speak out about the need for active female lives, understanding that girls needed interests to occupy their leisure time. In one such treatise, *The Use of Leisure* (1900), the author opined that for the "modern" girl: "the cultivation of hobbies is one of the most valuable of arts. Next to religion, and a sense of humor, it is chiefly hobbies which help us along in the pilgrimage of life."[19] As girls embraced hobbies and outdoor pursuits, clothing styles accommodated these new activities as "bustles, corsets, stiff petticoats" became a thing of the past.[20] With these changes, girls' recreation began to resemble that of boys, and the Girl Scouts capitalized on these cultural shifts.

Despite girls' early enthusiasm for Scouting as if they were boys, Girl Scouts were an awkward presence in the movement. Baden-Powell himself had thought girls could benefit from Scouting and in 1907, he included a note about girls in his first Boy Scout pamphlet, but without giving much thought to the notion. He had begun receiving letters from girls as early as 1908, and in summer 1909, he started planning for a girls' version of Scouting.[21] His first suggestions for Girl Guides appeared in November 1909, at which time he was now envisioning a separate movement for girls. Mirroring the comments of the anonymous "A Returned South African," Baden-Powell argued,

Girls must be partners and comrades rather than dolls .... One sees the streets crowded after business hours, and the watering-places crammed with girls overdressed and idling, learning to live aimless, profitless lives; and, in some cases, they run to the opposite extreme and take up manly pursuits, which make them hard and sexless; whereas, if an attractive way were shown, their enthusiasm would at once lead them to take up useful woman's work with zeal.[22]

The attractive way Baden-Powell proposed was to be called Girl Guiding, a separate but complementary form of Scouting designed for girls. With different uniforms, altered organizational structure and emblems, Guiding was designed as a sex-appropriate answer to the thousands of girls clamoring for entrance to Scouting. Boy Scout officials estimated that the number of girls in the movement unofficially had reached 6,000 by 1909. In Guiding, girls would be taught to be women of character, just as Scouting inculcated healthy manliness for boys.

As Baden-Powell worked to develop an "appropriate" version of Scouting for girls, *The Spectator* picked up the issue in its columns. Violet Markham, who had been so complimentary in her description of Boy Scouts just three months earlier, wrote a scathing letter condemning Scouting for *girls* on December 4, 1909. Her outline of concerns with girls playing the Scout game echoed larger societal complaints with Girl Scouting and later, albeit to a lesser degree, Girl Guiding.

First, Markham worried about boys and girls Scouting *together*. She described her objection in detail, noting that "Girl Scouts and Boy Scouts roam the countryside together on what I can only describe as glorified larking expeditions, expeditions from which they have been known to return home as late as ten P.M." Markham allowed her readers to infer the deleterious affects on society that such "expeditions" could encourage. She also noted that the supervision, which she observed was rare, came from men, rather than "ladies." This concern, of girls mixing inappropriately with boys or becoming boyish, permeated many of the early debates on Girl Guiding, both in Britain and in the other areas where Scouting spread. In the United States, for instance, Boy Scouts of America executive James E. West issued threats, wrote scores of letters, and finally sued the Girl Scouts to try to end their use of the term "Scout." West thought Girl Scouts "sissified" the name, and like Markham, West "firmly believed that scouting was only for men and boys."[23]

In addition to her worries about girls mixing with boys, Markham's second complaint was that Scouting was too military for girls. She assumed that Scouting was aiming to train boys for military service, for which there was no apparent need to train girls, since they were noncombatants. Nursing training, she wrote, is excellent for girls, but "it is not necessary to associate these things with night attacks or ranging the countryside with a long pole."

Markham opined that the Red Cross could easily train girls without the help of the Scouts. This precise point, that Scouting was too militaristic, struck a particularly harsh chord for the organization in this period. The perceived militarism of the movement was one of its biggest problems as Scouting developed. In fact, Baden-Powell and his advisors spent much of their time combating the idea that Scouting was merely a feeder for the Territorials or other military organizations, while simultaneously encouraging military-style drill, rifle training and army scouting. Markham, in celebrating Scouting's militarism for boys and condemning it for girls, had hit on an especially vulnerable spot for the Scout movement, especially since the London Scout Commissioner, Sir Francis Vane, had very publicly chastised the movement for being overly militaristic, for which Baden-Powell dismissed him. Vane held a meeting of Scoutmasters in London to air his grievances about Scouting and to discuss creating a separate Peace Scout movement on December 3, 1909, the night before Markham's letter appeared. In fact, on the same day Markham attacked girl scouting in *The Spectator*, the *Daily News* and *Daily Express* ran headlines such as "Split in the Boy Scout Camp" and "Scouts' Revolt."[24]

Markham's final worry echoed her two earlier complaints and got at the heart of the problem she had with girl scouting. She fretted about girls becoming too masculine and neglecting their womanliness. Here, Markham did not hold back: "The whole spirit of excitement and self-advertisement bred by the movement is highly objectionable ... [g]irls are not boys, and the training which develops manly qualities in the one may lead to the negation of womanliness in the other." This charge, of destroying the womanliness of girls, was one that Girl Guiding and Girl Scouting around the world would fight for decades. An early Girl Guide remembered the prejudice that Girl Scouts and Guides met with in 1910 when she joined, writing: "Most people were firmly convinced that we wished to turn all the girls of the British Empire into hoydens, who would run about with Boy Scouts all day long, and be a universal nuisance."[25] Hoydens and tomboys, while problematic enough for many on an individual level, were symptomatic of the broader decay of home and empire that many organizations hoped to combat in the Edwardian period. Girl Scouting seemed to some a direct threat to what Markham called "the qualities which are essential to the nation [of] the wives and mothers of tomorrow."[26] These qualities of womanliness, gentleness, and nurturing, would be the very things added to Guiding in order to give it a "complementary" framework to the boys' movement.

The Spectator "heartily endorse[d]" Markham's concerns, urging Baden-Powell not to proceed with a girls' movement that might jeopardize the good work of Scouting with a "mad scheme of military co-education."[27] Other correspondents joined the journal in condemning Girl Scouting, and in one case, a letter to the editor called on parents who allowed their girls to join to be pilloried![28] To his credit, Baden-Powell stuck with his impulse to develop Guiding as a girls' movement, enlisting his 51-year-old younger sister, Agnes, to help provide a feminine face for the organization. In seeking to answer the charges being leveled against Girl Guiding, Baden-Powell, his sister, and other Scout leaders began a vigorous defense. Using Robert Baden-Powell's pamphlets from 1909 and 1910 as well as Agnes Baden-Powell's later 1912 handbook, *The Handbook for Girl Guides, or How Girls Can Help to Build The Empire*, leaders in the movement laid out the girls' version of Scouting for the British public over the course of nearly a decade of controversy.

In *The Spectator* itself, members and "friends" of the movement immediately responded to Markham's critique. A week after Markham's letter, a Scoutmaster condemned the critique as misinformed, and explained the new Girl Guide scheme. As he wryly commented, "Better a girl should become a 'tomboy' than an idle doll with poor morals." The Guides, he explained, would be run entirely by ladies, and although their activities included signaling and hiking, girls also learned cooking, washing up, childcare, music, art, and nature study.[29] The Boy Scouts' Managing Secretary also entered the fray, defending the organization: "Mixed troops of boys and girls are not countenanced . . . all we have done has been to register and take note of the large number of girls who have applied to us as anxious to take up scouting."[30] Other Scoutmasters and Scout officials followed with letters all making the same case, namely, that while Girl Scouting might be inappropriate, Girl Guiding was an entirely different thing altogether.

Again evoking the comments of "A Returned South African," Guiding envisioned a sort of "home frontier" for girls that would train them as homemakers, but in an imperial context that provided adventure rather than drudgery. Leaders genuinely believed that girls were both over-civilized and primitive, and they required Guiding to give them an outlet for both problems.[31] Guiding utilized the same powerful colonial imagery and language to appeal to children who longed for imperial adventure, but it also inculcated qualities designed to please parents hoping to "civilize" their children—friendliness, propriety, helpfulness, obedience, patriotism. The word "Guide" referred specifically to the Guides of India's northwest frontier, and early in the first Guide handbook, girls are encouraged to be "just as good as" these men and to sacrifice for home, country, and empire. Yet a few pages later, a whole section is devoted to the command, "Be Womanly." In short, girls were to be heroines in their everyday lives who fantasized about the glories of roughing it on the imperial frontiers, all the while training to be good wives and mothers at home.[32]

For many, the defense of Guiding and its connection with "ladies of quality" allayed fears and concerns, but Markham continued to question even this version of Guiding, noting that the term "B.P.'s Girl Guides ... inevitably suggests a troop of *vivandières* [camp followers] rather than a band of girls organised for the serious duties and responsibilities of life."[33] Markham's criticism reflected many concerns accompanying Guiding's appearance on the youth scene in Britain. In fact, until Agnes Baden-Powell wrote a long letter in June 1911, *The Spectator* editors themselves did not retract their condemnation of December 1909. Finally in this June 1911 issue, the editors made sure to endorse Guiding in strong terms, providing a benediction of sorts: "May Miss Baden-Powell and her helpers guide her Guides to all that is brave and womanly."[34] Agnes Baden-Powell and her committee of "ladies" tried to do just that from 1910, when they officially formed an executive board, until near the end of World War I, at which time Olave Baden-Powell, Robert's young wife, assumed control of the movement and reorganized the committee.[35]

As the Guides worked to develop an organization and to register/convert the Girl Scouts of Great Britain, girls in other areas of the world were also finding inspiration from *Scouting for Boys*. Groups of Girl Scouts and Girl Guides sprang onto the scene particularly early in the British Empire. For example, in New Zealand, one of Baden-Powell's military colleagues from the Boer War, Colonel David Cosgrove, started a "Girl Peace Scout" movement in 1909 in Christchurch. Adorned in khaki dresses and big floppy hats, the Girl Peace Scouts traveled with their own bugler and were never seen out without their staves and haversacks. Cosgrove authored an early handbook, and the movement spread slowly into other parts of the country. When the Girl Guide Association finally formed in New Zealand in 1923, these Girl Peace Scouts units traded in their khaki for blue and became Guides, thereby linking themselves to a burgeoning international movement.[36] In Canada, the first official Girl Guides were registered in 1910 in Toronto, after Mrs. A. H. Malcolmson traveled to England in 1909 and witnessed the Crystal Palace rally and its aftermath.[37] South Africa saw its first eight Guide companies formed in 1910, but they were exclusively for white children.[38]

Many of the earliest Guide movements in the British Empire and in other countries, such as Chile, Sweden, and Poland, began when women who witnessed Girl Scouting and Girl Guiding in action in Great Britain took the ideas home. Perhaps the most famous example of this phenomenon is Juliette Low, founder of the Girl Scouts of the USA. While some isolated Girl Guide and Scout troops and a competing movement, the Camp Fire Girls, had begun in the United States prior to Low's Girl Scouts, she is widely credited with developing Guiding in the U.S. setting. Low, a wealthy Savannah-born widow of an Englishman, spent part of each year in London and Scotland. While in the United Kingdom in 1911, she met Robert Baden-Powell, and she started her own Girl Guide unit among the poor, rural communities in Scotland where she had rented a lodge. Some of the skills she taught the Guides to help improve their livelihoods included poultry farming and wool spinning! When Low moved to London later in the year, she became involved in organizing urban Guide companies there, amassing useful experiences in a variety of Guiding settings.[39] Low spent time in London as a Guide Commissioner, she asked questions and discussed methods with the Baden-Powells, and she trained at Guide headquarters with other leaders.[40]

After this crash course in practical Guiding, Low returned to the United States, where she enlisted the help of Nina Pape, the headmistress of a girls' school in Savannah, to begin Guiding there. The early groups were known as Guides, but by 1913, the girls petitioned to change to the "somehow more American" Girl Scouts, with its connotations of American pioneer life.[41] Stalwart pioneer women such as Annie Tilis on the Florida frontiers joined other extraordinary females featured in Guide and Girl Scout literature, such as scientist Marie Curie or physician Louisa Garrett Anderson.[42] These appealing stories provided role models for girls and helped Low, with her connections to women of influence in both the United States and abroad, to build the Girl Scouts into a major force in world Guiding by the interwar period.[43]

So what exactly was Guiding, and what made it adaptable enough for girls in Britain and most other countries in the world? Guiding's successful formula was built on the Scout model, but with certain adaptations to make it better suited to girls. Guiding offered girls interested in the movement enough excitement to quench the adventurous fantasies they had conjured while reading youth literature of the period, such as boys' and girls' school stories.[44] Popular imperial stories by G. A. Henty and H. Rider Haggard fueled not just boys' but girls' imaginations as well, and many Guides saw their back gardens and nearby forests as jungles or deserts in far-flung reaches of the Empire. Besides, as Robert Baden-Powell pointed out in a Guide pamphlet, girls could also consider a life in the colonies, but only if they were prepared because, "in a Colony, a woman must know how to do many things which she finds done for her at home in civilisation."[45] Girl Guides were encouraged to consider building the British Empire by working in domestic service, teaching, or missionary work in the colonies. In fact, even if girls could not move to the Empire, they could still do their part to construct and maintain it by populating the colonies with patriotic white men.[46]

Girls could also, however, develop skills that would make them a force to fight the perceived decadence threatening homes in the early twentieth century. Guides trained as "comrades" and companions for men, rather than dependents, but they also received the necessary training as moral guardians of the home.[47] Guides were reminded early in the 1912 handbook that their greatest duty in life was to "bring up good citizens" for the country and to "teach them to be good, hardworking, honourable and useful citizens for our great British Empire."[48] In order to fulfill this duty, the book suggested that Guides learn housewifery and childcare, both essential to their citizenship in the nation and the empire. The dual focus on adventure (camping, hiking, signaling, tracking, outdoor life) and womanly attributes (cooking, sewing, nursing, childcare) attracted girls and appeased their parents' fears that Guides were, as Violet Markham put it, inculcating a "lawless spirit" in girls.

The core of the movement, as with Scouting, was the motto "Be Prepared" and the Guide promise and laws, as laid out in the original 1912 handbook:

Promise:

I Promise, on my Honour
To be loyal to God and the King;
To try and do daily good turns to other people;
To obey the Law of the Guides.

Laws:

1. A Guide's Honour is to be Trusted.
2. A Guide is Loyal.

3. A Guide's Duty is to be Useful and to Help Others.

4. A Guide is a Friend to all, and a Sister to every other Guide, no matter to what Social Class the other belongs.

5. A Guide is Courteous.

6. A Guide keeps herself Pure in Thought, Word and Deeds.

7. A Guide is a Friend to Animals.

8. A Guide Obeys Orders.

9. A Guide Smiles and Sings.

10. A Guide is Thrifty[49]

The Promise that girls made when joining Guiding was nearly identical to the Scout Promise, and they pledged to adhere to the same 10 laws that Scouts did, albeit with the substitution of "singing" for "whistling" in the law promoting smiling and whistling when faced with difficulties.[50] Whistling was considered far too vulgar for girls. The motto, promise, laws, and rituals of Guiding all reinforced the importance of proper and thoughtful behavior. Guides were taught to think of others, to be friends to those who were different from themselves, to obey authority, to be helpful and loyal, and to act with honor and integrity. According to early Guides, these were not just empty promises; Guides took these vows seriously. When Guiding modified the Promise in the 1990s, scores of former Guides wrote letters protesting the changes, saying that stripping the Promise and Law of meaning would destroy Guiding's uniqueness.

One Roman Catholic Guide, who joined in Ireland in 1919, remembered that "when I joined it [Guiding] was character-forming, aiming at honesty, caring for others and for what the rest of the Guide Laws stood for, friendship of the company, out of door activities, smartness and behaviour." She decried the modern emphasis on playing to the masses rather than attracting girls with something that could provide more than just an opportunity to lark about; in short, a program that would help them make a difference in their communities and nations. Likewise, other Guides from the early years of the movement stressed its importance in shaping their values and ideals, their sense of morality and their personal conduct. A working-class Guide from southeast London who joined in 1928, stated merely that Guiding "governed all my actions and thinking," while another girl from the same area felt that Guiding provided a stable influence that inculcated good citizenship and morals. Over and over Guides from the first three decades of the organization saw the movement as different from other youth clubs because of its emphasis on character formation. A middle-class girl from Kent said bluntly, "If they took away the Promise, the Guides would be just another youth club."[51]

The Promise provided a serious intent, but the engine driving the movement was its activities, which included fitness training, handicraft, first aid, homemaking skills, hiking, and camping. With the first handbook in 1912, motherhood served as an important focus, but by the end of World War I, citizenship had become more central to the Guide ethos.[52] Through these shifts and the programmatic alterations, the activities remained quite steady with an overwhelming emphasis on active games, outdoor activity, homemaking, and handicraft. The 1912 manual provided a guide to possible activities for Girl Guides that included woodcraft (stalking, tracking, observation, and signaling), lifesaving and first aid, household skills (childcare, cooking, health, and sanitation), patriotism, and frontier skills (camping, seafaring, self-defense). Girls earned their child-nurse and sick-nurse badges, but they also did badge work in rifle shooting, swimming, and pathfinding. Their excitement at having an opportunity to show off their talents was hard to contain, as one Guide reminisced that, "A runaway horse was a dream come true," and another remembered her company leaping into action when a man fell in front of them and broke his leg: "The very chance we had pined for, and we took it joyfully. I often wonder, did we look indecently gleeful as we joined hands and held back the crowd."[53] A 1914 *Punch* cartoon depicting eager Girl Guides "doctoring" boys involved in a fight mocked this almost "indecent" thrill at the opportunity to use emergency skills, but for girls, the experience was indescribable. This glee at the misfortune of others was not exactly in the spirit of the Guide laws, but it does point to the real sense of urgency and importance Guide training provided for girls.

As they prepared to spring into action, Guides were often easily identifiable by their distinctive blue uniforms and broad-brimmed hats, and prior to the war it was unusual enough to see girls in military-style uniforms that they sometimes created a stir. Joan Denny Cooke remembered "the first time that I went out in uniform, wondering whether I ought to salute soldiers and policemen! Everyone I knew was saluted as a matter of course, Guides or public."[54] While Guides were not encouraged to salute the world at large, they were taught to value the uniform as a status symbol. Guides usually owned their uniforms, which they purchased themselves, unlike in many other youth clubs such as the Girls' Brigade.

Uniforms provided a sense of belonging for girls, but they also served to identify Guides to the outside world, giving them a public presence.

Uniforms were an important part of the movement's ideology, because they were advocated as great levelers; Winn Everett, daughter of Guide official Percy Everett, said in a 1993 interview, "It did not matter if you were poor or rich, because you all looked the same."[55] Another Guide from Northamptonshire also recalled her company as multiclass: "Our company (Althorpe) had aristocracy in the Spencers, middle class—those of us from Northampton—and poorer class (at that time) from the village children; and it all worked extremely well."[56] As an organization that aimed for cross-class membership and that hoped to break down the walls of class prejudice, Guiding relied on the uniform to create regimentation and smartness, but also to erase obvious class differences. Unfortunately, the uniform could never provide that camouflage, especially as most poor Guides could only afford a few uniform pieces or had to rely on home-made versions and hand-me-downs.[57] Poorer Guides suffered acute embarrassment when their uniforms pointed to their status; a Doncaster girl's homemade blue cap proved not to be colorfast in a rainstorm, turning her face blue. Similarly, an orphan felt betrayed when her homemade uniform wasn't good enough at a rally. She later wrote, "We had thought that dressed in Guide uniform, we could mix with anyone in the world and become part of it, but no!"[58]

Notwithstanding the limitations of "uniformity" in the movement, Guiding aimed to attract girls from all class backgrounds. While many of the earliest Guide companies were predominantly from middle-class or upper-class backgrounds, Guiding did attract some working-class girls from the beginning of the movement, especially in companies attached to churches or settlements. For example, Rev. W. T. Money found himself enlisting the aid of his sister to run a Guide troop in his Greenwich church for "rough" girls, while he started a Scout troop for the boys.[59] Schools and other educational institutions also saw the advantages of Guiding for keeping children interested and out of trouble. At Bayswater Jewish School (London), the Guides were well established by the First World War, and the Notting Hill High School for Girls (London) held a public meeting in 1912 to organize Guiding to help teach "the 'hard-up' women of London . . . to cook dinners," thereby boosting family life generally.[60]

Scout and Guide leaders spoke and wrote about the advantages of the programs for working-class and poor kids. Agnes Baden-Powell's letter to *The Spectator* in 1911 focused on "workgirls" and the role of Guiding in providing after-work and after-school activities to keep girls out of idleness and trouble. Cramped up and confined with work all day, these girls, many only 13 or 14 years old, craved excitement. Guiding, she noted, kept them off the corners of streets and in a healthy, open-air, controlled environment.[61] This emphasis on Guiding as social reform and education for the poor led some wealthy Guides to start companies in poor areas. Many working-class Guides around the country recalled meeting at "Captain's house," where they caught a glimpse of a life different from their own. In such cases, "Captain" often helped poor girls purchase uniforms or obtain camp equipment. Despite these experiments, the cross-class sisterhood remained a difficult dream to attain in Guiding until after the First World War, when the movement broadened its scope considerably, and its numbers rose to well over half a million in Britain (1930s).

Structurally, Guide companies had a captain to lead them with an assistant called a lieutenant, but the basic unit was the patrol, as with Scouting. Several patrols of six to eight girls (named after flowers) made up a company, and each patrol had a girl patrol leader. This structure allowed for adult supervision and guidance, but it was also designed to inculcate leadership abilities and cooperation among the girls themselves. In *The Patrol System for Girl Guides*, patrol leaders are encouraged to help "each girl in the patrol feel that she is an essential part of a complete and self-contained unit."[62] Patrol leaders were elected by their peers or appointed by the captain, and they were supposed to keep order and "smartness" among their fellow Guides. Girls sought to "foster patrol spirit," which led to a competitive element in Guide life as patrols often competed to be "top patrol" in conduct, badge work, and smartness.[63]

Guiding's flexibility regarding religion was also an important part of its success and longevity. Unlike the Girls' Friendly Society, which was entirely Anglican, or the Girls' Guildry, which focused on religious instruction, both Guiding and Scouting were broad-minded in their approach to religion.[64] Early movements included various Protestant groups as well as Roman Catholic and Jewish companies in Britain, and as the organizations traveled into the empire, soon Hindu, Muslim and Buddhist youth joined as well. In a book aimed at reassuring parents about Guiding's religious aims, the Girl Guide Association in 1927 explained that, "So far from being irreligious, it [Guiding] looks upon the faith of each individual child as the most sacred thing the child possesses, to be guarded against all interference."[65] This plea for tolerance and privacy was central to the Guide religious ethos and shaped by Baden-Powell's own vague approach to religiosity. He counseled faith in a higher power, but often focused more on good deeds and morality. Guides were encouraged to find God in nature, and Guides' Own (religious ceremonies for Guide companies) often emphasized an interdenominational spirituality that little resembled any organized religion.[66] Baden-Powell, in commenting on the 1920 Girl Scout (USA) handbook, laid bare his hopes for Scouting: "Leaving aside all clothing and ritual we offer to the girl the elemental points within her grasp, namely the realization of God the Creator through a closer intercourse with Nature, and of the God of Love through service."[67] Despite the fact that leaders in the movement often disagreed with this ecumenical stance, Scouting's founder's broad-mindedness allowed Guiding to move beyond its Christian roots into a world movement, although not without controversy as Guiding grew and expanded.

Finally, as with Scouting, the Baden-Powells used marketing and publicity to launch Guiding and tirelessly worked to place it in newspapers, public events, and educational institutions. This marketing onslaught was purposeful, for as Percy Everett, Robert Baden-Powell's right-hand man in Scouting and the long-time financial officer for the Guides, noted in a memo to B-P, "the only way to get the public to come in large quantities and so cover expenses is to keep the pot boiling in the papers."[68] Everett himself was on loan to Scouting from publisher C. Arthur Pearson specifically to help with marketing; it was perhaps a surprise to Everett when he got so ensconced that he stayed in both Scouting and Guiding the rest of his life.[69] The marketing blitz that Pearson, Baden-Powell and Everett devised for the initial Boy Scout scheme had worked marvelously well, and so Baden-Powell wanted to employ the same tactic for Guiding. Both Agnes and Robert Baden-Powell gave public lectures, addressed organizations and clubs, and visited with other youth workers in the country to publicize Guiding.

As part of the publicity push, ladies of standing, especially wealthy women with country estates, were enlisted as patrons and commissioners in the young movement, providing wealth and resources (both time and money) for its development, but also donating space for camping and other recreational activities. As patrons signed on, their names were advertised to help enlist more members and more patronage. Agnes Baden-Powell turned first to friends and acquaintances, many of them in her age cohort, for support of the fledgling Guides. Among the early shapers of Guiding was Mrs. [Carrie] Lumley-Holland, a wealthy widow with experience in charitable work and a forceful personality.[70] Lumley-Holland and other "women of quality," such as the Countess of Carrick and Dr. Mary Davies, set about organizing the Guides, finding commissioners, patrons, and Guide leaders. They sought funding from wealthy donors and forged a particularly strong bond with the Royal Family in Britain, beginning in 1911 with Princess Louise, Duchess of Argyll as Guiding's first Royal Patron.[71] By January 1911, they had more than eighty regional secretaries helping to organize and register Guide companies.[72]

Guiding also began to build up its own literature that included fictional books, nonfiction guides, and magazines. Exciting adventure tales, such as *Terry, the Girl Guide* (1912), appeared alongside books on badge hints, patrol work, and games. Catalogs of Guide paraphernalia also became widely available and stores offered Scout and Guide equipment sections. The organization's first serial publications were included as part of *Home Notes* (a Pearson's journal) and *The Golden Rule* (another small publication), but it was not until January 1914 that its own magazine aimed at leaders, *The Girl Guides Gazette*, appeared on the scene. The first magazine targeted specifically at girls rather than leaders was *The Guide*, first published in 1921.[73] This profusion of literary production along with the Guide committee's early newspaper articles, speeches, and fundraising events did much to help market the young Guiding vision.

As Guiding expanded around the United Kingdom and the world, its organizing committee attempted to establish clear rules and to protect the movement. For example, in the United States, Juliette Low launched the national Girl Scout scheme in 1913 and then immediately began applying for patents to protect the uniform, insignias, and training materials. Low financed much of the early Girl Scout organization with her own personal fortune (with assistance from other women of wealth) and helped it get off the ground.[74] She incorporated the organization as "the Girl Scouts Inc." in 1915 and established a new national headquarters in New York City in 1916.[75] As with Guiding, U.S. Girl Scouting formed an executive board of prominent women, which helped publicize and finance Scouting. British Guiding, too, had by 1916 a Charter of Incorporation, a book of *Policy, Organisation and Rules* and an annual reporting structure. Importantly, in both Girl Scouting and Girl Guiding, the development of more professional structures and administrative offices led to employment opportunities for women;

Guiding and Scouting headquarters were staffed almost exclusively by women until quite recently in the organizations' history.

Perhaps most key to Guiding's success was its emphasis on service—to friends, family, employers, countries, humanity, God. Service imbued the organization with a mission and a sense of importance that girls did not take lightly. Dozens of Guides interviewed about their involvement with the movement in its first 30 years pointed to this factor as most important and long-lasting. The Promise and Laws set the organization apart from other activities or clubs for young people, at least in the minds of those who joined Guiding. Girls wanted their lives to mean something, and they wanted to be useful—Guiding offered them that chance. "A Returned South African" had recognized this yearning for useful activity, writing that "the truest happiness lies in the simplest and most primitive pleasures."[76] The Baden-Powells tapped into this need girls felt for the primitive— camping, woodcraft, hiking—but Guiding also thrived on the notion that girls could be active citizens through homemaking, service, and friendship.

It is no coincidence that Guiding's numbers, both in Britain and abroad, spiked during and after the two world wars, as girls sought to find meaningful service activities to prove their patriotism during war. Sustaining the movement beyond the wars proved more difficult. Juliette Low bemoaned this idea that girls sometimes only saw the importance of Girl Scouting during wartime, when they could visibly demonstrate their uniformed patriotism. In a letter discussing a plan to hire only volunteers for Girl Scouting, not paid workers, Low wrote:

> In fact in her ideas of having volunteer work, may be high & very much better than paid workers, but the instances she quotes of enthusiastic workers all had the [war] patriotism as their incentive. When we are at war even drones will work, for their country, but no one can count on such workers for Girl Scouts until the woman once begins to work, then she becomes the slave of the organization.[77]

Yet this emphasis on war service, while perhaps deplorable to leaders hoping to sustain a movement in peacetime, led not only to a widespread jump in membership numbers, but also to a visible role for Guides and Girl Scouts in war work throughout the world. World War I, in short, was a coming-of-age for Guiding and Girl Scouting. It marked a terrific period of transformation, both in leadership and vision, but it also launched the movements into a new internationalist mission, from which they never looked back. The idea sparked by a group of girls that picked up *Scouting for Boys* and formed their own Scout troops blossomed by the end of World War I into a major international movement with millions of members by the 1930s.

NOTES

1. "English vs. Colonial Life for Girls," Letter to the Editor from "A Returned South African," *The Spectator* 103 (September 4, 1909), 343.

2. "The Boy Scouts," *The Spectator* 103 (September 11, 1909), 373–374.

3. "Scouting for Boys," *The Spectator* 103 (September 25, 1909), 463–464.

4. Robert Baden-Powell, *Scouting for Boys: The Original 1908 Edition* (Mineola, NY: Dover Publications, 2007), 110–115.

5. Marguerite de Beaumont, "From the Beginning," *The Leader's Opinions: Magazine of the 5th Lone Guides* 4 (April/May 1921), 39; GGL.

6. Robert C. Harrison to Robert Baden-Powell, July 12, 1916, TC/42, Scout Association Archives, Gilwell Park (SAGP).

7. "The Boy Scouts," Letter to the Editor from Violet R. Markham, *The Spectator* 103 (September 25, 1909), 455.

8. Rose Kerr, *The Story of the Girl Guides* (London: Girl Guides Association, 1940), 52–55; Early Days of Guiding Box, GGL.

9. Elizabeth de Beaumont, "Reminiscences," 1931, Early Days of Guiding box, GGL; de Beaumont, "From the Beginning," 39; GGL.

10. "This is your Life Scrapbook—Dorothy Hattersley Clough," 1977; Guide records in possession of Sheila Marks, Ilkley (UK). Early camping in Britain varied considerably by location and parental concern—some camps were merely overnights in donated houses or barns, others were tent camps. The first documented Guide camps appear to have occurred in 1910.

11. Kathleen Davies-Cooke obituary, *The Times* (July 4, 1994).

12. Margaret C. White, *A History of The Girl Guide Movement in Sheffield* (Sheffield: County of Sheffield Girl Guides Association, n.d.), 1.

13. Kerr, *The Story of the Girl Guides*, 59.

14. Evelyn Goshawk, "Reminiscences," 1977, Early Days of Guiding box, GGL.

15. Undated transcript of interview with Sybil Canadine, Early Days of Guiding box, GGL.

16. Undated transcript of interview with Sybil Canadine, Early Days of Guiding box, GGL.

17. Nesta G. Ashworth, "One of Canada's Oldest Guides Started as a Boy Scout," clipping from Canadian Guiding magazine, ca. 1970, Early Days of Guiding box, GGL.

18. Sally Mitchell, *The New Girl: Girls' Culture in England, 1880–1915* (New York: Columbia University Press, 1995), 103–105. For more information on the

restrictions on girls' activities in late Victorian and Edwardian England, see Carol Dyhouse, *Girls Growing Up in Late Victorian and Edwardian England* (London: Routledge, 1981).

19. Lucy H. M. Soulsby, *The Use of Leisure* (London: Longman, 1900), 24–26.

20. Jennifer Hargreaves, *Sporting Females: Critical Issues in the History and Sociology of Women's Sports* (London: Routledge, 1994), 63–87, 94–100.

21. Tim Jeal, *The Boy-Man: The Life of Lord Baden-Powell* (New York: William Morrow and Company, 1990), 469.

22. Robert Baden-Powell, *Pamphlet A: Girl Guides* (London: Girl Guides Association, 1910).

23. Mary Aickin Rothschild, "To Scout or To Guide? The Girl Scout–Boy Scout Controversy, 1912–1941," *Frontiers: A Journal of Women Studies* 6:3 (Autumn 1981), 118.

24. Jeal, *The Boy-Man*, 404–407. For more information on the militarism issue, see Tammy Proctor, *On My Honour: Guides and Scouts in Interwar Britain* (Philadelphia: American Philosophical Society, 2002), 15; and an excellent article on the debate by Martin Dedman, "Baden-Powell, Militarism, and the 'Invisible Contributors' to the Boy Scout Scheme, 1904–1920," *Twentieth-Century British History* 4:3 (1993), 201–223.

25. Beatrice Swaine to Rose Kerr, November 2, 1930, Rose Kerr letters, Early Days of Guiding box, GGL.

26. "Girl Scouts," Letter to the Editor by Violet R. Markham and follow-up editorial comment, *The Spectator* 103 (December 4, 1909), 942.

27. Markham letter, December 4, 1909.

28. G. A. Seebohm Letter to the Editor, *The Spectator* 103 (December 11, 1909), 994.

29. "Girl Scouts," Letter to the Editor by Warrant Scoutmaster, *The Spectator* 103 (December 11, 1909), 994.

30. J. Archibald Lyle Letter to the Editor, *The Spectator* 103 (December 25, 1909), 1100.

31. Tammy Proctor, " 'A Separate Path': Scouting and Guiding in Interwar South Africa," *Comparative Studies of Society and History* 42:3 (July 2000), 606.

32. Agnes Baden-Powell and Robert Baden-Powell, *The Handbook for Girl Guides, or How Girls can help to Build the Empire* (London: Thomas Nelson and Sons, 1912), 16–24.

33. "Girl Scouts," Letter to the Editor by Violet Markham, *The Spectator* 104 (January 8, 1910), 51.

34. "Our Workgirls," Letter to the Editor by Agnes Baden-Powell and editorial response, *The Spectator* 106 (June 17, 1911), 922.

35. Proctor, *On My Honour*, 108–109; Jeal, *The Boy-Man*, 471–475.

36. Girl Guides Association of New Zealand, *Thirty Years of Guiding in New Zealand, 1923–1953* (Auckland: GGANZ, 1953), 7.

37. Anne Gloin, *Like Measles, It's Catching!* (Toronto: Girl Guides of Canada, 1974), 5; Dorothy Crocker, *All About Us: A Story of the Girl Guides in Canada, 1910–1989* (Kitchener, ON: Girl Guides of Canada—Guides du Canada, 1990), 5.

38. World Association of Girl Guides and Girl Scouts (WAGGGS), *Biennial Reports 1928–1930* (London: WAGGGS, 1931), 24; Kathleen F. Hill, *Brief History of the Guide Movement in South Africa* (unpublished), May 1951, WAGGGS, General—Girl Scout of the USA Archives, New York (GSUSA).

39. Kerr, *The Story of the Girl Guides*, 52–53; Rose Kerr, "Juliette Low Meets Sir Robert Baden-Powell and the Girl Guides of England," in *Juliette Low and the Girl Scouts*, eds. Anne Choate and Helen Ferris (New York: Girl Scouts, 1928), 65–71.

40. Laureen Ann Tedesco, "A Nostalgia for Home: Daring and Domesticity in Girl Scouting and Girls' Fiction, 1913–1933" (PhD diss., Texas A&M University, 1999), 39–40.

41. Rothschild, "To Scout or To Guide?," 116; Susan A. Miller, *Growing Girls: The Natural Origins of Girls' Organizations in America* (New Brunswick: Rutgers University Press, 2007), 14–17, 26–28; Tedesco, "A Nostalgia for Home," 40–42. There is some debate about when and how the name got changed, but the consensus seems to be that Low herself had some idea that Scouting might work better than Guiding in a U.S. setting and that the girls in her Savannah group asked for the change.

42. W. J. Hoxie, *How Girls Can Help Their Country: The 1913 Handbook for Girl Scouts* (Bedford, MA: Applewood Books, 2001), 9, 115.

43. Charles Strickland, "Juliette Low, the Girl Scouts and the Role of American Women," in *Woman's Being, Woman's Place: Female Identity and Vocation in American History*, ed. Mary Kelley (Boston: G. K. Hall & Co., 1979), 257, 259–260. For an interesting article that touches on the "pioneer" myth, see Leslie Hahner, "Practical Patriotism: Camp Fire Girls, Girl Scouts, and Americanization," *Communication and Critical/Cultural Studies* 5:2 (June 2008), 122–123.

44. Since the 1880s, girls had been more interested in reading boys' adventure magazines and books. Gillian Avery, *Childhood's Pattern* (London: Hodder & Stoughton, 1975), 206–207.

45. As quoted in Mitchell, *The New Girl*, 123. Mitchell's book examines the development of girls' culture, literature, and organizations of the period with a focus on the development of "modern" notions of girlhood.

46. Michelle Smith, "Be(ing) Prepared: Girl Guides, Colonial Life, and National Strength," *Limina: A Journal of Historical and Cultural Studies* 12 (2006), 8.

47. Allen Warren, "Mothers for the Empire," in *Making Imperial Mentalities: Socialisation and British Imperialism*, ed. J. A. Mangan (Manchester: Manchester University Press, 1990), 97–98.

48. A. Baden-Powell and R. Baden-Powell, *How Girls Can Help to Build the Empire*, 24, 298, 313.

49. A. Baden-Powell and R. Baden-Powell, *How Girls Can Help to Build the Empire*, 25–26, 38–41.

50. Originally there were nine Scout laws, but they were quickly adapted to include "A Scout is Pure in Thought, Word and Deed."

51. Oral Interviews and written surveys by author with Sidney Brock, Phyllis Lockyer, Peggy McGill, and Jeanne Holloway, 1993.

52. Warren, "Mothers for the Empire," 104.

53. Oral interview by author with G. Winn Everett, 1993; Ida Edwards as quoted in Kerr, *The Story of the Girl Guides*, 66.

54. Joan Denny Cooke, "Reminiscences," ca. 1930s, Early Days of Guiding box, GGL.

55. Oral interview by author with G. Winn Everett, 1993.

56. Letter from Miss Eileen Jennings (1917) quoted in *Guiding in Northamptonshire*, 26, GGL.

57. Tammy Proctor, "(Uni)Forming Youth: Girl Guides and Boy Scouts in Britain, 1908–1939," *History Workshop Journal* 45 (Spring 1998), 103–134.

58. Winifred Renshaw, *An Ordinary Life: Memories of a Balby Childhood* (Doncaster: Doncaster Library Services, 1984), ch. 35; G. V. Holmes, *The Likes of Us* (London: Frederick Muller Ltd., 1948), 97–98.

59. Kerr, *The Story of the Girl Guides*, 57–59.

60. "Girl Guides Movement," *Jewish Chronicle* (December 14, 1917), Press Cuttings 1910–1922, GGL; "The Task before the Girl Guides," *The Times* (January 16, 1912).

61. Agnes Baden-Powell, "Our Workgirls," 922.

62. Roland E. Philipps, *The Patrol System for Girl Guides* (London: C. Arthur Pearson, 1920), 26.

63. *Pages for Patrol Leaders* (London: Girl Guides Association, 1930), 26.

64. Tammy Proctor, "'Something for the Girls': Organized Leisure in Europe, 1890–1939," in *Secret Gardens, Satanic Mills: Placing Girls in European History, 1750–1960*, eds. Mary Jo Maynes, Birgitte Søland, and Christina Benninghaus (Bloomington: Indiana University Press, 2005), 241.

65. Girl Guides Association, *Religion and the Girl Guides* (London: Girl Guides Association, 1927), 9.

66. Proctor, *On My Honour*, 139–143.

67. Robert Baden-Powell to Jane Rippin, June 10, 1919; Girl Guide box; GSUSA.

68. Percy Everett to Robert Baden-Powell, August 27, 1909; Miscellaneous history, GGL.

69. Jeal, *The Boy-Man*, 390–391.

70. Kerr, *The Story of the Girl Guides*, 69–70.

71. *1910 . . . And Then? A Brief History of the Girl Guides Association* (London: Girl Guides Association, 1990), 7.

72. Kerr, *The Story of the Girl Guides*, 78–79.

73. Kerr, *The Story of the Girl Guides*, 99–100. *The Girl Guides Gazette* became *The Guider* in January 1928.

74. Gladys Denny Shultz and Daisy Gordon Lawrence, *Lady from Savannah: The Life of Juliette Low* (Philadelphia and New York: J. B. Lippincott Company, 1958), 310. Low's U.S. Girl Scouts were not the only groups to depend upon women of means to sustain them. For example, Lady Mary Pellatt "financed almost entirely" Canadian headquarters until after World War I. Kerr, *The Story of a Million Girls*, 32.

75. Tedesco, "A Nostalgia for Home," 41–43.

76. "English vs. Colonial Life for Girls," Letter to the Editor from "A Returned South African," *The Spectator* 103 (September 4, 1909), 343.

77. Juliette Low (Great Stanhope St., London) to Anne Choate, December 8, 1922; Personalities folder, Storrow, Helen Osborne (Mrs. James) Correspondence, GSUSA.

2. War

When 16 German Girl Guides (part of the *Jungdeutschlandbund*[1]) in their handsome dark green uniforms and "sou'wester hats" arrived in London for a 10-day visit with the British Girl Guides in April 1914, they were met by members of the Girl Guide Committee and whisked away to a series of outings, events, and rallies. Over the next week, they visited Guide companies, theatrical productions, and tourist attractions such as the observatory at Greenwich and Kew Gardens. More than 1,000 London Guides gathered for a rally in South Kensington to fête the visitors, and a reception at the Imperial Institute also drew a crowd. The German Guides, seeking a connection with their British counterparts and an insight into the methods and activities practiced in the birthplace of Guiding, expressed their unconcealed delight with the visit in an interview with a *Times* reporter, noting particularly how much they appreciated the kindness that greeted them. The visit, which all hailed as a success, ended with plans for a group of British Guides to visit Germany in August 1914.[2]

While merely a minor incident in the history of the movement, the German Guide visit of 1914 points to several important changes that Guiding underwent between 1914 and 1920. First, the visit was one of the first of its kind for the fledgling organization, an official public exchange of people and ideas across national boundaries; this would become a crucial element of Guiding's success and development from the period of World War I to the present. Second, the existence of German Girl Guiding in any form indicated the spreading interest in the movement beyond the boundaries of Great Britain and its empire and beyond the English-speaking world; it spoke to a broader interest in many countries in developing the potential of youth. Guiding's nascent international movement would only strengthen and expand with the advent of war. Finally, the German Guide visit also highlighted the catastrophe about to divide Europe. With the outbreak of war in August 1914, the British Guide trip to Berlin was cancelled, and the German girls were cut off from their newfound friends.

The First World War undeniably transformed world Guiding. The Guide organization's focus, leadership, activities, and membership all shifted with the 1914–1918 war period, and the immediate postwar period marked some of the most important growth in its history. War functioned as the opportunity Guides had been waiting for since their founding; finally they had a real chance to prove their usefulness. Guides around the globe sprang into action, and girls who had not been interested in the movement prior to 1914 flocked to its membership. New countries joined the ranks of Guiding as well, and girls saw this youth organization as a way to serve their countries in a time of crisis. Even in areas not directly fighting the war, Guides embraced the call to war service, providing support to the Red Cross and other war relief agencies. Later they served to help alleviate the global influenza epidemic. Membership figures alone demonstrate the shift that took place with the war—in Great Britain, there were approximately 10,000 Guides in spring 1914; by 1920, this number had risen to more than 180,000. The U.S. Girl Scouts saw similar growth—at the end of 1913, membership stood at just under 600; by 1920, there were more than 50,000 Girl Scouts.[3] In short, war served as an unparalleled opportunity for Guiding.

With the entry of Britain into the war in August 1914, Guides immediately volunteered for a variety of service activities, some of them not as glamorous as the girls had imagined. Dorothy Scannell remembered her sister made a special bag with provisions, which she tied around her waist at night in order to "be prepared" for the call to active service in the war.[4] Rose Kerr, making reference to such preparations, wryly noted that,

> Instead of nursing at the front and carrying messages between the lines, they were set down to such dull jobs as darning socks, making bandages, washing up in hospitals, collecting waste paper. At all these jobs they worked quietly and steadily, and thereby converted to a belief in Guiding many of those people who had thought it merely a game for tomboys. It was certainly the way the Guides behaved throughout the war years which earned for them the large measure of public support which they enjoy today in Great Britain.[5]

Darning socks and making bandages may not have been the thrilling "Guide" work of those on the frontiers of the empire, but girls' war service instilled pride nonetheless. After all, Guides were in uniform too, and they knew their work was of importance to the nation. Cicely Stewart-Smith, a former Brownie who had left the movement in a huff, rejoined Guiding in 1917 after friends told her she could do war work.

She recalled in her 1923 diary, "This decided me, previous persuasions and talks of the high aims of the Guides did not move me but the idea of doing proper war work was really thrilling . . . perhaps it was because the whole world was in uniform then."[6]

Guide war work centered first around the internal life of the company, with emphasis on first aid, drill, and signaling. Guides practiced stretcher drill, and they marched to whistle and voice signals. The girls also learned Morse and semaphore. Stewart-Smith, for instance, practiced her Morse while crossing Kensington Gardens to go to school. She described the way she must have looked to others, "A long legged tense faced schoolgirl of twelve in blue coat and scarlet tam o'shanter is seen walking towards the Bayswater Road. Suddenly she yells 'PIP' jumps gives 2 strides and a jump calling the while dot-dash-dash-dot."[7] Guide companies also held public rallies to demonstrate their proficiency in drill and signaling, such as the large Guide review before Queen Alexandra in July 1918 at the Guards' Drill Grounds. So many Guides showed up for this rally that the march past took nearly an hour. Newspaper reports of the display complimented the girls' "discipline" and called them the "anti-thesis of the flapper."[8]

The mention of Guiding as a counteracting influence to flapperdom was a common accolade by the end of the war, and it points to Guiding's ability to walk the line between daring and respectability.[9] In Britain, but also other countries with Guide and Girl Scout movements, girls and women faced a different challenge in establishing themselves than boys. As Mary Aickin Rothschild has noted in her study of U.S. Girl Scouting, "Whereas Girl Scouting combined traditional roles with new roles for women, Boy Scouting stressed only traditional roles for men."[10] This meant that the female organization had a tougher job in mediating the forces pulling it in opposing directions. Guiding sought to provide adventure and meaningful public service while avoiding the labels of "flapper," "hoyden," or "tomboy."[11] The topsy-turvy nature of wartime, with women serving as police, munitions workers, and auxiliary service forces, helped in this project by providing a safe space for girls' war service.

The Guide War Service badge, introduced in May 1915, received a spot of honor on the uniform above the right breast pocket. Other badges were sewn on the right sleeve, and even the big three of early proficiency badges, Ambulance, Child Nurse, and Sick Nurse, belonged on the sleeve, albeit on the left side for emphasis.[12] This special placement for war work helped highlight how important Guides saw their service to country and empire during the 1914–1918 conflict. War service, as indicated in the badge requirements, included more than 60 hours of supervised service at a hospital, Guide hostel, or public department. In addition, Guides had to fabricate socks, mittens, shirts, and other garments for refugees or other war-related organizations. Finally, to earn the badge, Guides had to work "directly for the Government in connection with the war," in farm work, dairy work, market gardening, light machinery for armaments, etc.[13]

Guiding also reached into many areas of public life with individual and company war service. Whole companies of Guides volunteered to entertain convalescing soldiers, to collect waste paper, or to tend war cemeteries. Guides served with Voluntary Aid Detachments as orderlies, and they staffed hostels. They made "comforts" for soldiers and worked with refugees. Guides even worked in some of the most important government offices in the nation, such as the censorship bureau and MI5, the counterespionage bureau. In the case of MI5, Guides replaced Boy Scouts who were deemed too unruly. From September 1915 until the end of hostilities, a Girl Guide company worked daily from 9 A.M. to 7 P.M. as messengers at MI5. All the 14- to 16-year-old girls had to pledge "on their honour not to read the papers they carried," and each received payment for the work. To keep up the Guide side of their activities, the girls paraded every Monday on the roof of MI5 before their captain.[14]

Guides performed messenger work in other civil service offices as well, their uniformed presence helping to publicize the movement further. One sign of this public presence came in 1916 with the film, *Girl Guides at Work*, which showed "the varied forms of work pursued by the sisterhood."[15] The half-hour film played in theatres around Britain. In addition, honor guards composed of uniformed Scouts and Guides became common sights, and Guide visibility thus increased enormously during the war. This was true in other countries as well, with Guide and Girl Scout war service celebrated by the media. In the United States, historian Charles Strickland argued that "there can be little doubt that the international conflict stimulated the interest of Americans in the new organization for girls."[16] In fact, Girl Scouts began their war work in 1914, long before the U.S. entry into the war in April 1917. Like the Guides, they participated in Red Cross drives, knitted garments, and made dressings. They worked in agriculture and helped can and preserve foods.[17] By the time of President Wilson's inauguration in March 1917,

Girl Scouts were even invited to parade with other service organizations, while the Boy Scouts were confined to behind-the-scenes crowd control.[18]

One of the Girl Scouts' most important yet controversial services during wartime was their participation in the Liberty Bond campaigns, selling more than $9 million in bonds, mostly in public venues.[19] Philadelphia Scouts sold nearly $1.36 million in war bonds, while smaller groups around the country sold thousands of dollars worth of bonds.[20] In fact, Girl Scout service in the war bond campaigns led directly to the U.S. Treasury's issuance of a bronze Girl Scout War Service Medal in September 1918.[21] Girl Scout national headquarters sought to publicize these war activities whenever possible, holding public rallies to demonstrate the girls' signaling and marching abilities, trumpeting their patriotism to the nation.[22] Their national magazine, *The Rally*, featured in its first issue in October 1917 a Girl Scout parody song to the tune of "I Didn't Raise my Boy to Be a Soldier" called "Why Don't You Raise Your Girl to be a Girl Scout?" The lyrics clearly demonstrated Girl Scout identification with the war and their place in it: "You needn't think we're afraid of danger/We'll even make fine soldiers if we may/We know there'll be a day, when mothers will say/'I want to raise my girl to be a Girl Scout.'" In summing up the Girl Scouts' war years, historian Susan Miller notes: "In short, the Girl Scouts played soldier, and they did so with expertise and aplomb."[23]

In some areas, Guiding's war service turned more revolutionary. In Poland, the Guide movement that began in 1911 (officially separating from Boy Scouting in 1913) was in a tricky situation, because Poland was partitioned between Austria, Germany, and Russia. In some areas, Guiding was outlawed so it had to operate in secret. Hela Geppnerowna, for instance, lived in the "forbidden" area of Warsaw, so to go to camp in the "free" area, she used a false name for traveling. Guide camps in the free zone were sometimes raided by police looking for girls from German and Russian Poland.[24] As one official history notes, "When the First World War broke out in 1914, contacts between regions became difficult because fighting was taking place on Polish territory, and a special Guide authority was established in Warsaw . . . [and] Polish Guides co-operated actively with all those who worked and fought for the independence of Poland."[25] Olga Malkowska, Polish Guiding's founder, stockpiled arms and ammunition in preparation for an uprising against the partitioning powers. She had to flee when the scheme became public, and she spent much of the war in the United States, Switzerland, and Great Britain.[26]

Her Guides in Poland engaged in dangerous and varied war work as "postmen, couriers, labourers, etc. In the typhoid and cholera hospitals at Cracow all the nurses were Guides, and in Zakopane a crèche for 25 poor children who had lost their parents was entirely run by Guides." Other Guides worked in epidemic hospitals in the besieged town of Przemysl, ran first aid organizations and served time as prisoners of war.[27] Unlike in Poland, where Guiding survived and thrived despite the hardships, in other war zones such as Russia, Hungary and Romania, Guide units that operated pre-1914 disappeared with the war and its aftermath.

In German-occupied Belgium, Guiding was born in the midst of war. A Roman Catholic priest founded a Guide company for girls in one of the roughest, most impoverished workers' quarters in Brussels, the Marolles. The priest, Melchior Verpoorten, hoped that scouting could provide a moral foundation for "girls of the street" and help them "to come into contact with another world" beyond their neighborhood. Father Melchior enlisted the help of women leaders and received public financial support from the Archbishop of Mechelen, Cardinal Mercier, actions which helped establish the new organization. As word spread, other Guide companies sprang up in Brussels and its suburbs. Given the war situation, Guiding faced challenges such as restrictions on travel, inadequate food and clothing supply, and curfews. Melchior himself was imprisoned in June 1917 by the Germans for trying to "prepare Boy Scouts for military life."[28] At the time of his arrest, about 70 Girl Scouts were meeting regularly.[29] Despite the hardships of the occupation, however, the war may have also forced Father Melchior and his early compatriots to include girls in the Scout scheme. Living in the "strongly feminized environment [created] by the absence of men and young men" and with intense pressure not to run uniformed youth movements for boys, girls may have emerged from the shadows. As Sophie Wittemans explains, "The war made him see the potential that young girls and women represented."[30] The war, too, made young girls take more responsibility for themselves and their families in the absence of and restrictions on males. In fact, during Melchior's imprisonment, one of his recruits, 24-year-old Marie-José Furquim d'Almeida, assumed entire responsibility for the troop. Thus, in Belgium, the hardships and displacements of war jump-started Guiding.

Although not living in such harrowing circumstances, Canadian Guides also performed war service, especially by 1917 with the advent of their "Greater Production" project. With permits from government authorities, Guide companies cultivated cereal crops and planted vege-table gardens around the Dominion; their proceeds went to purchase recreation huts for soldiers in France. Many Guide patrols also adopted animals, raising pigs, chickens, and other livestock.[31] Guides knitted socks, rolled bandages, babysat soldiers' children, helped in hospitals, worked in factories, and bought war bonds.[32] In Nova Scotia, Guides found themselves using their first aid skills after the devastating December 1917 explosion of a munitions ship in Halifax harbor that killed more than 2,000 people and wounded thousands more. Guides "went on daily duty for a month at 6:30 A.M. in the Emergency Hospital" and worked in child-ren's wards with disaster victims.[33]

Countries such as Canada, which had established Guide units prior to 1914, saw them spring into action with the war's outbreak, but as in Belgium, the war itself provided a spur to create Guiding companies in other parts of the world. Austria's first organized Guides began meeting in 1915 as an outgrowth of Boy Scouting, with eight or nine companies engaging in voluntary war work among the wounded, refugees, and sol-diers' families.[34] In Jamaica, girls' desire for war service led to the founding of the first company in Spanish Town in 1915 and to enthusiastic war work. The Jamaican Guides drilled, learned Morse and semaphore, and attended first aid lectures. The khaki-wearing Guides of Jamaica soon included both teen girls and young women above the official age limit, all eager to do war work. By 1916, there were six active companies in Kingston alone.[35]

Sometimes within countries Guide companies formed as a result of war work, as with Guides attached to munitions factories or government offices. Such companies met in the evenings after 10 and 11 hours of work in munitions, and these groups tended to include older girls and young women. For instance, the 2nd Hayes Munitions YWCA Company [Britain] had members who ranged in age from 18 to 30.[36] Some of the Guide munitions companies not only worked all day in factories and met for Guide meetings, but they also volunteered their time with the Red Cross and at YMCA canteens.[37] Joan Denny Cooke (later Fryer) organized Guide companies in a factory in Coventry. She remembered sus-picion at first among the girls, who worried Guiding "was out to make them good." Cooke went slowly and as girls were attracted to the games, dancing, drill, and first aid classes, the company grew to four patrols. They spent most every evening after work engaging in Guide activities, and almost all the Guides in the company earned War Service badges for volun-tary war work in their free time.[38]

Special war awards and distinctions for individual Guide service also helped publicize the work of the Guides in Britain and abroad. These awards often featured war heroines or martyrs, as in the case of the Nurse Cavell badge, which was created in 1918. Guides who had demonstrated "special pluck in saving life, self-sacrifice in work for others, endurance of suffering, or calmness in danger" earned this badge, which was named after a British nurse shot in 1915 by the Germans for helping allied soldiers escape occupied Belgium.[39] After the war, Guides participated in the memorial service and funeral procession that accompanied the return of Nurse Edith Cavell's body to Britain, cementing their connection to her legacy. Cavell, who was widely known through British war propaganda, was a perfect choice for a Guide badge because of the public perception of her as a self-sacrificing, patriotic nurturer.[40]

Around the world Guides and Girl Scouts "did their part" to "Be Prepared" for the work the war brought. Guide leaders recognized the valuable public relations they could garner from war service, and they took opportunities wherever possible to remind the public of the service girls' rendered during the conflict. Juliette Low told Americans in 1919 that "the value of Girl Scout training is shown in the war work they accomplished," while in the UK the Girl Guides held a victory rally at Albert Hall in London in 1919 to celebrate their part in the war.[41] In most ways, Guide war work boosted the reputation and public persona of the movement around the world, providing the organization with solid patriotic and service credentials as it moved into the sometimes fraught postwar environment.

One of the unintended consequences of Guide war service was a sense that the organization needed to grow and change with the times. This led to newly professionalized and regulated institutions in most countries with Guide or Girl Scout organizations. Rather than relying on intermittent funding or makeshift camp and training facilities, rather than using borrowed or outdated handbooks and materials, leaders began to institutionalize their methods, rules, and indeed, the organizations' very existences. This led, perhaps unsurprisingly, to clashes among leaders and members over the "spirit" of Guiding. A Guide from Darlington expressed her disappointment with the changes, noting "We felt like pioneers, and there were not all the rules and regulations there are now."[42] Those who had enjoyed the thrill of pioneering and forging the new did not always want to accept the bureaucracy and "red tape" required of large-scale organizations. In short, war spread to Guiding itself as national leaders attempted to channel the burgeoning organization into "proper" and professional lines.

Robert Baden-Powell fired the first shots when he began meeting with the Guide executives frequently in 1914. After attending several meetings, at a September 1914 gathering Baden-Powell laid out plans for changes. In particular, "the general feeling of the meeting was that the movement is at present not making the progress which might have been expected of it; also that the present national crisis affords an opportunity for the exercise of its functions such as is not likely to occur again."[43] With this preface, Baden-Powell suggested reorganization along Boy Scout lines, and by 1916, he had almost completed the imposition of the Scout administrative structure on the Guides. First, the Guides received a formal Charter of Incorporation from the Board of Trade on September 24, 1915, and in 1916, they published both their first annual report (with census) and first *Policy, Organisation and Rules* book. In 1917, Guiding opened its first shop for equipment and literature, and it moved into new headquarters after a 1916 fire forced a change. As the organization developed on paper, it also grew in actual personnel, with a network of county, then divisional commissioners, trained Guiders and trainers. By the 1920s paid personnel would expand beyond the four employees on the payroll during the war. When the armistice came in 1918, Guiding had a membership and organizational presence far exceeding its informal roots nearly a decade earlier.[44]

At the same time that Robert Baden-Powell was working to establish this structure, his young wife, Olave Baden-Powell, began interesting herself actively in the Guides, first as a County Commissioner (March 1916), then as Chief Commissioner (October 1916) and finally as Chief Guide (1918). The small group of elite women that had been running Guiding since its founding seemed outmoded to Olave, and with the help of her husband, she reorganized headquarters and moved Agnes Baden-Powell into a merely honorary role. Olave described in her autobiography the need to replace her sister-in-law:

> She was a very gifted woman and extremely clever but thoroughly Victorian in outlook. She organised a Committee from among her elderly friends . . . [t]hese ladies did their best but they were not really in touch with the younger generation; their ideas were based on the old-fashioned women's organisations. . . . . As the war progressed and women played a greater role in the national effort, it was inevitable that the Girl Guides

should feel a need for a more up-to-date approach. As yet there had been no organisation on a national scale, only sporadic local growth. Robin [Robert Baden-Powell] began to receive letters from all over the country begging him to do something about Guiding. It meant a clean sweep of the Committee.[45]

The "clean sweep" turned out to be quite brutal, with most of the committee dismissed from the movement entirely only to be replaced with younger, active Guiders. Agnes tried to remain a part of the Guide leadership, but Olave and Robert increasingly marginalized her. As late as 1931, the battle still raged, with Robert writing to Girl Scout executives in the United States to "warn them" about Agnes's secret unsanctioned trip to the United States and Canada. He explained that Agnes "with increasing years" had become "prone to desire notoriety," and that he did not want her speaking in any way for the Guides.[46] Eventually, Agnes was barred from Guide functions and dismissed from all official roles. Agnes and her brother and sister-in-law spent the last decades of her life in an uneasy relationship.[47]

As part of her planned transformation of Guiding, Olave also removed the long-time office secretary, Miss Macdonald, and set out to organize the training program.[48] As part of this plan, she authored a small book on Guiding in 1917, *Training Girls as Guides*, which was not designed to replace Agnes' book. Instead, her slim volume served as a manifesto about women's and girls' roles in the war and its presumed aftermath. Writing as war raged in Europe and revolution transformed Russia, Baden-Powell focused on what she saw as the moral and civic dangers of wartime. She wrote not to the girls themselves but to leaders, whom she hoped to recruit to lead girls away from the moral peril facing them. Baden-Powell explained that whether it was drill or home skills, Guiding aimed to teach:

> The spirit of true citizenship in its highest sense with all that it embraces of humanity and the brotherhood of man, a still better thing, and it seems to me to be the essence of what we want to instill into young minds . . . [but] to tell young people that "citizenship is the direction of individual energy for the benefit of the community under the guidance of constituted authority" would be utterly futile.

Such a practice, Baden-Powell opined, would surely result in a group of "vacant little faces." However, "the day the little Guide joins her company and puts on her uniform for the first time this fact wants no explaining—it becomes a delightful and thrilling reality for her..”[49] Guiding offered girls the opportunity to actively embrace citizenship and Scout ideals by wearing their uniforms, living in the patrol system, and learning activities that taught the law and promise. No one need explain these things to girls; instead, they would absorb the lessons through action. This emphasis on active learning-through-doing with young and vigorous Guide leaders to shape the young girls was at the heart of the change Olave envisioned.

With these goals in mind, Olave and Robert replaced the London Girl Guide Officers' Training School (GGOTS nicknamed GOATS) and directly sparked the resignation of Agatha Blyth, its founder and beloved leader. The school, formed in 1915 with Blyth providing her own home as a training space, volunteering her time and bankrolling the whole scheme, was popular with Guiders because they learned by “practising the same rules the children observe.” Organized into patrols, the adult leaders got to revisit their teen years for training and learning, but also just for fun. While Blyth's program was successful, it was an essentially private venture, not under the control of any of the Baden-Powells, and it was insufficient in size to deal with the national aspirations for training that had emerged. Olave and Robert alienated Blyth, leading to her resignation from the movement entirely. The Baden-Powells then created a new Training Department, led by one of Olave's close friends, Alice Baird. Although many in the Guide organization were outraged at what they perceived as callous treatment of Blyth, Agnes Maynard took over the London Training program, and her bonafides as a genuine pioneer of Guiding helped smooth the edges of the conflict. As Edith Moore later reflected in a 1932 letter to Blyth, “perhaps this cruder [vision] was necessary to awaken a popular response.”[50] The transformation undeniably led to a successful Guider training scheme by 1919 that was controlled and shaped by the national headquarters.

As Olave reorganized training and expanded the county leadership structure, her husband authored a new official handbook, *Girl Guiding* (1918), which launched a second phase in Guiding's history. The earlier emphasis on imperial defense and drill began to disappear as the Guide program moved toward training citizen-mothers in a new international environment.[51] The emphasis in Baden-Powell's revised manual was on complementary development; boys and girls trained to be useful citizens in the nation, but in different ways. An explicit family model was at the heart of this picture of training, as Baden-Powell explained in *Girl Guiding*:

> Husbands and wives have been described as the boot and the doormat . . .
> [b]ut there is another side of the picture where a man and woman are pals
> and comrades and that is the right way to look on marriage . . . the true
> intense happiness that comes with the home, the married comradeship,
> and the children. There a woman . . . can be the making or the marring
> of the man. She can be his true GUIDE . . . . For our nation just now, if
> we will look ahead there is need for every soul, man or woman, boy or girl,
> to work.[52]

Robert laid out practical ways for women to be citizen-mothers in the
reconstructed postwar nation, while Olave called for "true womanliness"
to help rebuild the war-torn world and to lessen the opportunity for
social upheaval.[53] As the war ended, Guides created a "New Mother"
that combined badge work in homemaking and mothering skills with
camping, hiking, and international outreach; girls enjoyed the adventure
of the latter but fulfilled societal expectations of women with the
former.[54]

This new approach is readily apparent in two of the popular postwar
badges offered to Guides in the period: Sportswoman (1919) and
Domestic Service (1917). These badges aimed to please both the 1920s
"modern" girl and her parents. The Sportswoman badge required girls
to memorize Henry Newbolt's poem "Vitae Lampada" (1912), with its
rousing call of "Play Up! Play Up! And Play the Game." They also had
to learn two sports (rounders, tennis, cricket, hockey, basketball, or
lacrosse) and show proficiency in tracking, stalking, dispatch running,
flag raiding, and observation.[55] The badge took some of the "war" skills
and combined them with women's sporting endeavors and interwar body
culture to create a new focus for Guide athletics.[56] Meanwhile, the
Domestic Service badge (one of the most popular badges earned in the
interwar period) aimed to make girls "splendidly useful." Appealing to
the new field of home economics and "scientific" household management, the Guide leadership asked girls to see themselves not as servants,
but as "ministers." In the description of the badge for girls in *The Guide*
magazine, girls are told, "We have ministers of Religion, ministers of
State, and why not ministers of the Hearth? . . . to the intelligent girl
who can organise her work well, and who takes an interest in the scientific
aspect of her duties, domestic service will prove very fascinating."[57]

Making housework fascinating was a tall order, but for girls looking for
meaningful work to replace their wartime freedoms, a badge urging them
to be scientists, managers, and ministers in the home was a welcome

addition. To earn the badge, Guides learned to develop housekeeping timetables, proper dusting, sweeping, chimney/stove care, furniture care, and arranging and table design. However, the key to the badge was learning "the spirit of home-making" that would allow Guides to someday "guide" her husband and make his home a welcome haven.[58] Girls did earn this badge as well. Oral history interviews and records from the 1920s suggest that the badge was one of the first earned by girls after their required tests—it became a core of the Guide program in the interwar period.[59]

Beyond changes in organization and badges, Guiding had also expanded its scope during the war by including sections for younger girls, older girls, and girls with special interests or needs. Although younger and older girls had shown interest and sometimes attended Guide meetings, these girls were not officially recognized until the establishment of the junior section in 1914 (first called Rosebuds, later Brownies) and the senior section in 1916 (first called Seniors, then Rangers). By 1920, the age hierarchy had solidified, with the Brownie section for girls under 11, the Guides for girls aged 11 to 16, Rangers for girls over 16, and Guiders (leaders), who were aged 18 and older. Each group had unique uniforms (although Rangers wore the Guide uniform with a different tie), badges, promises, and handbooks; sections were organized around age-specific tasks and games. Figure 2.1, a comparison of Brownie and Guide First-Class status, makes the age structure apparent.

Notice that Guides not only had more difficult tasks than Brownies, but they also had to develop mentoring and leadership skills as part of their First-Class test. Unlike Brownies and Guides, Rangers did not earn additional First-Class badges, but they were able to earn stripes for qualifying or pursuing a profession. They were also expected to perform public service and help run their Guide company.[60]

While the war brought a broader age range in Guiding, it also led to the development of specialized sections of Guiding. For example, school Cadet companies for older girls formed during the war in high schools and universities, and they were designed to help recruit educated women leaders for the Guides. More popular, however, were the Sea Guides (called Sea Rangers after 1927), which developed as a special branch for older girls interested in boating and other sea pursuits. Led by a demobilized "Wren" (from the Women's Reserve Naval Service), Veronica Erskine, the Sea Guides began in 1920. Many women who had served in the WRNS gravitated to the Sea Guides, making it a popular and

Figure 2.1 Requirements for Brownie and Guide First Class (1921)

Brownie First Class	Guide First Class
Know alphabet in Morse or semaphore, and be able to send and read three letters out of four correctly.	Must already have become Second-Class Guide by passing those tests.
Know the first two verses of "God Save the King."	Intelligence:
Know eight points of the compass.	—State briefly the history and aims of the Girl Guides.
Clean knives, forks and spoons.	—Judge height, weight, distance, numbers, and compass directions up to eight points.
Knit a pair of wristlets or muffler.	—Have one shilling in Savings Bank.
Lay and light a fire; make tea and a milk pudding.	—Train recruit to pass her Tenderfoot test.
Fold clothes neatly.	Handcraft:
Carry a message of twelve words in her head for over five minutes and deliver it correctly.	—Hold Cook, Needlewoman, and Child Nurse badges
Apply a triangular bandage.	Health:
Perform the whole five body measurements in the Handbook, and know their objects, or those given on the new Guide Chart of Physical exercises, such as the Brownie may perform herself.	—Perform physical exercises in Second-Class test and instruct Tenderfoot in the same and in the health rules.
	—Must be able to swim fifty yards, or, in **very** exceptional cases, hold the Domestic Service badge, and have a knowledge of *Swimming Self-Taught*.
	Service:
	—Hold the Ambulance or Sick Nurse badge renewed every other year.
	—Have an intimate knowledge of the neighbourhood with a radius of half a mile from her Guide Headquarters and draw at the examination a rough sketch map which would enable a stranger to find his way from any one given point to another, and be able to direct a stranger to the nearest doctor, fire, ambulance, telephone, police or railway station, or post or telegraph office pillar-box, etc. from any point within that district.

Source: Robert Baden-Powell, *Girl Guiding* (London: C. Arthur Pearson, 1921), 41, 128.

media-friendly (if numerically small) branch in the interwar period. One of the most famous Sea Rangers of the interwar period was Princess Elizabeth (later Queen Elizabeth II), who helped popularize and publicize this branch, especially in the lead-up to the Second World War.

The final area where Guiding developed new branches was for girls with special needs. Early in the movement's existence, Lone Guides sprang up for children who lived in remote and inaccessible areas (these were particularly popular in Australia's outback, for example), but it wasn't until 1919 that an official Lone Guide branch developed in Britain. In another newly formed section, girls who were isolated not by distance but by physical disabilities that confined them to home could join Post Guiding by 1921, which provided correspondence courses to help them practice Guiding. For girls in institutions for the deaf or blind, in hospitals, mental asylums, or tuberculosis sanitaria, Extension Guiding was created in 1920. Although deaf and blind companies had been enrolled earlier, as part of Guiding's professionalization, leaders thought a segregated branch would improve services for "handicapped" girls. New literature and alternative tests were developed to adapt the Guide programs for special needs children, and headquarters sponsored camps specifically designed for each disability, such as all-deaf camps.[61]

As the British Guides reorganized, so too did other Guide groups around the world, and the British were by no means the only national organizations facing growing pains during the war and just after it. In the United States, junior and senior Scout sections emerged, training for leaders was instituted, Low authored a new handbook for Scouts during the war, and Scouting was incorporated under U.S. law in 1915. As in Britain, the Scouts reorganized, moving headquarters (to New York City) in 1916 and developing a Board of Directors and a new financial plan.[62] In addition, almost identical battles to those in Britain were waged over bureaucratization, personnel, and program.

For example, Helen Storrow, a wealthy Boston woman who had started a training school for leaders and who had donated land for camping and training, ran an almost military-style leadership training camp, complete with full drill and camping. She participated in the development of a national training scheme in 1917 and served as its first "Commandant." In 1919, Storrow moved the leader courses to Long Pond, the training school she donated to the Girl Scouts. She also served as first National Vice-President of the Girl Scouts.[63] Storrow's contribution to Scouting was voluntary, as she had the leisure and the money, and she felt strongly that volunteers were more devoted to the movement than paid employees. When Lou Henry Hoover, the new Girl Scout President, moved in 1922 to develop a larger staff of paid professionals, especially in training, Storrow resigned. She explained her logic in a letter to a friend: "Scouting inspires great enthusiasm, we all feel it, it appeals to the best there is in us . . . to have a professional person come in to do the work makes it easy, but lessens the feeling of personal responsibility."[64] As in the case of British Guiding, the issue revolved partly around personalities, but more importantly around the kind of future Girl Scouting would have in the United States. Hoover felt that trained, paid professionals would better support the nationally expanding organization and put it on a firm footing. As Sarah Louise Arnold, another Scout leader, noted of the Hoover/Storrow debate: "I believe that both are guided by high purposes; but their line of attack is totally different . . . while Mrs. H. is stating the entire case, and covering the field . . . the Big Scout [Storrow] dashes to the home base, and has time to say what she thinks of the field!"[65] The tragedy of the situation, as Arnold and others noted, was that both Hoover and Storrow had the well-being of the movement at heart, but their visions seemed impossible to reconcile. These struggles over the meaning and spirit of Scouting and Guiding between 1917–1922 were the first major disputes within the movement, but they would not be the last as the century progressed.

Juliette Low, shocked at Storrow's resignation, wrote privately to her goddaughter that while she understood Storrow's objections, she also recognized the need for more paid roles to entice women into the organization. Low, unlike Agnes Baden-Powell, more quietly loosened her hold on the Girl Scout leadership, recognizing that a paid professional staff could achieve great things in conjunction with volunteers. In fact, Low willingly gave up her active position as President in 1920 and refused all other positions except the honorary role as "The Founder." This turned out to be a shrewd move on Low's part. Jane Deeter Rippin, who became National Director in February 1919 and an important driving force behind Girl Scouting for the next decade, had great organizational skills as a former social worker, and under her leadership, the Girl Scouts bureaucratized as the Guides were doing in Britain around the same time. One of her first ambitious goals was to raise $1 million for the organization to get it on a solid financial footing. The drive launched in 1920 brought good public awareness, but less money than planned.[66] While Rippin dealt with the organizational changes, Low continued to work for Girl Scouting for the rest of her life, but in a more behind-the-scenes way. She used her newfound freedom from the day-to-day running of the U.S. organization to spend time shaping the emerging international Guide and Girl Scout groups. It was at her urging and with American money that the Guide international council agreed to meet in the United States in 1926, for instance. Low also focused much of her time in publicizing and promoting Scouting, while fending off external threats to its existence.

That external threats existed, of course, only complicated and raised the stakes in the internal conflict raging. Girl Scouts, engaged in the ongoing battle with the Boy Scouts over the use of the term "scout," also had to contend with the Camp Fire Girls, a competing youth organization for girls. The Girl Scouts assumed an entrenched position and refused to budge under combined pressure from the Baden-Powells, the Boy Scouts of America, and the Camp Fire Girl leadership regarding their use of the word "scout." When Girl Guide leaders in Britain tried to suggest that Scouting was too masculine, Storrow firmly wrote back in 1920:

> Our name, Girl Scouts, is very dear to us, and seems to us the logical name. The terms scout and scouting apply to girls and their activities as appropriately as to boys, and represent the same law and ideals. The idea that we are trying to make boys out of the girls is soon dissipated when the girls show their increased usefulness at home, and demonstrate womanly activities at their rallies . . . I wish most heartily we might share the same name. Would the Guides consider changing? I wish they would.[67]

While insisting on the name Scout, the Girl Scouts did want to retain close relations with Guiding. They also tried to cooperate with other girls' and women's organizations when possible. However, despite repeated "talks" the Girl Scouts refused any amalgamation with the Camp Fire Girls, whose program they viewed as too different, and they vowed to remain Scouts, not Guides. Several historians have traced the conflict between Girl Scouts and Camp Fire Girls, which continued well into the twentieth century.[68]

The Camp Fire Girls (CFG), founded by Luther and Charlotte Gulick in 1911, had as its motto "Woman is the conservator of the home." Its program dressed girls as Indian maidens, and its activities stressed camping and getting close to nature. When the CFG was born, Boy Scout leaders enthusiastically supported it as an "appropriate" outlet for girls interested in learning scout training.[69] When Low began the Girl Scouts, she spoke with CFG leaders about amalgamation, but in reality, each organization wanted the other to disappear. The CFG saw the Scouts as too military and unwomanly, while the Girl Scouts saw the CFG as "sentimental, impractical, and irrelevant." Girl Scout leaders by the end of the war wanted to depict their members as "eager and active" doers in society, which they saw as quite different from what the CFG promoted.[70] The Girl Scouts kept their name and in the process created a precedent for use of either the term "Guide" or "Girl Scout" among girls in the international Guiding community.

All of these debates suggest how far Guiding had come as an organization in just under 10 years. Because the substantial growth of Guiding and Girl Scouting during the war years had provided opportunities for female leaders, recruitment of new faces and ideas had changed the tone of the organization. An important shift occurred in the leadership by the early 1920s that was partly generational and partly due to temperament and interest. The storyline of pioneers leaving the organization and misunderstandings among leaders is repeated multiple times across national boundaries in the interwar period. In describing these shifts in Brazil, a Guide leader wrote: "Unfortunately the Council, owing to a misunderstanding, resigned, and a new one was formed, on which, however, several of the former elements remained . . . . Many of the pioneers had dropped out for one reason or another; some had married, others had left Rio or had take up jobs, and the companies, which had perhaps grown too quickly, collapsed through lack of leaders."[71] The generation who had pioneered Guiding and Scouting, such as Low, Storrow, Agnes Baden-Powell, and Blyth, gave way to a younger crowd in active leadership roles, such as Olave Baden-Powell, Baird, Anne Choate (Low's goddaughter), and Rippin. By no means did women of age and experience disappear from the movement, for their respectability and experience as well as their wealth and connections were significant factors in the ongoing success of Guiding and Girl Scouting. Younger women, however, overwhelmingly assumed paid roles in the organization, which was (and continues to be in some countries) almost entirely staffed by females.

As national organizations solidified and the war ended, Guides and their leaders began looking to make connections with Guides in other countries. Informal letters and visits resumed, and articles started appearing in Guide publications about the movement's growth around the world. Perhaps the most important development, however, came with Olave Baden-Powell's suggestion in February 1919 that an international council convene to discuss the growth of Guiding worldwide. The first of these meetings was held in Oxford in 1920, and thereafter biennial meetings considered international issues facing Guiding. After some years of this operational structure, in 1928 the World Association of Girl Guides and Girl Scouts was formed, with a paid secretariat, a world magazine, and a membership fee structure.[72] What began as a meeting of Guide and Girl Scout leaders from 15 countries to discuss transnational Guiding turned into an organization that today oversees more than 10 million Guides in 144 countries.[73]

In opening the second international council meeting at Newnham College, Cambridge, in 1922, Robert Baden-Powell laid out his hopes for world Guiding: "I ask you to Aim High—to Look Wide. You are an unique sisterhood, wide in extension, deep in thought, high in aspiration."[74] Guiding aimed to transcend narrow nationalist agendas and to create a multinational peaceful sisterhood. These goals differed considerably from those expressed during the movement's founding years, but World War I had helped convince Guide leaders that peaceful internationalism and citizenship were more important than the defensive imperialism of the pre-war period. Guiding's ambitions were grand. In his follow-up speech at the 1924 international conference, Robert Baden-Powell did not mince words about what was necessary:

> The present unsatisfactory conditions in the world are the after effects of the war—that war that was to have ended wars . . . . We civilised peoples with our education and our Churches have little to be proud of in having permitted this reversion to primitive methods of savagery for settling our disputes. The great war was a great disgrace . . . but out of the present ruin a foundation may be constructed on which to build a finer edifice.[75]

Baden-Powell envisioned a world with "civilized" European peoples leading the world to peace, and the early years of the international council reflected this idea. Britain and the United States clearly dominated decision-making about World Guiding for much of its early history. Yet Baden-Powell and other Guide leaders had also caught a glimpse of something beyond the narrow imperial ideal of "civilizing" the world:

> It may seem fantastic to imagine that a few thousand girls spread about the world, as ours are, can do much in producing universal peace and happiness, but if we so train those girls that each one is in herself not merely a well-badged guide but a real apostle of goodwill and service we shall go a

good way in helping to achieve that end . . . . It is only by ever widening and seeing with others' eyes that we can succeed.[76]

While the dream of a truly worldwide and egalitarian sisterhood was far from a reality in Guiding in 1924, the rhetoric became an important recruiting tool for Guiding as it expanded into new countries. In short, combining an older imperial zeal with a burgeoning internationalism that echoed the mission of agencies such as the League of Nations, Guiding used its newly founded World Association to create the largest girls voluntary organization in the world.[77]

By the end of World War I, Guiding and Girl Scouting were international institutions that had gained recognition and respectability among many members of the public. Signs of their newfound respect abounded, especially in Britain. Olave Baden-Powell, for instance, was invited to France in 1918 as part of a group of representatives from women's organizations to investigate charges of "immorality" among the Women's Army Auxiliary Corps. Traveling with Baden-Powell was the former opponent of "Girl Scouting" in the pages of *The Spectator* in 1909, Violet Markham.[78] The inclusion of the Chief Guide and Markham together in an enquiry into respectable conduct for women clearly pointed to the progress Guiding had made since Markham's comments about Guide "unwomanliness" almost a decade earlier. In fact, some of the women involved in supervising female auxiliaries during the war would become high profile members of Guiding, including Dame Helen Gwynne-Vaughan (Women's Army Auxiliary Corps) and Dame Katharine Furse (Women's Royal Naval Service), providing even more of a connection with the female service establishment in Britain.[79]

Yet despite the honors and the reorganization of the war period, Guiding still faced challenges in the years to come about its "womanliness" and respectability. The Guides of Luxembourg even published a pamphlet near the end of the war titled, *What the Guides are NOT*, hoping to dispel persistent rumors. The pamphlet text says a lot about the concerns adults still had about Guiding:

- The Guides are not only a sporting society; we practise various sports, but our main objective is a moral one.
- The Guides are not a movement turning girls away from their religion.
- The Guides are not a military movement . . . but are essentially a democratic movement.

- The Captains are not officers, but comrades and older sisters.
- The Guides are not girls playing at being boys; we aim at developing the finest qualities of womanhood, self-sacrifice, courtesy, helpfulness, etc.[80]

Guiding spent the interwar years battling internally and externally over many of the same issues raised in this pamphlet, demonstrating how far Guiding still had to go to achieve widespread acceptance.

Growth, consolidation, and bureaucratization during and just after the war had made Guiding into a solid organization by its tenth anniversary in 1920. Yet as it expanded to more diverse populations in countries around the world, the disputes over the "spirit" of Guiding grew increasingly complex. Issues of religious and racial inclusiveness, class prejudice, and appropriate sexuality in the movements tore at the notion of international sisterhood, while official and unofficial threats from politicized youth movements on the left and right challenged the nonpolitical claims that Guiding made. The war may have shaped the Guides into the lasting organization that it has proved to be, but 1918 did not mark the end of the disputes and challenges that Guiding faced as it moved into an uncertain future of economic hardship and polarizing politics.

NOTES

1. There existed a number of German youth movements before the war, some coeducational and some single-sex, many of whom were poorly organized. This group of German girls probably made contact with the British Girl Guides and called themselves "girl guides" in English to establish a connection for their visit. For information on the variety of youth organizations for girls in Germany, see Marion E. P. de Ras, *Body, Femininity and Nationalism: Girls in the German Youth Movement 1900–1934* (London: Routledge, 2008).

2. *Times* articles dated April 2, 1914, April 6, 1914, and April 10, 1914; Rose Kerr, comp., *The Story of a Million Girls: Guiding and Girl Scouting Round the World* (London: Girl Guides Association, 1937), 17–18. It is important to note that Rose Kerr only authored some of the sections in this book; most of the entries come from anonymous Guide leaders and are based on local archives.

3. Early Guide census figures are rough prior to 1916, but 8,000 "official" Guides were transferred from Boy Scout headquarters in 1911, and newspaper reports cite 10,000 Guides in 1914. After 1916, Girl Guide headquarters kept accurate official census figures. Girl Scout figures come from *Highlights in Girl Scouting, 1912–2001* (New York: Girl Scouts of the USA, 2002), 6–8.

4. Dorothy Scannell, *Mother Knew Best: Memoir of a London Girlhood* (USA: Pantheon, 1974), 56.

5. Kerr, *The Story of a Million Girls*, 18.

6. Cicely Stewart-Smith, "The Log of a Loafer in the Guides," 1923–25, GGL.

7. Stewart-Smith, "The Log of a Loafer in the Guides", GGL.

8. "Girl Guides Rally," *Times* (July 22, 1918); "Flappers Fall In," *Daily Mirror* (July 15, 1918).

9. Tammy Proctor, *On My Honour: Guides and Scouts in Interwar Britain* (Philadelphia: American Philosophical Society, 2002), 70–73.

10. Mary Aickin Rothschild, "To Scout or To Guide? The Girl Scout–Boy Scout Controversy, 1912–1941," *Frontiers: A Journal of Women Studies* 6:3 (Autumn 1981), 120.

11. For interesting work on the flapper controversy, see Richard Voeltz, "The Antidote to 'Khaki Fever'? The Expansion of the British Girl Guides during the First World War," *Journal of Contemporary History* 27 (1992), 631.

12. Robert Baden-Powell, *Girl Guiding* (London: C. Arthur Pearson, 1921), 162.

13. *Girl Guides Gazette* 2:17 (May 1915).

14. Tammy M. Proctor, *Female Intelligence: Women and Espionage in the First World War* (New York: New York University Press, 2003), 58–60.

15. Voeltz, "The Antidote to 'Khaki Fever'?" 631.

16. Charles Strickland, "Juliette Low, the Girl Scouts and the Role of American Women," in *Woman's Being, Woman's Place: Female Identity and Vocation in American History*, ed. Mary Kelley (Boston: G. K. Hall & Co., 1979), 258.

17. Juliette Low, "Girl Scouts as an Educational Force," *Department of the Interior Bureau of Education Bulletin* 33 (1919), 7.

18. Laureen Ann Tedesco, "A Nostalgia for Home: Daring and Domesticity in Girl Scouting and Girls' Fiction, 1913–1933" (PhD diss., Texas A&M University, 1999), 46.

19. Laureen Tedesco, "Making a Girl into a Scout: Americanizing Scouting for Girls," in *Delinquents and Debutantes: Twentieth-Century American Girls' Cultures*, ed. Sherrie A. Inness (New York: New York University Press, 1998), 25.

20. Susan A. Miller, *Growing Girls: The Natural Origins of Girls' Organizations in America* (New Brunswick: Rutgers University Press, 2007), 56–60.

21. Mary Degenhardt and Judith Kirsch, *Girl Scout Collector's Guide: A History of Uniforms, Insignia, Publications, and Memorabilia*, 2nd Edition (Lubbock: Texas Tech University Press, 2005), 52–53.

22. Leslie Hahner, "Practical Patriotism: Camp Fire Girls, Girl Scouts, and Americanization," in *Communication and Critical/Cultural Studies* 5:2 (June 2008), 126.

23. Miller, *Growing Girls*, 79–81.

24. Kerr, *The Story of a Million Girls*, 132, 138.

25. *Trefoil Round the World* (London: WAGGGS, 2003), 252–253.

26. "Olga Drahonowska Malkowska, 1888–1979," Information Sheet, Poland box, GGL.

27. *Girl Guides Gazette* 6:72 (December 1919) and 7:79 (July 1920).

28. Geneviève Iweins d'Eeckhoutte, "De l'oeuvre aux fédérations le guidisme catholique en Belgique, 1915–1960: Chronique d'un mouvement," in *Guidisme, scoutisme, et coéducation: Pour une histoire de la mixité dans les mouvements de jeunesse*, eds. Thierry Scaillet, Sophie Wittemans and Françoise Rosart (Louvain-la-Neuve: Bruylant-Academia, 2007), 213–217.

29. "Belgian Girl Scouts," *New York Times* (March 14, 1920).

30. Sophie Wittemans, "Les conditions d'émergence d'un mouvement Guide unisexe puis coéduqué en Belgique: Analyse épistémique," in *Guidisme, scoutisme, et coéducation*, 43–48, 61.

31. Anne Gloin, *Like Measles, It's Catching!* (Toronto: Girl Guides of Canada, 1974), 20–21.

32. Dorothy Crocker, *All About Us: A Story of the Girl Guides in Canada, 1910–1989* (Ottawa: Girl Guides of Canada, 1990), 9.

33. Kerr, *The Story of A Million Girls*, 33.

34. Kerr, *The Story of A Million Girls*, 230.

35. TS Chronology and Daisy Jeffery-Smith, "When Girl Guides Wore Khaki," *Daily Gleaner* (September 25, 1955), Jamaica box, GGL.

36. "An Album of Thoughts and Doings" presented to Miss Helen Malcolm, October 1918, GGL.

37. Gloucestershire Girl Guides Log Book, 1919, GGL. The munitions companies included the 2nd Gloucester and the 4th Gloucester.

38. Rose Kerr, *The Story of the Girl Guides* (London: Girl Guides Association, 1940), 139–142.

39. Robert Baden-Powell, *Girl Guiding*, 162.

40. Katie Pickles, "Edith Cavell—Heroine, No Hatred or Bitterness for Anyone?" *History Now* 3:2 (1997), 1–8; Proctor, *Female Intelligence*, 100–106.

41. Low, "Girl Scouts as an Educational Force," 6; Girl Guide Victory Rally Programme (November 4, 1919), Headquarters Record Book (1919–1924), GGL.

42. Florrie Coapes to Rose Kerr (January 24, 1931); Early Days of Guiding box, GGL. Coapes had been Captain of the 1st Darlington Company since 1910.

43. Minutes of Meeting (September 29, 1914); History—Girl Guides (Organisation), GGL.

44. Kerr, *The Story of the Girl Guides*, 122–135.

45. Olave Baden-Powell [as told to Mary Drewery], *Window on my Heart* (London: Hodder and Stoughton, 1973), 108.

46. Robert Baden-Powell to Mrs. Frederick Edey (September 23, 1931); Girl Guiding box, GSUSA.

47. Tim Jeal, *The Boy-Man: The Life of Lord Baden-Powell* (New York: William Morrow and Company, 1990), 471–477.

48. Jeal, *The Boy-Man*, 476–477.

49. Olave Baden-Powell, *Training Girls as Guides* (London: C. Arthur Pearson, 1917), 66.

50. Proctor, *On My Honour*, 110–112.

51. Proctor, *On My Honour*, 108–110; Allen Warren, "Mothers for the Empire," in *Making Imperial Mentalities: Socialisation and British Imperialism*, ed. J. A. Mangan (Manchester: Manchester University Press, 1990), 104–106.

52. Robert Baden-Powell, *Girl Guiding*, 175–176.

53. Proctor, *On My Honour*, 109.

54. Proctor, *On My Honour*, 74.

55. *Policy, Rules and Organisation* (London: Girl Guides Association, 1919), 64.

56. On the explosion of "keep fit" and body culture in interwar Britain, see Jill Julius Matthews, "They had Such a Lot of Fun: The Women's League of Health and Beauty Between the Wars," *History Workshop Journal* 30 (Autumn 1990), 22–54.

57. "Domestic Service Badge," *The Guide* (September 24, 1921), 365.

58. *The Guide* ran a whole series of articles on the Domestic Service badge in 1921. Issues include: 1:23 (September 24 1921), 365; 1:25 (October 8, 1921), 389; 1:26 (October 15, 1921), 415; 1:28 (October 29, 1921), 439; 1:30 (November 12, 1921), 469; 1:32 (November 26, 1921), 505.

59. Proctor, *On My Honour*, 76.

60. R. Baden-Powell, *Girl Guiding*, 179–180.

61. Kerr, *The Story of Girl Guiding*, 154–165, 214–217; Doreen E. Woodford, *Seventy-Five Remarkable Years: A Record of Deaf People and the Girl Guide Movement 1910–1985* (Feltham, UK: British Deaf Society Publications, 2005), 1, 6, 39.

62. *Highlights in Girl Scouting, 1912–2001*, 6–8.

63. Obituaries and tributes to Helen Storrow; Personalities folder (Helen Osborne Storrow biographical data), GSUSA; *Highlights in Girl Scouting, 1912–2001*, 9.

64. Helen Storrow to Genevieve Brady (September 1922), Personalities folder (Helen Osborne Storrow Correspondence), GSUSA.

65. Sarah Louise Arnold to Ann Choate (1922), Personalities folder (Helen Osborne Storrow Correspondence), GSUSA.

66. Tedesco, "A Nostalgia for Home," 61–62; "Girl Scouts to Parade," *New York Times* (November 5, 1920).

67. As quoted in Tammy Proctor, "Scouts, Guides, and the Fashioning of Empire, 1919–39," in *Fashioning the Body Politic: Dress, Gender, Citizenship*, ed. Wendy Parkins (Oxford: Berg, 2002), 133.

68. See Miller, *Growing Girls*, and Tedesco, "A Nostalgia for Home," in particular.

69. Miller, *Growing Girls*, 14–20, 26–28.

70. Tedesco, "A Nostalgia for Home," 59.

71. Kerr, *The Story of a Million Girls*, 317–318.

72. Proctor, "Scouts, Guides, and the Fashioning of Empire," 128.

73. *Trefoil Round the World* (London: WAGGGS, 2003), v.

74. Kerr, *The Story of a Million Girls*, 378.

75. Robert Baden-Powell, "Address to the International Girl Guide Conference by the Founder" (1924), TC/39 Articles by the Founder (Girl Guides), SAGP.

76. Robert Baden-Powell, "Address to the International Girl Guide Conference by the Founder."

77. Proctor, "Scouts, Guides and the Fashioning of Empire," 131.

78. O. Baden-Powell, *Window on my Heart*, 115–116.

79. Jeal, *The Boy-Man*, 479–480.

80. Kerr, *The Story of a Million Girls*, 290.

3. Controversies

The 1921 letter began "Dear Lady Baden-Powell," before the 11-year-old author launched into the profound problem facing her. "Please may I be enrolled as a Lone Guide?," Katharine Rathbone queried. "I can make up beds and take care of babies, and set tables and all that sort of thing," she continued. The problem, however, was that Rathbone's family was moving from Jamaica to New York in the fall, and she was worried about becoming a Girl Scout rather than a Guide. She was concerned that "if I became an American Girl Scout I would have to pledge allegiance to the American flag, and that wouldn't be honourable if I love England best." The Chief Guide responded to Rathbone's dilemma by writing to the Girl Scout executive, Jane Deeter Rippin, asking her to take an interest in the case, but she also wrote directly to Rathbone:

> I think that it would be quite possible for you to join a Girl Scout Company there, have all the joy of doing the practical work, having the games and activities and all, and that the captain of any company that you joined would be quite ready for you to make a special seperate [*sic*] promise to the others if you wanted . . . you could quite well have a Union Jack couldn't you and make your promise to be loyal to King George even if you do happen to be living in America.[1]

Baden-Powell's answer to Rathbone demonstrated clearly some of the solutions that Guiding developed in the interwar period to the problem of diversity—whether it was nationality, race, religion, or class. As Baden-Powell explained to Rathbone, Guiding had increasingly embraced accommodation as a policy in the movement, allowing tinkering with uniforms, promises, activities, and organization in order better to grow in a diverse society. Guiding sought to negotiate the precarious rocks of the postwar world by expanding with care and flexibility. While this policy often foundered on racial hatred, class or caste divisions, ultranationalism, or religious discord, Guiding's flexible accommodationist approach was partly responsible for its success in a divided world.

With the international expansion and consolidation of the 1920s, Scout and Guide leaders sought to prove that the "fundamental needs of young people are much the same all over the world."[2] To realize these goals within international Guiding, leaders realized that they would have to be willing to address difference in a meaningful way in order to avoid the potential problems that they would face. The movements had some success in their development of schemes that could be adapted to meet the needs of different countries, but the issues of religion, race, and gender remained obstacles throughout the interwar period. Echoing a move in Britain to define who was really "British," Guides and Scouts in the interwar period could reconcile their conceptions of exclusion with their stated policies by erecting boundaries within countries. Girls could scout, but in different uniforms and with an independent organization. Non-whites could be Guides, but in separate divisions. Catholics could be Guides, but in restricted companies. Modifications and accommodations determined the character of Guide companies around the world.[3] Some of these modifications were small—rather than using patrol names that were flowers (as did British Guides), girls in Peru used Inca names and in Mexico, they relied on Aztec history for patrol nomenclature. Climate could also determine the need for accommodation, so Guides in Burma wore long wrap skirts with lightweight muslin jackets. They also eschewed hats for plaited hair slicked with coconut oil and arranged carefully with a flower (patrol emblem) tucked behind their ears.[4] These accommodations were easy compared to some of the more difficult and politicized questions that arose, creating the need for compromise.

One of the first and most lasting of these compromises came over the name Girl Scout. With U.S. Girl Scouts determinedly hanging onto their name, it was inevitable that this dispute would spill over into the international setting. Because Guiding had developed in multiple ways around the world, sometimes through the acquisition of *Scouting for Boys*, sometimes with the appearance of an English Girl Guide in a new country, sometimes with schoolteachers or missionaries who sought a coherent youth program, its naming practices were diverse. In France, for instance, Protestant Guides called themselves "éclaireuses" as the female version of the boy "éclaireurs," but the Catholic girls took the name "guides" to mirror the Catholic boys' "scouts" name. As in the United States, some girls in non-British settings chose to be Girl Scouts rather than Guides, often because of the different connotations of the terms in foreign languages. With Britain and the United States at odds over the naming issue, the two largest national movements often competed to "assist" new countries interested in the movement. For example, in February 1919, Olave

Baden-Powell wrote to Percy Everett advising him that they needed to send representatives to Brazil to help start Guiding, stating: "It is rather important that we should get there and start up real Girl Guides before the Americans start forming Girl Scouts."[5] Likewise, when Guiding moved into Siam in 1921, a flurry of correspondence between New York and London centered on whether British Guiding or American Scouting should be the model allowed. The Chief Guide again tried to explain Guide headquarters' position:

> It is not the name IN AMERICA that matters, but the misinterpretation that is ALWAYS put upon it in other countries. It so obviously shows that it is to all intents and purposes the same thing for the girls as "scouting" is for boys . . . . We have to reckon, in promoting this quite modern and Western idea, with Caste, Creeds of all kinds, Climate, Languages, Customs, Racial feelings and National feelings, as well as Politics and it really is most important that where it is being pushed it must be done by the right people in the right way![6]

While Baden-Powell's comments were bound to infuriate U.S. Girl Scout leaders with her reference to the "right people," she had described in detail the scope of the problem with international Guiding. Given all the obstacles she listed, however, both countries eventually realized that their competition over control of name was not helping international growth, so with the advent of the World Association of Girl Guides and Girl Scouts (WAGGGS) in 1928, a compromise was reached that allowed coexistence of the two names.

While this diversity of naming became an acceptable part of Guide international policy in the 1920s, it did not happen without protest, especially from the Boy Scout International Bureau. In a letter to Robert Baden-Powell in 1926, Boy Scout International Bureau Chief Hubert Martin reiterated his office's opposition to girls calling themselves "scout" or "éclaireuse." Martin explained to Baden-Powell that men were made to "scout" and women to "guide," and the modern girl's neglect of her own sphere was in need of correcting—but through Guiding, not by "ap[ing] men" in the Scouts. He finished by saying "It seems to me that the use of the term 'Girl Scout' is a big question of principle and that the persistence of its use is symptomatic of the tom-boy, aping the man, instead of concentrating on woman's most important sphere—the home."[7] Martin's concerns focus on two elements that Guiding combated in the interwar period—that it was creating women who "aped" men and that it was poaching on male territory. The second objection was fairly easy for Guiding to ignore, since their programs clearly differed from that of the boys and their uniforms also separated them from Boy Scouts. The first concern about tomboys or unwomanly women was a trickier situation for Guiding, partly because they were indeed allowing girls to be tomboys and to do the exciting things often reserved for boys. Girls liked Guiding and Girl Scouting precisely because it offered them a measure of freedom and adventure and "boyishness," while also teaching womanly activities.

At camps, the real boy spirit was unleashed as girls imagined themselves in the roles of pioneers—usually male pioneers. Camp was a fantasy world where conventions disappeared and girls escaped their mundane homes, schools, or jobs.[8] From the first camps in 1910, girls experienced a delicious sense of freedom, even if it was hard to bear the rain and bell tents. Descriptions from log books and oral histories emphasize the fun of "mud pools," midnight feasts, and camp tests. Some remember feeling "tough" after overcoming some hardship at camp.

Camping allowed girls to experience an imagined past, and as Susan Miller has argued about the United States, camp became "a stand-in for the frontier."[9] Frontiers took all kinds of forms, some of them the pioneer American past or the edges of the British Empire, some of them the fictional frontiers of Edwardian authors. For example, patrol leader Marguerite de Beaumont wrote a logbook for her tent at Houghton Camp in August 1920. The tent was dubbed "Never Never Land" and the girls inhabiting it were "Pirates." De Beaumont became Peter Pan, and the other five in her patrol took the roles of the crocodile, Captain Hook, Starkie, Tinker Bell and Smee. Significantly, none of the Guides took the role of Wendy, the little girl who became the surrogate mother in Barrie's story, rather they became boys and pirates and fantasy creatures.[10]

Single-sex camps allowed girls to have fun by taking control of their environments and by being self-sufficient, whether they were pitching tents and digging latrines in Britain or constructing their own wooden-sided, canvas-topped structures in Czechoslovakia.[11] Camping, at the center of the Guide program in many countries after World War I, differed dramatically from country to country because of natural and social climate, but in all cases it provided an adventure away from home for girls. Camp reports often emphasized the glorious feeling of being really dirty after sleeping "rough" or the way food tasted better outdoors or the hardships overcome by sheer determination. Girls faced more control of their behavior and sexuality than boys, and the home served to reign in young women; therefore camp felt like an opportunity to move outside the bonds that society used to police gender roles.[12] Guides talked and wrote about camp as an initiation into something new, and even those who hated camping recognized its value in teaching self-sufficiency. Betty Prance, who joined Guiding in 1928 in southeast London, tried to explain the attraction of camping, and of Guiding generally:

> [Camp] was smashing. In bell tents, 6 to a tent and all legs to the middle. We went on the back of a lorry with kit bags . . . when I got home, my mother said "I never saw you so dirty in my life!" . . . I think [Guiding] sort of followed the Scouts. They wanted to, you know, be after the origins of the Scout movement with Baden-Powell and that. I think after the First World War there were so many women who wanted to do something similar to what the Scouts had done.[13]

As Prance explained, Guiding *was* "aping" Scouting, but that was the point. Guide camps ran like Scout camps, and they sparked the same kinds of excitement for girls that boys discovered with Baden-Powell's program for them.

Girl Scouts in the United States reported similar feelings of excitement and self-reliance, as camping became increasingly important to their program after the First World War. While much U.S. camping took place in permanent camps owned by the organization rather than in farmer's fields as in Britain, the girls still felt a delicious sense of danger and excitement. Gean Morgan, a Girl Scout in Nashville, Tennessee, told a historian that she remembered carrying a mess kit and wearing her uniform "like a soldier" at the Georgia camp she attended between 1927 and 1931. She recalled being given a "bucket of water and one match" and then told "call me when the water is boiling." Morgan believed that such experiences as these as well as other parts of Girl Scout training made her self-sufficient and helped her "advance in the world and make something of [herself]."[14] Given her five years of camping memories, Morgan may well have agreed with Cicely Stewart-Smith, a British Guide, who wrote, "If I were given the choice of week at camp or a week at a Country House party, I should choose camp. I don't know why but I would and that's that."[15] Camp mattered to girls in the movement, and it created some of their most lasting memories.

Camp was not just exciting for girls, but for adults as well. If girls learned self-sufficiency, so did the women in charge of watching those girls. Female leaders had to deal with storms, floods, local hooligans, and unruly teenaged girls at camps, but they also had the chance to spend time with other women and girls in a supportive environment. When they attended adult training camps, they experienced many of the same thrills as the girls and the intoxicating sense of freedom from conventions. Logbooks from the Foxlease training center in the United Kingdom demonstrated these feelings in their descriptions of adult females at camp: "We all returned to our second childhood and became Brownies. A perfectly delightful trail, haunted by dragons and gnomes, was laid . . . afterwards we played a thrilling game in which Boggarts pounced out upon unwary Brownies and hauled them off to deep dark dungeons if they could not answer a question."[16] The freedom of camp was intoxicating for girls and grown women alike.

The same-sex bonding of Guiding, again especially at camp, was an important emotional connection for girls and women, and it helped forge not only close female friendships but also self-reliance in an age when women were taught to depend on men. Many former Guides and Girl Scouts counted "companionship" and "friendship" among the most valuable aspects of the movement, and girls found themselves remaining in Guiding well into their adult years so as to retain those connections. Some Rangers (the older Guide branch) in the interwar period remained active in their companies into their thirties and forties, but this caused conflict since some thought Guiding was for girls, not grown women. In a debate about the upper age for Rangers at the world conference in 1934, one French leader summarized the difficulty: "I quite see the point of people of forty getting something through the Rangers, but what about the poor people of eighteen being with those children of forty. It is rather bad for them."[17] Guiding eventually created in 1943 an organization for women over 21 who wanted to retain their Guiding ties but who could not lead companies, the Trefoil Guild. Other countries formed similar associations for "old Guides."[18] The long interest of some women in retaining their Guiding ties is apparent in the fact that many Ranger and Guide companies held frequent reunions; multiple units from the 1920s were still meeting monthly or annually in the 1990s!

Leaders did not want to deny this aspect of Guiding for older women, nor did they want to dismiss enthusiastic leaders who had embraced "unwomanly" lifestyles by choosing not to marry or to make their lives with other women. While Rangers often socialized with Rovers (senior Boy Scouts) and married them, it was not uncommon for leaders or older Rangers to develop relationships with other women in the movement.

Some of the most important Guide leaders of the first part of the twentieth century shared homes and work with other women, while others remained single and lived alone. In both cases, Guide leadership worried that the public might see these examples as undermining the citizen mother training that Guides aspired to give to girls. Yet for women seeking independence or alternatives to heterosexual marriage, Guiding was undeniably attractive and their participation helped it succeed as an organization by pouring energy, money, and time into the movement as leaders, trainers, and administrators. For example, at an imperial camp for Guide leaders at Foxlease in 1926, out of almost 300 women present, 84 percent of them were unmarried. Of the 46 married women at the camp, including Lady Baden-Powell, most held positions as commissioners, rather than as grass-roots Guide captains.[19]

Among Guiding's earliest leaders were several women who remained single, married late in life, were divorced or widowed at a young age, or spent their lives with other women. For these women, Guiding provided a supportive and meaningful community of women as well as a direction for their energies. Juliette Low, widowed in 1905 (just before a planned divorce), poured much of her fortune into Girl Scouting and most of her free time until her death. Katharine Furse, director of WAGGGS, had been widowed as well in 1904, after only four years of marriage. Likewise, Helen Gwynne-Vaughan's husband died four years into their marriage. Alice Behrens, the first Guider-in-Charge at Foxlease, worked tirelessly for the movement until her marriage late in her thirties to Scout leader, Arthur Gaddum. Unmarried "Monty" Montgomery served as Guide secretary from 1920 to 1935. Ida "Falk" von Herrenschwand ran the Guide training center "Our Chalet" for 20 years, and her replacement, "Pen" Wood-Hill, was also single.[20] All of these independent women saw Guiding as an outlet for their ambitions and interests.

Guiding also created a safe refuge for many lesbian women or women who had long-term "loving friendships" with women. Lady Helen Whitaker and Ann Kindersley were "constant companions" and both held important roles in the Guide executive, while Mrs. Walter Roch and Miss Clementina "Kit" Anstruther Thomson also developed a close relationship. Anstruther Thomson (1857–1921) was particularly significant in the Guide world, as an organizer, County Commissioner and trainer until her death in 1921.[21] Marguerite de Beaumont, who wrote a biography of Robert Baden-Powell, bought a home and horse farm in 1934 with Doris Mason, a fellow Guider and Boy Scout volunteer. The two women gave copious amounts of time and energy to the Girl Guide and Boy Scout movements while running their equine business and developing a network of close female friendships over their Guiding years.[22]

In an interview in 1993, Lady Marjorie Stopford and Miss Florence Cobb discussed Guiding and their life together, and their experiences provide an interesting window into the way Guiding helped them feel a sense of shared purpose. The two met through their Guiding activities in the 1930s in Hertfordshire, where both were Guiders. Marjorie (1904–1996), the daughter of the 6th Earl of Courtown, had joined Guiding in Ireland as a Lone Guide just after World War I, and Cobbie (1910–2003), who later became a schoolteacher, had become a Guide in 1920. Both women served as Guide captains and in a variety of active capacities for the movement well into the 1970s, and they were still active members of the Trefoil Guild in the 1990s. Marjorie even served on a Guide team to rehabilitate devastated war zones in Greece and Egypt in the 1940s (which Cobbie described as a terribly lonely period for her at home). Marjorie and Cobbie shared a house Marjorie inherited in Bushey Heath (Hertsfordshire) for almost 60 years until Marjorie's death in 1996, and for the two women, Guiding provided a focus for their energies. Guiding allowed the two to travel the world, meet interesting people, and help teach young women self-sufficiency. As Cobbie starkly stated, "I don't know what I would have done if I hadn't been in Guiding," and Marjorie simply added, "Agreed."[23]

The kind of devotion and energy that women such as Cobbie and Marjorie put into Guiding helped the movement succeed over the course of the twentieth century. Yet women such as these two put Guiding into a precarious position of explaining how it was that single women, especially those involved in relationships with other women, could teach girls to be useful wives and mothers for the nation. Given the anxieties about girls' possible rejection of marriage and motherhood following World War I, Guiding needed to explain its ability to inculcate both modern career girls and mothers for the nation.[24] Often in practice this meant that handbooks and other publications, especially articles in newspapers and popular magazines, overemphasized the domestic training of girls in Guiding. Olave Baden-Powell, for instance, wrote an article for *Home Chat* magazine in 1930 titled "A Successful Wife." In it, she explained that at first she could not help her husband with Scouting and Guiding much because "I had my babies to bring up." This was interesting, given that her involvement in Guiding began even before their third child was born!

But Baden-Powell was trying to make a public point about Guiding's ambitions to create wives who knew their place, and she emphasized it in her final comments in the article, by noting that her Guide work taught her that "the woman who learns to help her husband really does succeed in helping herself."[25]

Olave Baden-Powell was not the only Guide leader emphasizing Guiding's ability to train wives and citizen-mothers. In an article in the *Manchester Guardian* in 1932, the author listed all the reasons "Why Girl Guides Make the Best Wives," while a 1924 *Yorkshire Observer* piece explained why girls can be "sporty" and "modern" while "not neglecting home." In these articles and many others, Guiding was depicted as an organization that made "real women." These messages about girls' home duties showed up within the movement's publicity as well, but with a counterbalancing sentiment that "we have no right to let a girl think that to be a good wife and mother is the sole aim of women's existence . . . we are not out just to train good women—but good women citizens." This speech at the 1920 international conference was given by Mrs. Walter Roch and followed a speech by Lady Clinton that emphasized that "Woman has the strongest influence from the cradle upwards."[26] The two messages summarized the Guide strategy in the interwar years of combining citizenship and motherhood.

This mixture of citizenship, motherhood, and action marked the Guide movement profoundly in the interwar years, and the reality of the Guide movement on the ground was a great diversity of activities and training. Some companies drilled and signaled as an important part of their weekly routine, others went on cinema outings and practiced sewing, still others focused on camping and nature study. The decentralized nature of Guiding in Britain, and eventually in many parts of the world, gave great latitude and flexibility to individual captains, thereby sanctioning a diversity of experiences for girls. There were companies that focused primarily on domestic skills, but there were also company logbooks that demonstrated that some leaders spent little time teaching home skills. This does not mean that Guide headquarters did not try to maintain a focused program—trainings, camps, publications, and frequent visits/interactions helped to do just that.

The question of motherhood training was not just one of general morality, character building or even societal order, but it touched significantly on the question of religious belief as well. In fact, next to the issue of appropriate female behavior, religion became one of the primary debates for Guiding in the interwar years. From the beginning, parents had questioned the movement's stance on religion, especially the odd mix of nature reverence, general devotion to God and personal faith, but as the movement broadened its base and extended its membership beyond Judeo-Christian religious groups, these questions intensified. For instance, in Muslim companies, girls asked for the right to adapt their uniforms to make them more modest, in keeping with religious teachings about girls' clothing. In the British colony of Malaya, Guide Ibu Zain designed a modified khaki uniform that covered arms and legs, which helped make Guiding acceptable to girls and their parents. By the 1930s, Malaya had a thriving association, which was essentially nonsectarian and multiethnic, despite uniform accommodations for some girls.[27]

Beyond even this big question of world religious accommodation, however, splits developed within religions regarding the "spiritual question" in Guiding. These had to be addressed in order for Guiding to move forward. Countries around the world dealt with these splits, debates, and questions in different ways, but primarily there were two responses—separate sections or movements, and mixed sections with flexible rules. These solutions allowed Guiding to leap over religious hurdles in its path, but it also raised uncomfortable questions about the limits of uniformity, program, and sisterhood.

Debates over religion took on a variety of forms, but one of the most difficult to deal with was the fundamental problem that some leaders had with the nondenominational and vague religious affiliation of Guiding itself. In the Netherlands, for instance, Guides in the 1920s were given the choice of making their promise to God or of making a "neutral" promise that omitted mention of God.[28] Similarly in the United States, the executive council under the leadership of Edith Macy tried to emphasize Girl Scouting's "nonsectarian character" by giving positions on the Board to "women of different religious beliefs and different political allegiances."[29] British Guiding too had registered Roman Catholic, Jewish, and Protestant Guide companies in its first years, allowing "God" to be defined by individual girls when each made her promise.

Among more evangelical Christian groups, the lack of a clear Christian program made Guiding suspect. One of the solutions to this problem was to create separate "closed" sections of Christian Guides, often with similar program, uniform and badges, but with explicit promises to serve God. In Scandinavia, the development of such closed sections was particularly prevalent, with YWCA Guides, Salvation Army Guides, and specific Protestant sections (Baptist, Mission Covenant, etc.). Sweden even had a separate temperance section for Guides and Scouts. These entities usually met separately, but cooperated with other national Guide sections and worked together in federation in order to meet the requirements of world membership. For instance, in Sweden, there were five national organizations by the interwar period—Guides (founded 1912), Salvation Army Guides (founded 1916), YWCA Guides (founded 1921), Temperance Guides (founded 1927) and Mission Covenant Guides (founded 1931).[30] So in the Swedish case, the way to deal with multiple agendas for Guiding was to create multiple organizations.

Like Sweden, many countries dealt with religious and ideological divisions in the interwar period by creating multiple associations, and today those fractures in the movement remain. France serves as a useful example of the challenges of maintaining multiple organizations in one country. In the 1920s, when French Guiding solidified and developed, it reflected the multiconfessional nature of French society at the time. Historian Marie-Thérèse Cheroutre described the process Guiding went through in the interwar, as it "took the form of many autonomous associations but federated."[31] Federation, however, was never easy, and many agreements broke down when it came to creating an umbrella organization that all could except. Today the World Association recognizes five official organizations in France, and there are a further four organizations that are not recognized outside of French borders. The "official movements" are all segregated along religious lines, with the two main sections existing for almost a century: one Catholic (*les Scouts et Guides de France*) and one Protestant (*les Éclaireuses et Éclaireurs de France*). As France's demographics have changed over the last 100 years, rather than working toward combining these groups or making them more inclusive, the movement in France has proliferated new Scout sections, including Muslim Scouts, Jewish Scouts, and a small group of "unified" or unaffiliated Scouts. The other four unrecognized movements are almost all the result of schism within the larger recognized organizations, and they often reflect disagreements over questions of religion, coeducation and program. The French example demonstrates well the fragmentation of Guide movements within national contexts along the lines of religion and religious identity and the long-term impact of these decisions in the 1920s and 1930s.[32]

It was not just within countries that religious questions created divisions, but across national boundaries as Guiding tried to construct an international sisterhood. Roman Catholicism caused particular headaches for world Guide and Girl Scout leaders, as some Catholic families saw Guiding as undermining familial and religious teaching. Among non-Catholic Guides, there was also prejudice against Roman Catholics, who were considered to be in thrall to the Pope. Robert and Olave Baden-Powell tried to ease these tensions by promoting Catholic Guiding, and they made a very public trip on pilgrimage to Rome with 118 British Roman Catholic Guides in March 1933. While there, the Baden-Powells had an audience with Pope Pius XI, who said he approved the movement and saw it as "a great family."[33] This endorsement helped ease the fears of Catholic parents about Guiding's intentions, but did not erase all the conflict that existed regarding Roman Catholicism and world Guiding. In fact, Baden-Powell himself was still writing privately to other Guide leaders that he worried about the dangers of "Rome (whoever that may mean)" killing the spirit of Guiding with too many restrictions. While he understood sectarian concerns, he noted that "personal or sectional ideas, however good their intentions, must trim themselves down to meet the great need of the whole."[34]

In Canada, battles over religion raged in the context of Quebecois Guides. Roman-Catholic French-speaking Guides in Quebec grew increasingly unhappy with the direction of the mainstream Guide movement, which already had a Christian offshoot in the form of Salvation Army Guides. Despite "careful negotiations" and pressure from London to combine together, the "Catholic Guides of Canada" voted in March 1938 in Montreal to constitute themselves as a separate body from the Canadian Guides Association.[35] The split reflected Quebecois nationalism as well as linguistic and religious tensions. Yet while Guide leaders saw this separation as a setback, they could still reflect with pride upon the diversity developed within the mainstream Guide association, which had more than 20 nationalities, YWCA companies, and dozens of religious affiliations amongst its members. One company, the 1st Winnipeg, had 20 "nationalities" all in one company.[36]

The diversity of perspective and religious belief in the Canadian Guide Association was not that unusual, as many countries chose not to create separate affiliated sections, but to integrate difference into existing associations. In areas where there were significant concerns about "mixed" religion groups, separate companies or patrols were created. India (together with modern Pakistan and Bangladesh) used such a Guide model in the interwar period, with separate companies divided by caste and creed, but with a unified association. As Olave Baden-Powell recorded in her notebook about India: "Guiding is perhaps the ONE platform upon which all kinds can meet—Mohammedans, Hindus, Brahmins, Parsees, Buddhists, Christians, and Jews."[37] Likewise, the All-Malaya Guide Camp of 1931 brought together girls whose backgrounds included Malay, Chinese, Japanese, Sri Lankan, Indian, American, British and Australian nationalities.[38]

As with the question of "womanliness," one of the places where religious matters could be volatile was the camp. Any national or international camp that aimed to bring together girls from different cultural and religious backgrounds had to incorporate accommodations for their beliefs. Kosher or Halal foods for Jewish and Muslim Guides had to be provided, worship facilities for all denominations were necessary, and appropriate privacy for daily religious rituals and prayer had to be taken into account. Yet these accommodations for religious faith sometimes led to a different kind of barrier crossing, as girls from different nations and from different racial, language, and ethnic backgrounds came together as communities of faith. A Roman Catholic mass at a Guide world camp might draw English Catholics from Britain and its empire as well as French, Belgian, Polish, Italian, Spanish, Latin American and U.S. girls. In addition, Catholic Guides from Martinique, Algeria, Syria, Tunisia, Indochina and Ivory Coast might join the service. For all the divisiveness that religion sometimes created in Guiding, it also provided the kind of bridge across cultures that Guiding hoped to build, serving as both unifier and divider in world Guiding. This ambiguity surrounding religion in the world movement was something most leaders could live with, but the more difficult question to overcome was that of prejudice based on skin color or nationality.

Unlike the myriad of religious accommodations possible in the movement, Guiding was faced with two clear options in racial, ethnic, and linguistic disputes—integration or segregation. Its choice was never clear, however, and as Guiding spread around the world, local conditions often determined how volatile issues would be handled. Nonetheless, British headquarters and then later WAGGGS did have to take a stand because, if the organization planned to stand for "international sisterhood," then it had to deal with perceived discrimination and prejudice in the movement. Particularly when a world gathering was planned, racial controversies often made for tense times among world Guide leaders. Several cases help to demonstrate the ways in which Guiding attempted to negotiate the treacherous waters of identity politics while promoting a world agenda of peace, cooperation, and sisterhood.

One approach to Guide diversity was to push for integration and assimilation into the dominant culture of Guiding. Several countries attempted this, most notably the United States in the 1910s and 1920s with its "Americanization" programs for Girl Scouts. Identifying new immigrants as particularly in need of Girl Scouting's teachings, Scout leaders wooed immigrant children with the same games, badges, and camps that attracted "American" girls. Immigrant girls who could learn Girl Scouting's mothering and self-reliance skills could then teach their parents and help integrate their families into the "one nation" of the United States. Using stories of brave "outsider" women from the past, the Girl Scout handbook provided immigrant girls with examples to follow and with a model of citizenship through loyalty and service. Girls learned flag drills (patriotism), housekeeping skills (mothering), and war work (loyal service) in the 1910s.[39]

Americanization programs, although largely abandoned by the mid-1920s, had served to integrate foreign-born girls into Girl Scouting with mixed companies and camps. While some accommodations had to be made, such as the allowance of cooler white uniforms in Hawaii rather than the standard brown khaki, Girl Scouting took hold in many U.S.-occupied colonies and protectorates as well by the end of World War I.[40] Despite integration of immigrants and the existence as early as 1920 of African American, Asian, and Native American girls in the Scout movement in various parts of the country, true equality and integration eluded the grasp of many Girl Scouts.[41] At summer camps and in local councils, girls of color were channeled into separate troops and accommodations. For example, black Girl Scout troops in Ogden, Utah, had to attend camp during special separate weeks set aside for them in the 1930s. This mirrored the national policy of opening its doors to all girls, regardless of race, religion, or political affiliation, while "encouraging segregation of troops."[42] Yet it also perpetuated racist policies in some local councils, especially when park officials denied their spaces to girls of color. The Girl Scout national headquarters, worried about alienating white Scouts, tried to help African American girls with behind-the-scenes funding and encouragement, not confronting prejudice directly. As Lou Henry Hoover explained it, "Nationally the Girl Scouts have no policy regarding the colored situation. It must be decided in each area by the Council thereof, because Boston and New Orleans, California and Florida, cities and small towns look at all with such different eyes."[43]

One woman who struggled with segregationist policies in trying to maintain an active Girl Scout program was Josephine Holloway, an African American social worker in Nashville, Tennessee, beginning in 1923. Nashville had developed a Girl Scout program among white girls in 1917 during the surge of patriotism that accompanied the war. The city's Scouts had embraced religious diversity, with troops attached to Jewish and Christian schools in the area, but race was a trickier question in the segregationist U.S. South. Holloway, assigned to work with girls at the Bethlehem Center, a social settlement in a poor area of Nashville, thought Girl Scouting might work well for her girls, so she wrote to national headquarters for assistance. Juliette Low herself trained Holloway in 1924 while she was in Tennessee at a youth conference, and Holloway earned her title of "Captain". Holloway created a successful Girl Scout program at the center among African American girls until she gave up her job (and Girl Scouting) upon her marriage in 1925.[44]

Between the time of Holloway's marriage and her return to Girl Scouting in 1933, Nashville created a local Girl Scout council, which dealt with requests for troops and other local matters. When Holloway applied to start a new troop, this time for her six-year-old daughter, it was the council's first request for an "official" African American troop under the new structure, and the council turned Holloway down, citing financial concerns. Because segregationist laws in Nashville meant that African American girls could only function in separate units, the council felt it could not afford to start a whole new unit, or so it argued. It took until 1942 (again during a wartime expansion) for African American Girl Scouting to develop officially in Nashville. Wartime conditions, but also a concerted effort by national Girl Scout headquarters to combat prejudice, helped increase African American participation—nationally by 252 percent in the five years following 1942.[45]

Meanwhile Holloway had been running "unofficial" Girl Scout troops since 1933 for her daughters and other girls in the African American community. Holloway's daughter may have helped get official status for her mother's troops by approaching Eleanor Roosevelt in 1942—when Roosevelt gave a speech in Nashville—and asking her to help get recognition for African American Girl Scouts. Once the doors opened, Girl Scouting skyrocketed among African Americans in Nashville; by 1944 there were 13 troops with more than 250 girls. The council hired Holloway as a "field advisor for Negro troops" to deal with the expansion.[46] Despite these advances, discrimination did not end, and Holloway had to fight for camp facilities, equal access to funds, and other benefits of national membership. African Americans remained in segregated units and facilities until the early 1960s.[47]

Segregation and its destructive influence on Guide pretensions toward egalitarian world sisterhood made an appearance in many British colonies and former colonies as well. In these situations, where British headquarters had official control over the movement's growth, racial tensions became particularly problematic for leaders in London. As personnel changed, so too did perceptions regarding race, and often new arrivals in racially segregated societies wanted to use Guiding to help create societal change. In South Africa even before official apartheid policies were legislated, the national Guide association refused to allow African girls in the movement. Instead, African and mixed-race girls were channeled into a separate movement, the Girls Wayfarers Association (created in 1925), which featured different uniforms, handbooks, and programs. Many individual Guides and Guide leaders helped the Wayfarers, but they had to do so without wearing their Guide uniforms, as it was against association rules to assist the Wayfarers in an official uniformed capacity. This strict segregation reflected white Guiding's fears about political repercussions if it "mixed" girls of different races. Olave Baden-Powell tried to explain the fears, especially as members around the world questioned this undermining of Guide stated policies toward egalitarian sisterhood. Her explanation only complicated the issue, showing clearly the continuing racial stereotypes at work among Guide leaders in the interwar period:

> The reason for this [segregation] is that the feeling of insecurity where the natives are concerned and the very real dangers to white girls, lack of control, etc. make it quite definitely not safe for black and white girls to meet on equal footing . . . . As you know, our policy is one of complete sisterhood and it would not be possible to lay down defining laws within the Movement which would secure the complete safety of the white girls and the peace of mind of their parents.[48]

In effect, Baden-Powell argued that to retain egalitarian sisterhood within the movement, some girls must be kept out. The holes in this argument were apparent, and as pressure continued to build for a solution in South Africa, the Wayfarer-Guides were created in 1936 as a closed Christian branch. Because this branch still treated the Wayfarers as separate, a large group of Wayfarers seceded, creating their own Transvaal Wayfarer

Association.[49] South Africa's apartheid laws that solidified into a national program by the 1940s made any real equality impossible, and the country retained a racially divided Guide program into the 1990s.

While South Africa might be a unique example given its government-legislated apartheid program, other colonies faced some of the same arguments about the suitability of Guiding for so-called "native" girls. One of the best examples of these conflicting views regarding race in Guiding was the Bahamas, a British colony. In this case, Olave Baden-Powell was astonished to find in 1926 that there were no "colored" companies, partly because "in the other Islands there are coloured companies," and mixed-race Guiding existed even in nearby places such as Jamaica.[50] Yet, in the Bahamas, and in other islands such as Bermuda, Guiding was for white girls. Intermittent letters about the situation reached Baden-Powell and London Guide headquarters, but it was not until the late 1920s that the issue really exploded. Guider Evelyn Shedden tried to create "colored" Brownie and Guide companies in the Bahamas in 1928, but her official request was turned down by the local council. Trying to appeal to a broader sense of history and world sisterhood, Shedden had phrased her request carefully, noting that: "As in the early history of the Guide movement, it was the [coloured] girls themselves who asked for [a Guide company] ... you are acting here in the interests of the whole Guide Movement."[51] Like Josephine Holloway in the United States, Shedden was undeterred, and she ran unofficial "colored" companies. However, the girls longed for official Guide status. She briefly considered getting help from the South African Wayfarers and even got copies of their literature, but Shedden soon realized that they lacked what she wanted—official worldwide sisterhood and recognition for her Guides. In an appeal for a "trial company," Shedden expressed her frustration: "It was like kicking against a brick wall of prejudice."[52] When Shedden was turned down yet again, she decided to build up an excellent and popular "unofficial" company to demonstrate the girls' fitness for the Guide program.

Shedden had to leave the Bahamas in 1930 (although she returned in the mid-1930s), and Olave Baden-Powell commiserated in a letter with her lack of success in breaking the "colour bar": "I always hate the colour bar in guiding. It is a weak link in our sisterhood but one cannot go against public opinion unless you have good courage and strength behind you, and I doubt the time being ripe in Nassau."[53] Baden-Powell's shifting statements and ambiguities about segregation and discrimination in

Guiding point to the very difficult job she and other leaders faced—retaining public opprobrium while keeping faith with Guide principles. The policy of embracing local solutions might have kept public opinion quiescent, but it undermined the larger message Guiding sought to inculcate.

As was often the case with Guiding disputes, the "color bar" question in the Bahamas waxed and waned throughout the 1920s and 1930s, coming to a head finally in the mid-1930s. The newly instituted World Association magazine, *The Council Fire* (1928), published letters and reports about Guiding around the world, which included discussions of the color bar. Guides could weigh in with their opinions, which helped create pressure for social change. By the mid-1930s, Guiding in South Africa had reached its solution of federation (Wayfarer-Guides), and Bermuda had opened its tents to non-white girls, so the pressure was certainly increasing in the Bahamas.

The new Governor's wife, American-born Alice Clifford, combined forces with Olave Baden-Powell and Princess Alice (Commissioner for Overseas Guiding) to help force the issue of colored companies again in 1934. As Clifford noted, "With regard to a native Company, I am personally greatly in favour of it . . . [but] it will unquestionably raise a terrific amount of feeling amongst the leading families here."[54] Baden-Powell tried to appeal to the leading families' sense of elite membership in the empire, writing to Guide Commissioner, Lady Norah Johnson, that Princess Alice was "very surprised to find that in the Bahamas, alone amongst the West Indian Islands, Guiding had not been extended to the native population."[55] This ploy did not work, and Johnson replied abruptly by throwing earlier Guide policy back at Baden-Powell: "We, who live here and know our people, believe that these lines are those best suited for local conditions. Perhaps you do not realize that conditions here differ radically from those which prevail in the West Indies."[56] As Princess Alice dryly noted in a letter to a friend: "Lady Johnston [*sic*] has the hide of an armadillo, & I frankly think it would be well to suffer everyone resigning & for a completely new start to be made while thanking her for what she has done."[57]

The Princess had interpreted the situation correctly, but had not anticipated the fallout that would come with Johnson's resignation. Her whole executive board and many leaders also resigned; lack of Guide leaders and financial resources, plus political pressure, then led to the suspension of Guiding in the Bahamas and the sale of all Guide property.[58] Guiding restarted on mixed-race lines (in separate companies), but not until more than a decade and a world war later, in 1946. At that time, the Governor's wife, Betty Murphy, "made it absolutely clear that there could be no question of the Girl Guides being started again unless the coloured community is included, and that there is equal opportunity for coloured and white ... no racial discrimination."[59] This new policy in the Bahamas reflected a growing shift in Guiding worldwide to rely less on "local conditions" to dictate Guiding's principles and more on universal ideals of equality and human rights.[60]

In addition to questions of race and religion, Guiding also faced threats from nationalist and politicized youth organizations in the interwar period. Some of these organizations, such as Catholic or Socialist youth movements, had competed with Guiding from its inception, but particularly worrisome for Guide leaders were new ultra-nationalist youth groups in countries such as Germany, Italy, and the Soviet Union. These governments had banned Guiding and installed their own versions of youth service organizations, based on badge work and incorporating similar language of loyalty and service, but strictly based on national lines. Nationalist youth movements boomed in many countries after World War I, with *Voortrekkers* in South Africa (1931), *Komsomol* in the Soviet Union (1918), *Opera nazionale balilla* in Italy (1926) and the *Bund Deutscher Mädel* in Germany (1930), to name just a few. These uniformed youth organizations sought to use many of the Guide techniques of drill, activities, outdoor life, and motherhood skills to mold young people, but with a narrowly nationalist purpose. For the Italian and German youth movements, in particular, shaping youth was a governmental project, and in each case, girls' physical fitness and outdoor activities were aimed to build strong mothers for the nation.[61] As Austrian Guide President, Archduchess Ileana, wrote in a 1935 article on the subject: "A great wave of nationalism is sweeping over Europe today. All countries seem suddenly to have realized that the young play a great part, or will do so in the future."[62] For Guiding, the difficulty was in making its particular approach appealing in the charged interwar political atmosphere.

Guiding struggled to know how to cope with these sectarian movements. On the one hand, Guide leaders wanted to "grow" their international sisterhood, and if there was one recognized girls' association in a country, perhaps Guiding should reach out to those girls. Guides in some countries had already felt the restrictions imposed by nationalist officials, with banning of Guiding in such countries as Germany,

Hungary, and Romania, but also in Denmark, which tried to counter nationalist youth by banning ALL uniformed youth in 1933. Brazil as well dissolved the Guide movement in 1940 to try to block nationalist penetration of the youth organizations.[63] On the other hand, mandatory nationalist organizations ran counter to the very spirit of Guide internationalism and voluntary membership, so Guide officials argued that no affiliation was possible or even desirable. In the World Association constitution, countries with explicitly political agendas or who discriminated openly against girls could not in theory be members, and the national association wanting membership in WAGGGS had to agree to the following:

a) Adhere to the principles of the original Promise and Law as laid down by the Founder;

b) Have a movement open to all girls without distinction of creed, race, class or nationality;

c) Have a self-governing Movement independent of any political organisation and not supporting any political party;

d) Have adopted the Trefoil (the symbol of the threefold Promise as its Badge);

e) Have undertaken . . . to begin work on a Constitution . . .;

f) Undertake to pay annually the Tenderfoot Membership Quota to WAGGGS, and to send an annual report to the World Bureau.[64]

Given these very clear rules, no formal affiliation of a nationalist youth organization with WAGGGS was even possible. Any outreach would have to have been unofficial and informal, and a few cursory visits of Guides to nationalist youth organizations were reported in the 1930s. However, most Guide leaders were reluctant to sponsor even informal connections, and no real outreach took place. Besides, the truth was that the nationalist movements themselves had little interest in Guiding, dismissing it as embracing bourgeois liberal values and vague internationalism.

Katharine Furse, Director of WAGGGS, tried to lay out the problem Guiding faced in an article for *The Council Fire* in 1937. She pointed out the contradictory problems, namely, that as a nonpolitical movement it was difficult to cooperate with "political" movements. However, if Guiding continued to isolate itself from these "huge new bodies of young people," was it also playing at politics? She wondered if by spurning politicized ultra-nationalist movements Guiding was in fact undermining its own stated goal of peaceful cooperation and world outreach. Furse admitted this was a "real tangle," and noted that one of the best suggestions she had heard from a Guide recently, was that WAGGGS should promote a "prayer for world peace" among Girl Scouts and Guides in all countries.[65] Using friendship and prayers for peace as glue seemed like a possible solution in 1937, but by 1939, even this brief hope was gone.

Nationalism, race, religion, language, and ethnicity all created tensions within Guiding's international sisterhood in its first few decades. Guide leaders at the local and national level struggled to face these difficulties and to create policies that would be true to the ideals of Guiding while appeasing public opinion and attracting girl members. The thorny nature of these questions led to bitter debates among Guide leaders, and eventually to the formation of a special research and advisory council, "Quo Vadis" (Where are you headed?) in 1931. The brainchild of France's Madeleine Beley, this council was made of up of leaders from 12 countries. It met for a long session in 1933 to discuss "the conditions of little girls" all over the world, with focus on whether Guiding "can help them all." The group came up with five general suggestions to keep Guiding's ideals alive and to keep it "up-to-date." First, Quo Vadis suggested recognizing more explicitly that Guiding's purpose is character training, and to this end, perhaps simplification of some Guiding methods might be in order. Second, the group realized that activities were a core of the Guide program, but that often Guides could not connect the activities to the ideals, a problem needing fixing. Third, leader training had to be key at the local, national, and international level. Fourth, the council thought it should remain as an advisory body that the world committee could call on when necessary for "special projects." Finally, Quo Vadis recommended that Guiding not be insular. As its Chair, Margrethe Parm, wrote in her report: "We must have our windows open; co-operate, give-and-take, must be our policy. We must never become shut up in watertight compartments."[66] The trick, as Guide leaders well realized, was to open the watertight compartments without sinking the whole ship. As war threatened again in the late 1930s, the urge to cooperate and to promote international peace and sisterhood became hard to maintain as the patriotic nationalism of a wartime world took hold.

NOTES

1. Katharine Rathbone to Olave Baden-Powell (May 4, 1921); O. Baden-Powell to K. Rathbone (May 24, 1921); O. Baden-Powell to Jane Deeter Rippin (May 27 1921); Girl Guides box, GSUSA.

2. *WAGGGS Information* (London: WAGGGS, 1938), 11.

3. Tammy Proctor, "Scouts, Guides and the Fashioning of Empire," in *Fashioning the Body Politic: Dress, Gender, Citizenship*, ed. Wendy Parkins (Oxford: Berg, 2002), 129–131.

4. "Guides in the Heart of Burma," *The Council Fire* 10:2 (April 1935), 6.

5. Olave Baden-Powell to Percy Everett (February 8, 1919), ST1/C15/Shelf 1/Box 4: Countries B—Brazil, GGL.

6. Olave Baden-Powell to Miss Clendennin, June 2, 1921, WAGGGS, GSUSA.

7. Hubert Martin to Robert Baden-Powell (August 13, 1926); forwarded to Sarah Louise Arnold (August 15, 1926), WAGGGS, GSUSA.

8. Tammy Proctor, *On My Honour: Guiding and Scouting in Interwar Britain* (Philadelphia: American Philosophical Society, 2002), 76–77.

9. Susan Miller, *Growing Girls: The Natural Origins of Girls' Organizations in America* (New Brunswick: Rutgers University Press, 2007), 8.

10. Marguerite de Beaumont, "Log of a Lilywhite Cadet," Houghton Camp August 1920, GGL.

11. Rose Kerr, *The Story of a Million Girls: Guiding and Girl Scouting Round the World* (London: Girl Guides Association, 1937), 260.

12. Mica Nava, "Youth Service Provision, Social Order and the Question of Girls," in *Gender and Generation*, eds. Angela McRobbie and Mica Nava (London: Macmillan, 1984), 11–12.

13. Author interview with Betty Prance, Plumstead, Kent, April 5, 1993.

14. Elisabeth Israels Perry, "From Achievement to Happiness: Girl Scouting in Middle Tennessee, 1910s–1960s," *Journal of Women's History* 5:2 (Fall 1993), 81–82.

15. Cicely Stewart-Smith, "The Log of a Loafer in the Guides," 1923–1925 logbook, GGL.

16. Log of Greenfinch Patrol, Foxlease, August 29, 1922, GGL.

17. "Extra Session for Discussion of Rangers" at 8th World Conference, *The Council Fire* 9:4 (October 1934), 180.

18. *1910 . . . and Then? A Brief History of the Girl Guides Association* (London: Girl Guides Association, 1990), 20.

19. Imperial Camp Roster, 1926, Foxlease box, GGL.

20. Tim Jeal, *The Boy-Man: The Life of Lord Baden-Powell* (New York: William Morrow and Co., 1990), 478–487; Kerr, *The Story of a Million Girls*, 179; Anne Hyde Choate, "Our Chalet," *The Council Fire* 27:1 (January 1952), 3.

21. Anstruther Thomson had earlier had a decade-long relationship with Violet Paget (who wrote under the name Vernon Lee); the two worked, published, lived, and traveled together during the late 1880s and 1890s. For more information see Sally Newman, "The Archival Traces of Desire: Vernon Lee's Failed Sexuality and the Interpretation of Letters in Lesbian History," *Journal of the History of Sexuality* 14:1/2 (January/April 2005), 51–75.

22. Boy Scout diaries of Doris Mason (1925–1934), TC/296, SAGP; "Miss M. de Beaumont—an appreciation," *Newbury Weekly News* (August 24, 1989).

23. Author interview with Lady Marjorie Stopford and Miss Florence Cobb, Bushey Heath, Hertfordshire, March 24, 1993.

24. Penny Tinkler, *Constructing Girlhood: Popular Magazines for Girls Growing up in England, 1920–1950* (London: Taylor & Francis, 1995), 6.

25. Lady Baden-Powell, "A Successful Wife," *Home Chat* (September 27, 1930), 663–664, 705, TC/219, SAGP.

26. *Manchester Guardian* (April 15, 1932); *Yorkshire Observer* (January 19, 1924), Headquarters Record Book 1925–1930; and *Monmouth Post* (November 29, 1917), Press Cuttings 1910–1922, GGL. "Report of the Girl Guide International Conference at St. Hugh's College, Oxford, 23–28 July 1920," 6, 12, GGL.

27. Janice Brownfoot, "Sisters Under the Skin: Imperialism and the Emancipation of Women in Malaya, c. 1891–1941," in *Making Imperial Mentalities*, ed. J. A. Mangan (Manchester: Manchester University Press, 1990), 61–66.

28. Kerr, *The Story of a Million Girls*, 92–93.

29. Kerr, *The Story of a Million Girls,* 151.

30. *Trefoil Round the World* (London: WAGGGS, 2003), 303–305.

31. Marie-Thérèse Cheroutre, *Le scoutisme au féminin: Les guides de France, 1923–1998* (Paris: Les Éditions du Cerf, 2002), 46–48, 57.

32. Anne Jouan and Agnes Leclair, "Les huits grandes familles du scoutisme francais," *Le Figaro* (July 30, 2007), 7.

33. Robert Baden-Powell TS account, March 2, 1933, Founder's Files, TC/26, SAGP; "Chiefs in Rome," *The Council Fire* 8:2 (April 1933), 21; Rose Kerr, *The Story of the Girl Guides* (London: Girl Guides Association, 1940), 209.

34. Robert Baden-Powell to Katharine Furse, September 5, 1935, WAGGGS, GSUSA.

35. Olave Baden-Powell to Sarah Warren (October 6, 1937); Priscilla Marceau to Mrs. H. D. Warren (April 10, 1938), ST1/C15/Shelf 1/Box 5/Countries—Canada, GGL.

36. "Canada," *The Council Fire* 9:2 (April 1934), 95.

37. Olave Baden-Powell notes, "India," n.d., ST1/C15/Shelf 2/Box 8/Countries—India, GGL.

38. Brownfoot, "Sisters Under the Skin," 65. Brownfoot argues that this diversity in Guiding helped create social change for women in Malaya.

39. Leslie Hahner, "Practical Patriotism: Camp Fire Girls, Girl Scouts, and Americanization," *Communication and Critical/Cultural Studies* 5:2 (June 2008), 122–125.

40. "Girl Scout Troubles," *New York Times* (August 30, 1920).

41. Mary Aikin Rothschild, "To Scout or To Guide? The Girl Scout–Boy Scout Controversy, 1912–1941," *Frontiers: A Journal of Women Studies* 6:3 (Autumn 1981), 116.

42. Laureen Tedesco, "A Nostalgia for Home: Daring and Domesticity in Girl Scouting and Girls' Fiction, 1913–1933," (PhD diss., Texas A&M University, 1999), 65–66.

43. As quoted in Nancy Beck Young, *Lou Henry Hoover: Activist First Lady* (Lawrence: University Press of Kansas, 2004), 169.

44. Elisabeth Israels Perry, "'The Very Best Influence': Josephine Holloway and Girl Scouting in Nashville's African-American Community," *Tennessee Historical Quarterly* LII:2 (Summer 1993), 73–76.

45. Perry, "'The Very Best Influence'," 76–78.

46. Perry, "'The Very Best Influence'," 78.

47. Perry, "'The Very Best Influence'," 79, 81.

48. Olave Baden-Powell to anonymous correspondent, December 9, 1929, Box 1229/South Africa: Native Affairs, Wayfarers/Pathfinders file, School of Oriental and African Studies, London (SOAS).

49. For an in-depth look at South African Guiding, see Tammy M. Proctor, "'A Separate Path': Scouting and Guiding in Interwar South Africa," in *Comparative Studies in Society and History* 42:3 (2000): 605–631.

50. Olave Baden-Powell to Lady Cordeaux, April 20, 1926, ST1/C15/Shelf 1, Box 2 Bahamas, GGL.

51. Evelyn Shedden, Memo on Coloured Companies, ST1/C15/Shelf 1, Box 2 Bahamas, GGL.

52. Evelyn Shedden to Miss Hill, March 20, 1928; Evelyn Shedden to Olave Baden-Powell, June 22, 1928, ST1/C15/Shelf 1, Box 2 Bahamas, GGL.

53. Olave Baden-Powell to Evelyn Shedden, November 8, 1930, ST1/C15/Shelf 1, Box 2 Bahamas, GGL.

54. Alice Clifford to Olave Baden-Powell, July 5, 1934, ST1/C15/Shelf 1, Box 2 Bahamas, GGL.

55. Olave Baden-Powell to Lady Norah Johnson, June 15, 1934, ST1/C15/Shelf 1, Box 2 Bahamas, GGL.

56. Lady A. Norah Johnson to Olave Baden-Powell, July 4, 1934, ST1/C15/Shelf 1, Box 2 Bahamas, GGL.

57. Princess Alice (Countess of Athlone, Commissioner for Overseas Guiding) to Nellie [unknown surname], June 9, 1934, ST1/C15/Shelf 1, Box 2 Bahamas, GGL.

58. Lady A. Norah Johnson to Olave Baden-Powell, October 8, 1934 and GGUK Overseas Fact Sheet (Bahamas), ST1/C15/Shelf 1, Box 2 Bahamas, GGL.

59. Lady Betty Murphy to Lady Clarendon (Overseas Commissioner), October 29, 1945, ST1/C15/Shelf 1, Box 2 Bahamas, GGL.

60. Racial disputes certainly did not disappear, but by the 1960s, most Guide movements had moved to be more inclusive and welcoming.

61. Tammy M. Proctor, "'Something for the Girls': Organized Leisure in Europe, 1890–1939," in *Secret Gardens, Satanic Mills: Placing Girls in European*

History, 1750–1960, eds. Mary Jo Maynes, Birgitte Søland, and Christina Benninghaus (Bloomington: Indiana University Press, 2005), 239–253.

62. Archduchess Ileana, "Guiding and Nationalism," *The Council Fire* 10:3 (July 1935), 6.

63. Margaret Clark (Commissioner for British Guides in Brazil), "Report," July 16, 1940, ST1/C15/Shelf 1 Box 4: Brazil, GGL.

64. WAGGGS, *Constitution and Bye-Laws* (London: WAGGGS, 1936), 4–5.

65. Katharine Furse, "Prayer for World Peace," *The Council Fire* 12:2 (April 1937), 2.

66. Margrethe Parm, "Quo Vadis Council Meets," *The Council Fire* 8:3 (July 1933), 34–35.

4. War Again

On July 25, 1939, nearly 4,000 Girl Guides and Girl Scouts from around the world made their way to Gödöllö, Hungary, where a large camp was being erected for the first Pax Ting (Peace Parliament), Guiding's version of the Boy Scout Jamboree. Representatives from 23 nations were in the 8 sub-camps, and girls spent their days eating, working, visiting, playing games, and displaying their handicrafts.[1] The event was a triumph for Hungarian organizers, who were able to host the gathering despite an increasingly tense political situation in Europe. The Pax Ting, as its name suggests, was the culmination of 30 years of development toward peace and international sisterhood since that contingent of "Girl Scouts" had shown up at the boys' Crystal Palace rally in London in 1909. As the main organizer, Antonia Lindenmeyer of Hungary wrote before the event: "We hope . . . this great event will be a gathering worthy of its high aims, a deepening of our world-wide sisterhood, an increase of strength and confidence, a making of real friendship in this time of world crisis."[2] Her hopes went unrealized, however, and by the time the articles reporting on the Pax Ting appeared in *The Council Fire* in October 1939, much of Europe was at war.

The Guides, despite their dreams of peace and unity, were not unprepared for the crisis when it came. Polish Guides, who numbered nearly 75,000 in 1939, had turned to national defense and first aid training in the 1930s. Girls made first-aid outfits, learned to create emergency gas masks, and practiced identification of different sorts of airplanes. Polish Guides who had traveled to Hungary for the Pax Ting, returned to a German invasion, complete with aerial bombing and foreign troops. In fact, one of the casualties of German blitzkrieg in September 1939 was a Guide hut bombed by the Luftwaffe; 12 Guides died.[3] Like the Polish organization, Belgian Guiding had begun preparing for the possibility of war in May 1939, developing activities and a program "Pour Servir," that would allow Guides to assist wives and children of soldiers. Having lived under occupation and the constraints of war during World War I, Belgian Guides wanted to "be prepared" for such an eventuality again.[4]

French Guides also had barely settled back into their home routines when their country went to war with Germany in 1939. Guides and

Éclaireuses in eastern France helped with the mass evacuation of border zones, served at comfort stations, helped move luggage, distributed clothes, and interpreted for refugees.[5] This could be daunting work for teenaged girls and their leaders. The area of Hénin-Liétard in northern France, for instance, used the local Éclaireuse volunteers to help cope with an influx of 30,000 miners and their families from German-speaking Lorraine. Some of the families were in dire need indeed, and the Éclaireuses found themselves providing furniture, lodging, money, clothing, food, and social assistance. Often the refugees were ill, with diseases such as tuberculosis, or they were just too elderly to deal comfortably with such displacement. The Éclaireuses' program of assistance undoubtedly helped ease the transition of the refugees, and perhaps helped the girls themselves understand the situation they themselves would face months later with the occupation of their own homes by invaders.[6]

It was not just in areas facing invasion that the Guides stepped up to serve their nations. As in the First World War, World War II ignited interest in Guiding among girls, giving them a focus for their desire to serve in wartime. Throughout the world, Guides mobilized, again earning War Service badges and again boosting public opinion of their program. However, the war also transformed international Guiding and Girl Scouting, marking in many ways a profound shift in their program and ideals. The war coincided with a generational shift in which many of the great personalities and leaders of the early movement died (or were "called to higher service," as Guides and Scouts understood it). The Guide organization that emerged from World War II was both stronger and more visible, but also weakened by the destruction of its ranks during the war and by the Cold War tensions pulling at its international sisterhood. Guiding needed to retool its image for the postwar world, and the Guide movement crafted in the 1940s and 1950s had different ideals than its precursors.

For Guiding, one of the most immediate results of the declaration of war in Europe in September 1939 was a fracturing of the World Association. The World Bureau, housed in London, continued to operate and to publish its magazine, but world conferences were postponed indefinitely and "as a precaution" another WAGGGS office was set up in New York.[7] In addition, many national Guide organizations were lost to contact with WAGGGS. First Poland, Bohemia, Moravia, and the Baltic areas were cut off, then Denmark, Norway, the Netherlands, Belgium, France, and Luxembourg. In fact, by July 1940, the World Bureau was reporting that

"A curtain has fallen between them and us . . . we hear little . . . but we know that in all these Guiding is being carried on in a fine spirit in spite of great difficulties."[8] The loss of the mainstay of European Guiding to the World Association forced it to change its focus, and international Guiding activities shifted to the Western hemisphere. The United States took the lead in organizing camps for Guides and Girl Scouts, hosting a large camp in August 1940 with representatives from 23 countries in the Americas. The Director of the World Bureau also undertook a recruiting and inspection tour of Western Hemisphere units in spring and summer 1941, hoping to build numbers there. She visited Cuba, Mexico, Guatemala, Panama, Venezuela, Brazil, Argentina, Uruguay, Chile, Peru, Colombia, Trinidad, British Guiana, and Jamaica over the course of five months.[9]

The second immediate impact of war on Guiding was a fluctuation in membership figures. In Britain, membership figures had declined in the late 1930s, and with older girls enlisting in war service and younger girls being evacuated from their homes in air raid target zones, numbers continued to slide. From a high in 1933 of more than 625,000, Guide numbers in Britain dropped to just over 400,000 in 1941 and only rebounded slightly in the latter years of the war to approximately 500,000. However, well over 1,000 new Guide companies were formed during the war in Britain, including some among evacuated children.[10] In a marked contrast with Britain, in the United States, Girl Scout numbers soared from just under 700,000 in 1941 to 841,830 by 1943, then to more than one million in 1944. Between 1935 and 1945, Girl Scout membership more than tripled.[11] Likewise in France, where the Nazi occupiers had outlawed Guiding in its zone and all activities had to be clandestine, numbers rose from 23,000 in 1939 to almost 53,000 by 1946.[12] In fact, in most of the world, Guide numbers increased with the war.

Finally, the war retooled the focus of Guiding away from its interwar activities of pacifism and internationalism, as girls worked for their nations at war. By the 1930s, Guiding had embraced a multifaceted set of activities that combined service work, especially among those facing deprivation because of the worldwide economic depression of the 1930s, with outdoor exercise, handicrafts, and home training. Much of the military drill and signaling of the 1910s had receded as Guide troops participated in the consumerism and mass culture activities of the 1920s and 1930s. Cinema outings, fashion shows, and domestic science training had displaced (but not entirely eliminated) rifle demonstrations, drill with staves, and Morse demonstrations. Scrapbooks and logbooks from the period catalogue the activities of Guide groups. The 3rd Wimbledon spent the six months between August 1923 and March 1924 doing regular weekly Guide work, but their special activities included: camping, playing cricket, going to a film about bird life, participating in an intercompany sports event, giving a concert at a "cripples' home," sponsoring a jumble sale as a fundraiser, and going on a nature ramble.[13] The 13th North Kensington reported a company shopping outing, a netball game, a visit to a pantomime, and a dance with a "jazz band" among its 1925 events.[14] This was a far cry from the games of "Capture the Flag" and the semaphore competitions that Guides a decade earlier might have featured.

Yet first-aid training and tracking did not disappear entirely. A company that hosted a fancy dress party and practiced country dancing might also play Morse games or organize a tracking event. The 3rd Southall, for example, sponsored a tracking and map-making outing in May 1931, where half the girls laid a trail for the other half of the patrol to follow, while the following summer their activities revolved more around hiking, pony rides, and a visit to the beach.[15] This mix of Guide events can perhaps best be seen in the local "shield" competitions that girls competed for around Britain. These represented a smattering of important Guide skills, and the patrols who were best all-around won the shield. The 1925 shield competition that the 1st Chislehurst participated in required skill in the following: legends, first aid, knots, bottle game (physical fitness), Morse code, skipping, and obstacle race. This same company set as its aim in 1927 for all the girls to earn three particular badges, Child Nurse, Hostess, and Domestic Service.[16] As the experiences of interwar British Guides demonstrate, "scouting" and preparedness had not disappeared from Guiding's program, but the emphasis had shifted more to home skills, games, and citizenship training.

With the outbreak of World War II, the militarization and war preparedness of the early years of Guiding rose to the fore again, but with an overlay of interest in international relief work and refugee care. Guides in Britain, for instance, saw not a faceless mass of war victims and refugees in Poland or France, but the faces of the Guides they had met at the Pax Ting or read about in Guiding literature. In frontline and occupation zones, in concentration and internment camps, and in war jobs, Guiding continued where possible, despite privation, hardships, and outright danger. In a few areas, Guiding had to cease; in Fiji, the American Army's creation of a military base there in 1942 ended Guiding for the duration of the war.[17] Likewise in Aden, Guiding was suspended from 1938–1945 because of the war.[18] Yet, surprisingly few countries saw Guiding disappear entirely, and in more than a few cases, Guides continued as underground groups.

For Guides in the line of fire, their scouting training had immediate practical uses, particularly the law about smiling and singing in the face of difficulties. In Belgium, the German occupation of 1940 led to a chipping away at the Guide program as the war progressed. In 1942, semaphore and Morse code were outlawed, and then in 1943, marches, parades, meetings, and uniforms were controlled. With the interdiction against fires after dark and the rationing/shortages of the war, Guide camping was a challenge.[19] However, Guides did find a use for their camping skills. They ran camps, authorized by occupying authorities, for children of prisoners of war between 1942–1943.[20]

France also faced challenges with the German invasion of 1940 and the subsequent division of the country into zones: occupied, forbidden, annexed and "free" [Vichy]. In the first two zones, youth movements were outlawed outright, and in the last two, youth were targeted for nationalist "new orders." In this charged atmosphere, Guiding continued to operate clandestinely in the occupied zone, but the Guides de France decided to divide its leadership, with co-Chief Guides in Vichy and the occupied areas. The Vichy Chief Guide was Marguerite-Marie Michelin, former Vice President of Guides de France, and Marie-Thérèse de Kerraoul, President, became the Chief Guide in the occupied zone. This structure worked well for part of the war, with de Kerraoul even traveling to Morocco and Tunisia early in the war to visit Guides. However, the war intervened in July 1944, when Michelin was arrested and deported to Nazi concentration camps first in Germany, then in Czechoslovakia.[21]

Guides under Nazi occupation often took risks out of loyalty to their nations, enlisting in resistance efforts, running escape routes, or working in espionage networks. In France, Guides were particularly active in the northeast regions, where girls as young as 12 carried messages and collected intelligence for sabotage and intelligence work.[22] Many Guides spent time in prison or were deported for such wartime activities. One example of such danger was the group "Pure Blood," which included Lucienne Welschinger, Guide District Commissioner in Strasbourg (annexed zone), and 5 Guides aged 18 to 20. The group helped about 400 fugitives escape between 1940 and 1942 before they were arrested and sent to prison in Germany. All remained imprisoned until the end of the war except one Guide, Alice Daul, who escaped in February 1945. She used her Guide training to help her successfully move 600 miles through enemy territory to the Swiss border and safety.[23]

Polish Guides organized even more tightly for resistance efforts, creating an underground organization known as the "Trefoil Union," later changed to "Be Prepared." The Guides tried to help those displaced by war, focusing on childcare, assistance for Jews, homeless shelters, medical facilities, and humanitarian aid. They also worked with fellow Boy Scouts (known as the "Grey Ranks") to resist Nazi occupation, participating in the Warsaw Uprising and other anti-Nazi demonstrations. Many Polish Guides and leaders faced arrest, deportation, and even execution over the course of the war. One of the pioneers of Poland's Guide movement, Jadwiga Falkowska, died in the Warsaw Uprising.[24] Polish Guiding survived the war, despite multiple losses, and reestablished itself in 1945–1946. Re-formed Guide units tried to set up letter writing schemes with British Guides, as the 6th Krakow did in February 1945. The girls wanted to make it clear to their British sisters that they had been active despite Guiding's ban, writing: "Do not think that Scout and Guide work ceased during the War. Many of our present Guides worked in the Underground among countless dangers. Many of them perished in the Camps . . . many were killed in the Warsaw uprising."[25] As this letter suggests, Polish Guiding suffered a great loss of leaders and girls during the war.

Hungary, the center of the Guiding world in 1939 with its Pax Ting, suffered as well during the war. At first, in 1939, Hungary proved a refuge for Guides fleeing from Poland and surrounding areas, and Polish Guide troops flourished among refugee encampments in Hungary. Hungarian Guides worked hard for war relief, and their creation of a special Social Help badge sparked increased interest among girls in war work. One successful program was a summer camp in which Hungarian Guides "sponsored" Polish refugee girls as their guests as camp.[26] However, with the Nazi invasion in October 1944, Hungarian Guides were ordered to disband, and officials tried to move the more than 100,000 Scouts and Guides into the nationalist youth organization, *Hungarista Orszem*, but with little success. The movements continued discreetly, where possible, and bided their time until early 1945 when they could again meet, albeit still under suspicious eyes, this time of the Red Army.[27]

Even in Britain, where the war came from the skies rather than from invading armies, Guides sprang into action almost immediately. When evacuation of London children was announced on September 1, 1939, the Girl Guides were among the first women's organizations to help with the logistics and crowd control at rail stations.[28] Led by the example of their two princesses, Elizabeth and Margaret, both of whom were active members in the Guide world, British Guiding kept up its company activities and camping, where possible, while also engaging in national war service.[29] At first, much Guide energy was directed toward assisting with evacuation, but as the war progressed, their work included agriculture, salvage, messenger services, nursing, childcare, and sewing. Guides also tried to lend a hand during emergency situations, showing great valor and resourcefulness during air raids and aerial bombing. There are countless accounts of Guide heroism such as this one from Belfast in northern Ireland. Guides were staffing emergency feeding centers in the city when bombs devastated the neighborhood, cutting water and gas supplies. Guides made the best of the situation: "For the first ten days the Guides cooked all meals on a camp fire outside the hall, using their own camp equipment. The centre remained open sixteen days and during that time approximately four thousand people were fed."[30]

In addition to general war service, there were several special war initiatives among Guides and Guiders. One such initiative was the Home Emergency Service, started among Rangers. This program targeted older Guides and young leaders for "pre-service training" that would provide them with the necessary skills for joining a number of government-sponsored schemes, including the Land Army, Civil Defense, Army auxiliaries, etc.[31] Another unusual Guide scheme emerged in Scotland, the brainchild of Olga Malkowska, who had come to England on an evacuation train from Poland in September 1939, after her school was bombed. Once in Scotland, Malkowska started another school, run on Guide lines, for Polish evacuee children. The school was funded and furnished by Guide donations—nearly £650 was donated as well as toys, clothing, school materials, and furniture.[32] Service took many creative forms, for example, one of the best publicized Guide contributions to the war was the commitment to "equip and maintain" carrier pigeons for the army.[33] Sometimes Guide war efforts were small in scale; Katharine Furse and Betty Fry, both executives in the World Association, set up a small cottage and held open house for those in need of temporary shelter and help.[34]

Other parts of the British Empire also sprang into action after the outbreak of war. Guides in Trinidad and Tobago worked at "odd wartime jobs" such as "cleaning silver paper, picking silk cotton, sewing, [and] knitting," and Guide headquarters itself became a refugee center in 1941.[35]

Barbados developed a Guide Emergency Service, which among other things had a "Flying Squad" of six Guides, so named because they had to be "ready at a moment's notice" to render aid. In particular, they "provided hot soup, tea and coffee for all survivors brought ashore from ships torpedoed in the vicinity of the Island."[36] In Malta, Guides worked with casualties during and after the many aerial bombing raids of the island. Despite dispersal of the population, Maltese Guiding reformed their units as necessary wherever girls were congregated.[37] Guides around the empire banded together for war work, most notably with collections for the purchase of a lifeboat and two air ambulances; girls from Canada, South Africa, Australia, New Zealand, India, and multiple other colonies collected the funds during Empire Week in 1940. The total collected (with British donations) topped £40,000.[38]

Guiding also continued or developed in some of the most unlikely places, namely, internment and concentration camps. A Polish Guider reported after the war on her Guide company's attempts to function while in a Nazi concentration camp. One of the "tests" they devised was also a way to pass the time during inspections, when they were forced to stand in formation for hours. A Guide was chosen to "lead an excursion" between two known points in Poland, then:

> Standing in formation she would describe in detail the whole expedition: numbers, preparations, equipment, the sights seen on the way and the lessons learnt; the geography, history and ethnographical peculiarities of the region; the flora, fauna and legends. This proved so entrancing that even the non-Guides took part, and for a time everyone forgot the horror of her life, the senseless standing in all weathers, the cold, weariness and hunger.[39]

As in Poland, Guide companies arose in other detention facilities around the world. By 1942, the Japanese had occupied several areas with significant British populations, including Malaya and Singapore. Many British and European nationals were imprisoned for the duration of the war in internment camps or prisons.

At one such center, Changi Prison in Singapore, a Guide company formed among girls in the prison during their first year of internment in 1942. Olga Henderson, 10 years old when interned, remembered the Guide company as a highlight in an otherwise dismal three years of "malnutrition, beriberi and malaria." Years later she told Guiding magazine, "In prison . . . I looked forward to Guides. It was sort of a family.

I remember saying our Promise, singing and lying down at night learning the constellations." Yet she also recognized that there were dangers: "We hid from the Japanese prison guards and were always waiting to disperse. We had a lookout."[40] The 20 girls in the company left a lasting legacy of their company behind bars when they stitched together a quilt from scrap materials, signed in embroidery by each Guide. The quilt was presented to their captain, Mrs. Elizabeth Ennis.[41]

Another Guide group that persevered through internment was the 1st Chefoo (which had Brownies, Guides and Rangers) in Shandong province, China. The company, which began in a school in 1932, was imprisoned in a concentration camp in 1942. Their logbook survived the war, and it demonstrates the extraordinary attempts to keep up morale in the face of war and confinement. The November 2, 1942, entry for the Brownie logbook pleads for cheerfulness in the face of adversity: "We are in need of smiles. Have you got them ready, Brownies?" For their December 25, 1942, concert, the Brownies sang a song about their detention: "We might have been shipped to Timbuctoo/We might have been shipped to Calamazoo/Its not repatriation nor is it yet stagnation/Its simply Concentration in Chefoo!"[42] When the girls were moved from their detention in private homes to Weihsien Camp (a concentration camp for British, American, Dutch, Belgian, and other Europeans civilians), the logbook again provides a forcibly cheery commentary: "Hullo—what's this? Behind bars? Yes—its Weihsien Camp! Well I guess there's a good deal of fun to be got out of this. Just the place to learn some badges."[43] In such situations, Guiding provided children and youth with a sense of identity but also with activities and a focus for their energies.

In the United States, the Girl Scout national council provided small grants from the Juliette Low Fund to help facilitate Girl Scout troops in Japanese-American internment camps. In the camp at Rohwer, Arkansas, a visiting Girl Scout official attended a 1942 rally with 150 girls, which was "outstanding in the enthusiasm and eagerness of the girls."[44] By the end of 1943, all the Japanese-American internment centers had Girl Scout troops, and the total number of girls enrolled hovered around 750. With the end of the war, the Girl Scouts even tried to get lists of girls and their relocation assignments, so that they could hook them up with Girl Scouting in their new homes.[45]

Similarly, in Canada, Girl Guiding developed among Japanese-Canadians interned by their government in camps. Two Canadian Guiders drove on mountain roads through snow to help organize

Guiding in the camps of British Columbia. As they wrote in a January 1943 report:

> We go forth in road trucks . . . to a community of Buddhist Japs, we stuck three times, got at right angles to the road, precipice of 1000 feet below; but in Sandon a Buddhist Japanese lassie met us, beaming, she had collected 50 Guides, and some 10 possible Guiders and had told them they now belong to a world-wide movement and they must not let it down . . . . These Japs feel Canadian, they talk of "those darned Japs," and they take the first promise most willingly and seriously.[46]

As in the First World War, many national leaders felt Guiding could be used to assimilate and control foreign populations, and enthusiasm for helping Guiding grow in internment camps arose partly as a way of "boosting morale" and shaping loyal citizens. The principle of Guide training as important for all girls appears less in these descriptions than the notion that Guiding helped create patriotism, even among suspicious populations.

In nations engaged in war, but far from the actual fighting, such as Canada and the United States, Guiding and Girl Scouting were important ways for girls and women to serve, even if not at the front lines. Canadian Guides jumped into war service with both feet. One way they tried to contain their efforts, however, was to focus on other children and teens, whose lives had been devastated by war. For example, they made clothing for children living in bombed-out areas of Britain and sent books and toys to kids in refugee camps. Canadian Guides also tried to reach out to evacuees from regions such as Czechoslovakia, who had settled in towns across Canada. Guiding sought to develop Guiding companies for girls in these situations and to staff youth centers for evacuated and refugee children.[47] As in Canada, American Girl Scouting also organized and embraced war service quickly when war came to the United States.

After the bombing of Pearl Harbor in December 1941, Girl Scout headquarters contacted all local councils in the United States, reminding them that "Girl Scouting is Defense." Girl Scouts "paid" their country in service hours, with more than 15 million hours of logged war work by mid-1944. Among the work they undertook after Pearl Harbor:

> . . . salvage; childcare; Victory gardening and canning; farm-work; distributing recruiting posters and pamphlets . . . ; hospital work; war relief; . . .

selling War bonds and Stamps; working for the Red Cross; making service kits, cookies and scrapbooks and collecting records, books and furs for the USO, the armed forces, convalescent soldiers and sailors . . . .[48]

Constance Rittenhouse, National Director of Girl Scouting, asked girls to "give more than ever" in a publicized speech to Girl Scout professionals on December 9, 1941.[49] In answering that call, New York Girl Scouts organized "Victory Service" bureaus around the city to help coordinate war service among members. These bureaus, led by adult volunteers, were responsible for matching up girls looking for work with important community tasks.[50] A war service badge was again issued, as in the First World War, and girls were provided with lists of jobs that they could do to "help their country." One of the more unusual but ultimately successful jobs that Girl Scouts undertook was the collection of milkweed pods, which were used to construct life jackets. The Scouts collected almost 8,000 pounds of milkweed after the call for it was made in their magazine, *The American Girl*, in July 1944.[51] Girl Scouts collected other items as well, including scraps, rags, and grease; in 1943, Girl Scouts even canvassed New York apartment houses collecting silk stockings.[52]

American Girl Scouts had to adapt their program to wartime conditions just as those in war zones had to alter their activities as a wartime contingency. The U.S. "Sea Guide" branch, the Mariners, switched its activities in 1942 to land to comply with orders protecting waterways from pleasure boating. Some took up telephone work, while others developed their first-aid skills. In California, Mariners took up a project to help the Forestry service, by sewing "fag bags" for motorists to use in National Parks with the object of preventing forest fires from discarded cigarette butts. The approximately 5,000 Girl Scout Mariners met this wartime challenge by adapting their program and by waiting for restrictions to be lifted.[53] Unlike the Mariners, who saw their activities contracted, the Wing Scouts expanded in 1942 to encompass more girls. Created in 1937, the Wing Scouts allowed Girl Scouts to train in aviation. Younger girls learned general principles of flight and built model airplanes, while older girls and young adults studied about careers in the field, piloting, and maintenance.[54] Perhaps the most difficult problem facing wartime Girl Scouting was its own popularity. In 1944, the waiting list for troops was estimated at about half a million girls, and the national executive issued a desperate call for leaders, which was only partly successful in meeting the demand.[55]

As with the varied work of Canadian Guides and U.S. Girl Scouts, Guides in New Zealand also contributed to the war effort by staffing canteens, hospitals, nurseries, and factories. Girls collected reading materials for soldiers, sewed, knitted, and raised money for recreation huts and air ambulances. The Guides also performed some special tasks for the armed services, including roping 3,000 large camouflage nets and collecting/cleaning 95 tons of rags for army, navy, and air force use.[56]

Even in neutral countries, wartime service through Guiding was practiced. In Sweden, the government actually encouraged youth to join Scout and Guide troops, especially at times when schools closed because of fuel shortages. This led to swelling troops and active war relief work. Conferences, camps, and meetings continued as did war work with refugees.[57] In Switzerland, the Guider-in-Charge ("Falk") of the international Guiding center, Our Chalet, continued to run Guide camps at the facility when fuel was available. Many of the Swiss Guides who won prizes at their annual meeting donated them to the World Bureau to help those in war-torn countries.[58] On the fringes of war, Iceland (first under British then American occupation) continued its Guiding activities, despite the presence of large numbers of soldiers.[59]

One of Guiding's important contributions to the rebuilding of the war-torn world came with its international relief work. In her call for such work, Rose Kerr wrote in *The Guider* in February 1941:

> Whatever happens Europe will be left weak and exhausted and will need an army of peace, an army mainly composed of women who will be in the front line, ready to bind up the wounds and to heal the infirmities of those who have suffered. For this destiny no preparation can be too arduous, no training can be begun too early . . . . If we can begin collecting now an army of goodwill—perhaps a picked body of Scouters and Guiders, Rovers and Rangers—what can they not do to bring healing and comfort to a stricken world?[60]

In answer to Kerr's question, in 1942 Rangers and Guiders from Britain, New Zealand, and Australia began intensive training as relief workers. They would go as volunteers, but with room and board, transport, and uniforms provided by the army and with a small sum of weekly pocket money from Guiding. This group, known as the Guide International Service (GIS) and led by long-time Guider, Miss Rosa Ward, was a founding member of the Council of British Societies for Relief Abroad when it began developing teams for a variety of relief settings. Funding for the teams came from

Guides in Britain and its empire and from Girl Scouts in the United States, with well over £100,000 in cash raised. Other countries sent all kinds of gifts in-kind.[61] The first team, RRUY7, left for further training in Egypt in 1944 and actual relief work in Greece in January 1945. The Guide team arrived in the midst of the Greek civil war, terrible physical destruction, and humanitarian crises; therefore, much of their work took place among displaced people. The team provided transport, medical assistance, and most importantly, ran a hostel.

Thousands of Guides volunteered for GIS service, but those chosen typically had good camping and Guiding credentials, with widespread experience in first aid, cooking, outdoor life, and special skills (language, medical training, etc.). Most importantly, only Rangers and Guiders 21 years and older who were "good mixers" were chosen.[62] RRUY7, which stood for Relief and Rehabilitation Unit, included a crack mechanic, Georgie Hall, a registered nurse, a caterer, and two "sanitation" experts. The team of eight women was complemented by two male Scout leaders, who served also as drivers and sanitation helpers. One of the most celebrated members of the first team was classics scholar, Alison "Chick" Duke, who had impressive language fluency. Duke was given the role of "interpreter" and Greek tutor. Although only 24 years old in 1939, Duke had led the British Guide contingent to the Pax Ting, proving her resourcefulness and responsibility.[63] Hall, Duke, and the expedition leaders, Marjorie Pilkington and Muriel Lees, were all well known to the Guiding world by the time they were chosen as the first team.[64] Plus, as the first team realized after arriving in Greece, their Trefoil badges marked them as part of an international sisterhood, so they were known at least by reputation among the Guides and their families in the countries where they were headed. In fact, team RRUY7 found itself helping Greek Guiding to restart during the year they spent in Greece.[65]

Some of the members had emergency training already, working with Guiding's mobile teams in Britain who helped with the Blitz. As a group, however, they needed to train to work as a team and to try to meet a variety of conditions in the field. Much of the early training for British teams took place in the mountains of Wales in winter. Hauling laden carts across rough terrain, the GIS volunteers hoped to simulate the harsh conditions they might face abroad. Another aspect of preparation included "psychological" conditioning, so the fledgling GIS members served tea to hundreds of patients at a mental hospital to get exposure to mental illness and distress.[66] All volunteers had to attend lectures on language, culture, and practical matters, all had to obtain driver's licenses, and all had to take a course in truck driving and maintenance.[67] The training was intensive and lasted for months. Lady Marjorie Stopford, a member of the first GIS team, remembered this preparation as being full of "nasty jobs" like assembling and reassembling trek carts and climbing walls. Stopford, like many of the team, was not a teenager when engaging in this hard physical training; she was 40 years old when the team shipped out to Egypt.[68]

Despite rigorous and lengthy training, the team found appalling conditions and considerable challenges on the ground. Having come into the country on the heels of the civil war armistice, the Guide relief workers found themselves in difficult political terrain, in the midst of territory that had only recently been controlled by the Greek Popular Liberation Army (ELAS).[69] Duke, with her language skills, often traveled far into the mountains with members of the team, where she was met with extraordinary circumstances. She and her colleagues were snowed in, waiting for British troops to relieve them, when ELAS guerillas from the surrounding mountains came down and asked them to accept their surrendered arms.[70]

As this ambiguous and potentially dangerous situation developed in Greece, the first team arrived in January 1945. Their initial task was to collect information on the needs of the populace:

> At one village at the moment they reckon 90 people are now starving . . . . At another village 150 families are starving. All have scabies and there is much pneumonia and dysentery . . . . In another, many of the houses have no roofs and the people still live in them . . . . Some are living in beehive shelters . . . [others] have built rough shelters from odd wood.[71]

In other words, the task for the GIS was daunting. Subsequent teams faced similar or sometimes worse conditions in the areas where they were deployed. The bulk of the British teams was sent to the Netherlands and to Germany to work in displaced persons camps and hospitals, although one unit was a special laboratory unit that worked on testing for diseases. The Dutch and German GIS squads often entered their assigned zones just behind the liberating armies. Near Amersfoort, Netherlands, the GIS team arrived in ruined villages within hours of their capitulation to Allied liberators. As one member recalled, "When our trefoil badge was recognized the cry 'Padvinsters! [Scouts]' echoed down the line . . . that night a GIS billet was inside a concentration camp . . . in a building used as the SS officers' mess."[72] Other GIS members were sent to Belsen in July 1945, where half of the former camp there was still quarantined because of typhus. The GIS participated in the transformation of the Bergen-Belsen concentration camp of 14,000 people to a displaced persons' camp called "Hohne" over the course of 1945.[73] This work, while fulfilling for GIS members, was distressing and difficult; they really had had no way of properly training for such sights.

With primarily British Guides making up the GIS teams in Europe, the Australian and New Zealand Guides of GIS were most often assigned to Singapore and Malaya. As with their counterparts in Europe, the GIS teams in Asia found unpredictable situations. For example, the Australian team sent to Singapore and Malaya in 1946 faced the unhappy task of entering a rural area, rife with banditry, in order to set up a small-pox inoculation program. While there, they became a de facto mobile medical unit, despite their lack of formal training in medicine. In this case, their Guide first-aid training came in handy.[74]

Altogether 13 teams traveled to various locations in Europe and Asia, with just under 200 female volunteers and another 100 or so male Scouters. The first team spent 18 months abroad between 1944 and 1946, while some other teams stayed for up to 5 years. The physically and emotionally challenging early relief work gave way to more administrative tasks by the late 1940s, and the last GIS members worked more in the areas of immigration advocacy, relocation assistance, and employment help. The final GIS members did not return home until 1952, and the last GIS meeting was held in 1954. Over the course of the decade, the GIS had made a name for itself as an important Guide humanitarian endeavor, but it had also fostered Guiding in the countries where it functioned. German Guiding, which had been outlawed for a generation of youth, had really not flourished since that early visit of German Guides to Britain in 1914. With the arrival of the GIS and the end of the Second World War, GIS volunteers helped create a new Guide movement in the British occupation zone of what would become West Germany. GIS member, Verona Wallace Williamson, helped identify and train German women as Guide leaders, with assistance from national Guide organizations in nearby countries that offered to host the women for trainings in practical Guiding.[75]

Other countries also sponsored Guide relief work, and the World Association as well had a training team for voluntary work among displaced people.[76] Although much smaller in scope than the GIS program, U.S. Girl Scouts sent relief teams around the world as part of the United

Nation's Relief and Rehabilitation Administration's (UNRRA) projects for displaced persons. Scout leaders traveled to Palestine, Yugoslavia, Germany, Japan, and Korea to work with the displaced from war. As with the GIS, Girl Scouts found themselves organizing local troops of girls in the areas where they were engaged in relief work, including in Japan and Korea, where prewar movements were reestablished.[77]

Once again, Guides had shown their usefulness during a wartime emergency, working tirelessly and sometimes at great personal peril to serve their nations and the broader ideals for which they strived. The end of the war brought relief and reorganization for many national Guide organizations, and it provided a chance to regroup and think about the future. In its letter to the World Association in May 1945, the Danish Girl Guides captured the spirit of elation that accompanied war's end: "most cordial greetings again—from *free* Denmark! . . . it was possible for the Danish Girl Guides to continue our work actively through the time of occupation . . . and [now] we are prepared to offer all our good will and strength to the great work which lies in front of us, to help to build up what has been destroyed."[78] Guides seemed poised to take their wartime energies into the reconstruction period. In order to assess Guiding's strength, provide visible support, and to gather stories of wartime heroism, the Chief Guide and the Director of the World Bureau, toured Europe in spring 1945.[79]

Yet despite heroic war work and a sustained commitment to the Guide program by many members during the war, the period between 1946 and 1950 saw the destruction of some of the most important Guide communities in the world. Olga Malkowska, Polish Guiding's founder, issued a warning to world Guiding in 1948: "The little vessels of our Guide and Girl Scout Movement are on very troubled waters. The fresh breeze has turned into a gale and the waves are tossing the little craft hither and thither, ready to swallow them up."[80] Her words were prophetic in her own country. Guides had increased in numbers during and after the war, and they took part in reconstruction and postwar social service work. However, the movement was officially outlawed by the new Polish government and membership from WAGGGS withdrawn in 1950.[81] Likewise in Hungary, Guiding and Scouting were disbanded by the postwar regime in 1948.[82]

For those national movements that survived, restarted, or thrived during the war, funding and leadership were still important concerns. The Girl Scouts of the USA were still appealing for leaders and funds in

1945, and they worked to accommodate girls who continued to wait for troop availability. Elsewhere, rebuilding of units and recruitment of leaders also continued. In France, Guide journals began appearing again in 1945–1946.[83] World meetings were held again, beginning in 1946. Once more, as after World War I, Guiding retooled itself for peace.

Coincidentally, the upheaval of the war period occurred simultaneously with the deaths of many of Guiding's pioneers. This shift in leadership opened the way for more radical programmatic changes and corresponded to a feeling among many young Guides that a new focus was needed to attract girls in the postwar world. Perhaps the most significant loss, at least in symbolic terms, was the death of Robert Baden-Powell in Kenya in January 1941. The loss of the Chief Scout and founder of both Scouting and Guiding, while not unexpected given his age and ill health, moved Guiding into a new era of its history. B-P's death was followed shortly after by Agnes Baden-Powell's in June 1945 and by Rose Kerr's in December 1944. Kerr, who had been instrumental in developing the international movement and who had written Guiding's first official history, had been one of the Guide movement's stalwarts almost since its inception.

In other countries as well, many of the chief personalities of the Guide and Girl Scout associations died before and during the war, as is evident from Figure 4.1.

Figure 4.1   Deaths of Some Key Guide Leaders up to 1945

Name of Leader	Date of Death	Country/Guide Association
Robert Baden-Powell	1941	Great Britain
Agnes Baden-Powell	1945	Great Britain
Lady Mary Pellatt	1924	Canada
Mrs. Ulbricht	1937	Denmark (YWCA)
"Bes" Flagstadt	1939	Denmark
Albertine Duhamel	1937	France (Guides)
Marie Diemer	1938	France (Guides)
Marguerite "Chef" Walther	1942	France (Éclaireuses)
M. Cijfer-van Wijngaarden	1940	Netherlands
Jadwiga Falkowska	1944	Poland
Juliette Low	1927	United States
Birdsall Otis Edey	1940	United States
Sarah Louise Arnold	1943	United States
Lou Henry Hoover	1944	United States
Helen Storrow	1944	United States

Helen Storrow, Sarah Louise Arnold, and Birdsall Otis Edey in the United States had all been active since the First World War in Guiding. Marguerite "Chef" Walther was "an emblematic member" in the French Éclaireuses and a mainstay of the World Association. Many of the others listed were founders or important national presidents of their respective movements. Their deaths left holes in the leadership ranks, but also created unprecedented opportunities for transformation.

Those pioneers still standing at the end of World War II felt the pressure for change from a younger membership with new ideas about what youth education should mean. Some of the remaining adults who had given lifetimes of service to Guiding were pushed out in the 1940s. At the world conference in Evian, France, in September 1946, there was a shakeup in leadership that resulted in several resignations. The end result was that women such as Katharine Furse (WAGGGS), Arethusa Leigh-White (WAGGGS), Countess Maria Bernadotte (Sweden), and Madame Van Den Bosch (Netherlands) moved out of leadership roles in Guiding. While some resented the shift in personnel and the so-called "Evian putsch," others understood that they had to step aside for Guiding to grow.[84] As Elsa Kjederqvist of Sweden explained in a 1946 editorial:

> We who were young when Guiding was young are middle-aged now, and as we look back over the last thirty years we see more clearly than we did at the time the problems with which we contended—not always successfully. We older ones must now stand aside and let the young leaders go forward, taking responsibility and running their own show. Like parents who must learn to relinquish their children and allow them to be free and independent, so we must ask ourselves over and over again: "Am I standing in the way of the young?"[85]

Like Kjederqvist, Arethusa Leigh-White also realized that it was time to resign as World Bureau Director after eight years in the post. At Evian, she presented her resignation, saying, "I know that younger and stronger shoulders than mine are needed today, and perhaps a wider and more practical experience."[86] For some of these women, the war had just made them tired, and it seemed fresh energies were required.

With the end of the war and these important personnel shifts, the time seemed ripe for a reexamination of Guide methods and mission. The most widespread shift in Guiding history took place in the decade following the war as countries around the world sought to reformulate their programs, update their uniforms, and publish new handbooks. In the

Guides de France, for example, leaders spent eight years from 1945 to 1953 studying the movement and modern adolescents. After this intensive study, the movement transformed its program for younger girls, Jeannettes, and tried to make Guiding more "active."[87] In the United States, new uniforms designed by American fashion designer, Mainbocher, were introduced in 1948.[88] British Guiding also adopted a new uniform and hat in 1946, and Agnes "the Carpenter" Maynard, a pioneer Guider authored a new handbook, *Be Prepared!*, that same year.[89]

As Guiding approached its fortieth birthday, its leaders increasingly began to take stock of the girls in the movement, and more importantly, those girls who were not interested in Guiding. The 1950s would prove a test for national Guide movements as new conceptions of adolescent consumerism and interest emerged and as youth movement sought to "stay with the times." While the war consolidated Guiding's and Girl Scouting's reputations as national institutions and conferred new respectability, the postwar left some girls with the sense of strategic retreat into homes. Whether the correct way to appeal to girls of the 1940s and 1950s was to encourage stalking and camping or to embrace fashion trends and cosmetics became a question that Guides leaders had to address.

NOTES

1. "A Camp in the Forest," *The Times* (August 3, 1939), 10.

2. Rose Kerr, "The Pax-Ting," *The Council Fire* 14:4 (October 1939), 52.

3. "Nazi Bombing of Civilians. U S Ambassador's Testimony," *The Times* (September 14, 1939).

4. Geneviève Iweins d'Eeckhoutte, "De l'oeuvre aux fédérations le guidisme catholique en Belgique, 1915–1960: Chronique d'un mouvement," in *Guidisme, scoutisme et coéducation*, eds. Thierry Scaillet, Sophie Wittemans, and Françoise Rosart (Louvain-la-Neuve: Academia-Bruylant, 2007), 240–241.

5. Rose Kerr, unpublished typescript "Girl Guides in Countries at War," (December 1940), WAGGGS, GSUSA; Marie-Thérèse Cheroutre, *Le scoutisme au féminin: Les guides de France, 1923–1998* (Paris: Les Éditions du Cerf, 2002), 166.

6. "Secours aux refugies," *The Council Fire* 15:3 (July 1940), 40–41.

7. *Girl Guiding/Girl Scouting: A Challenging Movement* (London: WAGGGS, 1992), 16.

8. "News from our Scattered Family," *The Council Fire* 15:3 (July 1940), 33.

9. "The Western Hemisphere Encampment," *The Council Fire* 15:4 (October 1940), 49; "Tour of the Director of the World Bureau in the Western Hemisphere," *The Council Fire* 16:3 (July 1941), 36.

10. Note that census figures for the war years are inexact, especially because some Guide members were serving overseas. Figures provided by GirlGuiding UK. "Royal Visit to Girl Guides," *The Times* (November 15, 1939).

11. *Highlights in Girl Scouting* (New York: Girl Scouts of the USA, 2002), 18–19.

12. Cheroutre, *Le scoutisme au féminin*, 244.

13. Scrapbook, 3rd Wimbledon, 1923–1924, GGL.

14. Logbook, 13th North Kensington, 1925–1930, GGL.

15. Logbook, 3rd Southall Co (Fuchsia Patrol), 1928–1935, GGL.

16. Logbook, 1st Chislehurst, 1924–1929, GGL.

17. WAGGGS Membership Sheet, 29th World Conference, 1996, p. 6, ST1/C15/Shelf 1, Box 6 Fiji, GGL.

18. Girlguiding UK History Sheet—Aden, ST1/C15/Shelf 1, Box 1 Aden, GGL.

19. Iweins d'Eeckhoutte, "Le guidisme catholique," 241–242.

20. Clippings and logbooks, Guides Catholiques de Belgique Archives, Brussels.

21. Michelin was first in Ravensbruck, then Holleischen, a sub-camp of Flossenburg. Cheroutre, *Le scoutisme au féminin*, 172–174, 182, 231; Marthe Letourneux interview with Mme. Michelin (English translation), ST1/C15/Shelf 1 Box 6, France, GGL.

22. "History of French Guiding in the War," p. 10, ST1/C15/Shelf 1 Box 6, France, GGL.

23. Cheroutre, *Le scoutisme au féminin*, 232–234; Alice Daul, "Mon evasion," ST1/C15/Shelf 1 Box 6, France, GGL.

24. Andrzej Suchcitz, "The Grey Ranks (1939–1945)," (London: Polish Home Army Association, n.d.), accessed July 29, 2008 at http://www.polishresistance-ak.org. "Scouts Celebrate Centenary," *The Warsaw Voice* (August 22, 2007).

25. Memo from WAGGGS to Full Member Organisations, 1996, p. 8; Poland Information Sheet; 6th Krakow Guides to British Guides, February 1945, ST1/C15/Shelf 2 Box 13, Poland, GGL.

26. "Notes and News," *The Council Fire* 15:2 (April 1940), 17.

27. Piet J. Kroonenberg, "The Forgotten Movements III. Hungary," unpublished history, 1989, ST1/C15/Shelf 1 Box 7, Hungary, GGL.

28. "Keep Calm," *The Times* (September 1, 1939).

29. "Royal Visit to Girl Guides," *The Times* (November 15, 1939).

30. Rose Kerr, "When the Siren Sounds," *The Council Fire* 16:3 (July 1941), 44.

31. Winifred Lander, "Home Emergency Service," *The Council Fire* 17:3 (July 1942), 42.

32. "Polish Girl Guides," *The Times* (October 16, 1939); M. Chmielowska, "Madame Malkowska's School in Scotland," *The Council Fire* 17:1 (January 1942), 9; Olga Malkowska, "The Story of the Polish School," *The Council Fire* 19:2 (April 1944), 14.

33. *1910 ... And Then? A Brief History of the Guide Association* (London: Girl Guides Association, 1990), 15–16.

34. Katharine Furse, "The Future," *The Council Fire* 16:3 (July 1941), 33–34.

35. Girl Guides Association of Trinidad and Tobago, *Diamond Jubilee 1914–1974* (n.p.: GGATT, 1974), 37.

36. Memo on Barbados Guiding, n.d.; Mrs. Monica Skeete, "Guiding in Barbados, 1918–1968,"*Diamond Jubilee of Guiding in Barbados* (ca. 1968), 17, ST1/C15/Shelf 1 Box 2: Barbados, GGL.

37. History of Guiding in Malta and clipping (May 10, 1945), ST1/C15/Shelf 2 Box 10 Malta, GGL; "Notes and News: Malta," *The Council Fire* 16:1 (January 1941), 5.

38. Dorothy Crocker, *All About Us: A Story of the Girl Guides in Canada, 1910–1989* (Ottawa: GGC, 1990), 23.

39. "Guiding in a Concentration Camp," *The Council Fire* 21:2 (April 1946), 22.

40. Clipping, "Guiding under Guard," *Guiding* (November 2006), Changi Prison folder, GGL.

41. Betty Hall, "The Story of the Girl Guides Quilt from Changi," TS, Chester Grosvenor Guild, Changi Prison folder, GGL; Mrs. B. M. Hall, "Changi Quilts," *This England* (Autumn 2006), 63; Sheila Allan, *Diary of a Girl in Changi, 1941–1945* (Kenthurst, Australia: Kangaroo Press, 1994), 10.

42. Logbook of 1st Chefoo Brownies, 1942, ST2/S4/B2/Shelf 3/28/57, GGL.

43. Logbook of 1st Chefoo Brownies, 1943, ST2/S4/B2/Shelf 3/28/57, GGL.

44. Jane Schneider, "Ending the Silence: How One Determined Woman Managed to Keep Alive the story of Japanese Internment Camps in Arkansas," *Memphis Magazine* (February 2003) and News Letter of National Headquarters, February 25, 1942, p. 1, BOX: Defense—General (1941–1945) to General (Japanese Relocation Camps), FOLDER: Defense, General—Japanese Relocation Camps; GSUSA.

45. News Letter of National Headquarters, Nov–Dec 1943, p. 1, National Board/Executive Committee Minutes April 27, 1944, p. 84, and News Letter of National Headquarters, June 1945, p. 4, BOX: Defense—General (1941–1945) to General (Japanese Relocation Camps), FOLDER: Defense, General—Japanese Relocation Camps; GSUSA.

46. Miss Hannah and Miss Illingworth to Miss Paterson, January 1943, ST1/C15/Shelf 1, Box 5 Canada, GGL.

47. Canada Report for 1941 (1942), ST1/C15/Shelf 1, Box 5 Canada, GGL.

48. "Paid to the People of the USA," *The Council Fire* 19:4 (October 1944), 31.

49. "Defense Plea is Made," *New York Times* (December 9, 1941).

50. "10,000 Girl Scouts to Aid in War Here," *New York Times* (March 26, 1942).

51. Mary Degenhardt and Judith Kirsch, *Girl Scout Collector's Guide: A History of Uniforms, Insignia, Publications and Memorabilia*, 2nd Edition (Lubbock: Texas Tech University Press, 2005), 199–200, 203.

52. "Silk Stockings Needed," *New York Times* (February 28, 1943).

53. "New Jobs Started by Girl Mariners," *New York Times* (May 31, 1942); Bertha Stringer, "With the Girl Scout Mariners of Hingham, Mass., during the War Years," *The Council Fire* 21:3 (July 1946), 31.

54. Degenhardt and Kirsch, *Girl Scout Collector's Guide*, 195–197; "Schoolgirls to get Aviation Training," *New York Times* (July 5, 1942). In Britain, Air Rangers began in 1945 after a small experimental version in 1944.

55. Catherine Mackenzie, "Line for the Girl Scouts," *New York Times Magazine* (October 29, 1944), 33.

56. Girl Guides Association of New Zealand, *Thirty Years of Guiding in New Zealand, 1923–1953* (n.p.: GGANZ, 1953), 19–20.

57. "Notes and News: Sweden," *The Council Fire* 16:3 (July 1941), 34.

58. "Letters from Falk," *The Council Fire* 16:2 (April 1941), 26.

59. "Notes and News: Iceland," *The Council Fire* 19:3 (July 1944), 19.

60. Alix Liddell, *Story of the Girl Guides, 1938–1975* (London: Girl Guides Association, 1976), 25–26.

61. Liddell, *Story of the Girl Guides*, 28.

62. "Work for Girl Guides," *The Times* (November 11, 1942).

63. Alison Duke MA 22 July 1915–6 November 2005 (Girton College Life Fellows Directory) http://www.girton.cam.ac.uk/fellows-and-staff/life-fellows/alison-duke/, accessed July 30, 2008.

64. Phyllis Stewart Brown, *All Things Uncertain: The Story of the GIS* (London: Girl Guides Association, 1967), 14, 21–27, 31; Muriel Lees, *A Job in a Lifetime* (London: Girl Guides Association, 1976), 5.

65. Brown, *All Things Uncertain*, 33.

66. Catharine Christian, "Training with the G.I.S.," *The Council Fire* 18:2 (April 1943), 24–25.

67. Liddell, *Story of the Girl Guides*, 27.

68. Author interview with Lady Marjorie Stopford, Bushey Heath, Hertfordshire, March 24, 1993.

69. Muriel Lees, "A job in a lifetime," cited in Marion Sarafis, "Review," *History Workshop Journal* 13:1 (1982), 157–158.

70. Alison Duke MA 22 July 1915–6 November 2005 (Girton College Life Fellows Directory) http://www.girton.cam.ac.uk/fellows-and-staff/life-fellows/alison-duke/, accessed July 30, 2008.

71. "Guide International Service," *The Council Fire* 20:2 (April 1945), 16.

72. Brown, *All Things Uncertain*, 62.

73. Brown, *All Things Uncertain*, 66, 75–78.

74. Brown, *All Things Uncertain*, 140–146.

75. Elizabeth Hartley, "Rebirth of German Guiding," *The Council Fire* 24:1 (January 1949), 6. The U.S. Girl Scouts also started German Scout organizations in their zone as well.

76. Liddell, *Story of the Girl Guides*, 32–33.

77. Degenhardt and Kirsch, *Girl Scout Collector's Guide*, 203–204.

78. "Notes and News: Denmark," *The Council Fire* 20:3 (July 1945), 24.

79. Liddell, *Story of the Girl Guides*, 34.

80. Olga Malkowska, "Thinking of You All," *The Council Fire* 23:1 (January 1948), 1.

81. "Poland" in the *Ninth Biennial Report* (London: WAGGGS, 1946), 79; Memo from WAGGGS to Full Member National Organisations, 1996, p. 8, ST1/C15/Shelf 2, Box 13, Poland, GGL.

82. Piet J. Kroonenberg, "The Forgotten Movements III. Hungary," unpublished history, 1989, ST1/C15/Shelf 1 Box 7, Hungary, GGL.

83. Cheroutre, *Le scoutisme au féminin*, 243.

84. Katharine Furse to Constance Rittenhouse, May 5, 1948; Katharine Furse to Anne Choate, August 11, 1947; Constance Rittenhouse to Katharine Furse, March 30, 1948; Folder—Katharine Furse, Personalities box, Freeman to Futrell, GSUSA.

85. "Reflections," *The Council Fire* 21:3 (July 1946), 25.

86. "Report of the Business of the Eleventh World Conference," *The Council Fire* 21:4 (October 1946), 45.

87. Cheroutre, *Le scoutisme au féminin*, 247–253.

88. *Highlights in Girl Scouting, 1912–2001* (New York: GSUSA, 2002), 17.

89. Informational cards, GGL.

Scout and Guide founder Robert Baden-Powell poses with his wife, Olave Baden-Powell, who served as Chief Guide of the World. [By kind permission of Girlguiding UK]

Juliette Low, founder of U.S. Girl Scouting, presenting a pin to a member. [Courtesy of Girl Scouts of the USA National Historic Preservation Center & Juliette Gordon Low Birthplace]

An unofficial group of Girl Scouts from 1909 in Bristol with their leader, Miss Wise. [By kind permission of Girlguiding UK]

The 1st Weymouth Girl Guides (UK) collecting waste paper for the war effort during the First World War. [By kind permission of Girlguiding UK]

As Girl Guiding expanded internationally, diverse populations were drawn to the movement, as with this Belgian Girl Guide, Rosalie Pastijn, in 1919. [© Archives Guides Catholiques de Belgique asbl, Belgium, Fonds Melchior Verpoorten, 1915–1923. Used by Permission.]

It was not uncommon for whole families to be involved in Guiding and Scouting; these siblings belong to the Deldoncker family in Belgium, 1919. [© Archives Guides Catholiques de Belgique asbl, Belgium, Fonds Melchior Verpoorten, 1915–1923. Used by permission.]

American Girl Scouts in the 1930s demonstrate the Scout law promoting "kindness to animals." [Courtesy of Girl Scouts of the USA National Historic Preservation Center]

Brownies in Britain practice first aid in the 1920s. [By kind permission of Girlguiding UK]

Marguerite de Beaumont (third from left) with her Ranger Company at their "Daydream" camp at the British seaside in 1933. [By kind permission of Girlguiding UK]

A Brownie and Guide in Singapore, ca. 1930s. [By kind permission of Girlguiding UK]

A U.S. Girl Scout learning arts and crafts with her leader, ca. 1950s. [Courtesy of Girl Scouts of the USA National Historic Preservation Center]

4th Grahamstown Sunbeam Circle in South Africa, unknown date. [By kind permission of Girlguiding UK]

A British trainer working with Guides in the Bahamas, 1958. [By kind permission of Girlguiding UK]

Guides in Bangladesh (East Pakistan) at a rally, 1961. Many countries modify Guide uniforms to meet local cultural and religious traditions. [By kind permission of Girlguiding UK]

Guides from several countries share experiences at the Asian International Camp in Japan, 1963. [By kind permission of Girlguiding UK]

Sa'ad ibn Fahd al-Qahtani explains the flag to U.S. Girl Scouts in a troop in Saudi Arabia (their parents worked for Arabian American Oil) in the 1970s. [Courtesy of Girl Scouts of the USA National Historic Preservation Center]

Arden McHugh Braham with Courageous Camara, her Groovy Girls doll, which is one of several named after the Girl Scout laws. She will be eligible for the youngest branch of Girl Scouting, the Daisy Scouts, when she turns five years old. [By kind permission of Nancy A. McHugh]

5. Transformations

In his last message to Scouts and Guides around the world, published upon his death in 1941, Robert Baden-Powell exhorted leaders to "Look wide, and smile." With his usual talent for a yarn, B-P suggested that as Guiding moved forward, it might be best to think of mountain climbing:

> There are two ways of climbing a mountain: one man goes steadily upward, following the track that has been made by others or has been pointed out by the guide book; he keeps his eyes fixed on the track . . . . The other climber . . . looks wider. He looks ahead, and sees where the former track may now, owing to wash-outs, etc., be improved upon, and he varies his course accordingly. Occasionally he pauses to look around him and to realise the glorious view that is opening up and unfolding itself at every step.[1]

B-P's message to the Guides here is clear—don't be the dogged plodder who always sticks to the plan, but the intrepid climber, willing to stray from the path once in a while. Strive for the glorious view. This advice, oft-repeated in various ways through the founder's career, helped shape Guiding over its first half-century as it faced two world wars, major social and cultural change, and worldwide expansion.

This chapter takes a step back and examines the development of Guiding's programs and activities, the stops and starts, the deviations from the trail. Some of the shifts led to success and have remained crucial components of the movement today; other ideas had to be abandoned or changed as they grew outdated or merely did not work for girls. As the Guide movement celebrated its fiftieth anniversary, many of its activities and ideas were under scrutiny and were transformed to "stay current with the times." One easy way to chart these programmatic transformations is through the literature of the movement, specifically the handbooks, the badge lists, and the magazines. The constants in the life of Guiding were primarily structural and ideological, so weekly meetings, badge work, patrols, games, and songs remained at the heart of how Guiding was experienced. While some things in Guiding remained sacrosanct—service, scoutcraft, promise/laws, uniforms—as central principles, the methods and activities evolved over time.

In the earliest Girl Guide literature, the organizational aims are clearly outlined for possible leaders and members. Paramount goals included "character training" and teaching girls to be "self-helpful, happy, prosperous, and capable of keeping good homes and bringing up good children."[2] The method for achieving these goals was to emphasize games, active learning, crafts, and outdoor recreation. Baden-Powell's idea of teaching citizenship not through book learning but through doing marked this movement as different from school or religious institutions, and its use of the outdoors as a training ground brought a spark of excitement to many British girls of the Edwardian period.

For much of the first 10 years of the movement, military drill and defense preparation also featured prominently in the movement's ideals and methods, reflecting a larger societal preoccupation with preparedness and the expansion of women's access to activities such as shooting, driving, rambling, and signaling. As Sally Mitchell discovered in her look at girls' literature in the late Victorian and Edwardian eras, "military imagery pervades the period."[3] Girls were encouraged to be brave like soldiers and to imagine themselves in many of the heroic roles that boys were drawn to in their stories such as *The Prisoner of Zenda* and *The Scarlet Pimpernel*. Girls' fiction began featuring female heroines in similarly adventurous roles, especially nurses in wartime. Mitchell argues in her book that this rich fantasy life for girls made Guiding fit well in the broader militaristic and boyish cultural frame of the time for middle-class girls, helping foster the "new girls' mental life as a boy."[4] The war, when it came, provided a proving ground for all the fantasy adventures of service to country that girls had been internalizing through Guiding and popular literature.

With the interwar period, much of the overt militarization disappeared from Guiding as it shifted its methods to emphasize cross-class sisterhood and international peaceful outreach. Girls who had drilled and practiced Morse in the 1910s now incorporated nature study and international friendship initiatives into their Guide activities. Many companies that began their lives in the midst of war work had, by the early 1920s, shifted their focus to team sports, nature films, and rambling, among other things. The life of the company revolved around the same principles of character training, active learning, and outdoor recreation that had marked Baden-Powell's original scheme, but the form of the activities and the interpretation of the aims had changed. In particular, Guiding embraced more commercial leisure activities, mirroring a more general change in girls' lives in the 1920s. Girls spent more time in school, for instance, and they increasingly enjoyed new media such as radio, film, and phonograph records.[5]

As the movements grew, fundraising became a more central feature, with regular annual campaigns for funds emerging at the local, national, and international level to help expand and support activities. In Britain, Guides engaged in popular church fêtes and pantomimes, but in the United States, the Girl Scouts hit upon a fundraising scheme that has become one of their most recognizable features. Girl Scout cookies are a good example of how fundraising could become big business within the movements. As early as World War I, local Girl Scout troops sold cookies to raise funds, but these were homemade efforts. By the 1920s, as troops shared recipes and ideas, some local councils began engaging commercial bakers to produce and package the cookies as fundraisers for their Scout troops. Soon troops were competing in cookie sales in local regions. As the idea caught on, national headquarters sought to regulate and regularize this fundraising possibility, first licensing commercial bakers of Girl Scout cookies in the 1930s and helping market special "trefoil" design cookies. While World War II with its shortages of such basics as sugar stopped the cookie sales temporarily, they resumed in the late 1940s, becoming a national fundraising scheme with specific packaging and flavors by the 1950s.[6] Today most everyone in the United States has tasted a Girl Scout cookie at some point.

Fundraising and its possibilities led to tremendous changes in troops and companies as they began to use the funds for marketing, activities, and outreach. One of the principal ways in which Guiding had transformed was in its delivery of the movement's message. With the founding of a magazine for the girls themselves in 1921 (*The Guide*), Guide headquarters began to tap into mass cultural forms that it had only dabbled in during its first decade. The earlier magazine, *The Girl Guides Gazette*, was primarily aimed at leaders, with its advice on training and bits of headquarters' news. With *The Guide*, the organization hoped to attract middle-class and working-class girls with an affordable and interesting periodical, full of games, songs, stories, and advice. At first the magazine remained heavy on the Guide news and light on entertainment, but as the interwar period wore on, *The Guide* began to emulate the popular girls' story papers and magazines of the time. With its appearance in 1921, *The Guide* tapped into a broader move in Britain and the United States to produce cheap girls' periodicals for a cross-class audience.

Several long-running magazines were founded just after the First World War, including *Schoolgirls' Weekly* (1922), *Schoolgirls' Own* (1921), and *The School Friend* (1919).[7] Girls' magazines, in general, "proliferated" between the 1920s and 1940s in Britain. These magazines targeted girls of different social class background and helped invent a modern "teen" culture that had an impact on Guiding's program.[8] Some of these general interest magazines even targeted Guides; for instance, the *Schoolgirls' Own* featured a special "Girl Guides Corner" that allowed Guides to write to a "captain" with their questions.[9]

Playing to the emerging commercialized and consumer-oriented teen culture of the period as represented by popular mass magazines and playing to the original program Baden-Powell envisioned was a difficult task for Guide headquarters. Guiding depended on its serious notions of service to set it apart from other forms of mass youth culture, but leaders also wanted to depict their programs as being attractive and relevant cultural forms. In the United States, this dilemma led the Girl Scouts to move the magazine, *The American Girl* (founded in 1917 as the more militaristic *The Rally* and renamed in June 1920) toward issues pertaining generally to girls and away from Girl Scout material by the late 1920s and early 1930s.[10] While a typical issue from 1923 included Girl Scout activities, mail from Girl Scouts, stories and accounts from leaders, and insight about badges or international Guiding, by 1933, the magazine included mostly teen fiction, fashion tips, and some generic advice about girls' sports. Lou Henry Hoover, First Lady of the United States and Girl Scout Honorary President, decried this shift in 1929, telling another leader: "It is really a matter of very grave concern to me that we are constantly losing the Girl Scout impress on the magazine." As she noted, the Girl Scout items of interest had dwindled to "two 'badly done' pages."[11] In Britain, a Guide echoed this concern in her diary, writing "I want to ask why in the name of all that's sensible should Guide fiction be so extraordinary [*sic*] stupid," and she rhetorically longed for stories that are "a little less stereotyped and fatuous."[12]

Regardless of how engagingly written and believable these publications were, girls *were reading* them in the 1920s, so Guiding and Girl Scouting needed to produce such literature for its members to consume. The stories, often hair-raising adventure tales of self-assertive, daring, and transgressive girls, appealed to preteen and teen readers.[13] In a study of schoolchildren in London in 1933, more than one-half of the children surveyed admitted to reading at least "three 'storypapers' or comics per week," and another one-third of the children read six periodicals a week in their leisure time.[14] Many of these popular papers were produced by the same publishing houses and followed similar formulas, but they sold well and children liked them despite their homogenous nature (or maybe because of it). It was this market that Guiding also sought to gain with its publications. The Girl Scouts and Guides felt the need to use teenaged popular cultural forms to keep the attention of the older girls in the movement. Tips on fashion, fictional romances, dating advice, and "health" information sold magazines, which was important for Girl Scout and Guide retention and outreach. This new thrust toward consumption, mass culture, and teenaged popular forms only intensified with the post-World War II period, when the magazines competed for the female reading public. Guiding's strategy of emulating mass market magazines seemed to work, as circulation figures for *The Guide* expanded from just under 20,000 copies per week in 1925 to 40,000 subscribers in 1930. This number increased again in the 1930s after further format changes moved *The Guide* even closer to mass market women's and girls' publications.[15]

One of the features of the magazines from the 1920s into the 1960s was serialized romance and adventure stories, which sparked another media form—Guide novels. A number of Guide fiction books appeared in the 1920s, often parroting the popular girls' school or adventure story, with fantastic storylines of mystery, adventure, danger, and romance. Many female authors made their livings writing Guide fiction, including Dorothea Moore and Catherine Christian in Britain and Edith Lavell and Lillian Roy in the United States, to name just a few. Guide novels were not confined to the English-speaking world, but emerged in many nations with Guide movements. For example, Guide novels in French appeared first in 1930 with *Always Prepared!*, which like the English novels, presented Guide characters that were active, decisive, and full of energy.[16]

Guide fiction often contained an explicit message about appropriate morality and femininity, but it also allowed for hair-raising and outlandish escapades that kept girls' attention while they were absorbing the important "character" lessons. These books and stories mirrored popular publications in their emphasis on social mobility too, and many of the characters were outsiders (Americans or Canadians), scholarship girls at elite schools, or lower middle-class clerks. The dominant message in Guide fiction often focused on either a girl's ability to "make good" or to find redemption through a successful school career, a better job, a leadership position in Guiding, or an advantageous marriage. In this fictional fantasy world, selfish girls transformed into model citizens, and upper working-class girls discovered jobs in fancy boutiques or earned scholarships to high schools.[17] In many cases, the girls with poor home lives found their way with the help of Guide friends. A few parents in the stories are bad characters, but most are just neglectful, as with the parents in *Rosie the Peddler* (1925), who are "hard at work making fortunes" (father) or "busy giving magnificent parties" (mother). When their child, Rosemary, is abducted and sold to a peddler caravan, no readers are surprised at her lack of protection.[18]

The author of *Rosie the Peddler* provides a good example of the creators of Guide fiction and their messages. F. O. H. Nash wrote a series of Guide novels between the 1920s and the 1950s, including the popular *Rosie the Peddler*. Her work features girls in need of a lesson, often through multiple stages of their lives as Guides. In her "Audrey" series, Audrey moved from Guide, to camp, to school, to Sea Ranger over the four-book sequence. In each book, this middle-class girl learns a new life lesson through her Guide training, and in each, she encounters a new threat. The first book, *How Audrey Became a Guide* (1922) follows Audrey as she copes with a new stepmother (who is a Guide commissioner) and a visiting cousin (who is a Guide). After several selfish and mean acts, Audrey is converted, and she joins the Guides for a series of adventures that include saving a small boy from an evil itinerant tinker and befriending a "crippled" Guide. Audrey, now an enthusiastic Guide, learns new Guide skills and games over the course of the series, and she encounters even more mysterious characters and adventures in the second and third book. These books really mark her class status, especially *Audrey At School* (1925), which follows her promotion from a governess to the elite school "Boglemere Park." Now 14 years old, Audrey and her friends play cricket, devise pranks, and practice their Guiding; one of Audrey's friends even has a "rave" for another schoolgirl, although it was "discouraged at their school." This book reads much like any school story written for the popular market in the 1920s. The final book in the series comes much later, in 1931, when Audrey has moved into the senior branch—*Audrey the Sea Ranger*. In this installment, Audrey goes to Belgium with the Sea Rangers and participates in daring rescues, while also being abducted by smugglers. All these adventures are merely ways for Audrey to pass the time, however, as she waits for her boyfriend Jerry to finish at Cambridge and take the civil service exam. As with much of the Guide message, marriage and motherhood are the happy ending for Audrey, not an adventurous life at sea.

In addition to popular fiction, other forms of media were used by the Guides to promulgate their message. Publicity in the form of posters for events or fundraisers appeared in mainstream publications and on the walls of community buildings, churches, and schools. These forms of media were cheap to produce and ideal for circulating to companies and troops through the districts and divisions of the organization. Many were short and generic, such as "The Girl Scouts Hope Chest" (1925), which was a recruiting brochure produced in the United States. Its main message was an overt call to all girls, regardless of their aspirations: "The Girl Scout Influence prepares a girl either for marriage or a career by helping her to fill her hope chest with desirable qualities of mind, heart and spirit."[19] Guide and Girl Scout associations around the world printed pamphlets about particular aspects of the movement, but also sold equipment catalogs, songbooks, handbooks, and badge books. Use of media for outreach extended to all forms of printed materials, and the relatively new medium of radio became a home for Guiding as well by the interwar period.

Radio broadened these more traditional print sources and allowed Guide leaders to reach larger numbers of girls, especially in rural areas where contact between companies was difficult. Both Australia and Canada, for example, tried to bridge distances by sponsoring radio shows for Guides, and Lone Guides in several countries relied on radio for important ceremonies and procedures in their Guide lives. Radio also allowed the voices of Guides into the homes of the uninitiated. In the United States, Girl Scout leaders began broadcasting speeches by national leaders on National Broadcasting Company (NBC) airwaves in 1930 to publicize their program, capitalizing on their connection with such luminaries as the U.S. President's wife, Lou Henry Hoover.[20] Later as television developed, Guiding and Girl Scouting would use this technology to extend their message even further.

Guide leaders also began to utilize film for their weekly meetings. Some of these films were generic educational shorts about nature or history, but others were Guide films produced by national headquarters. One of the earliest of these productions, *Girl Guides at Work*, (1916) focused on Guiding's contribution to the war effort in Britain, while in the United States, Girl Scouts starred in and produced *The Golden Eaglet*

(1919), which toured the country and "enjoyed wide circulation." Like
Girl Guides at Work, The Golden Eaglet also celebrated Girl Scouts' usefulness, but it focused equally on war work and camping, useful daily skills
and adventure.[21] The storyline reflected many of the Guide fiction
scripts, with bored teen Margaret Ferris lamenting that "there's nothing
to do" at the start of the film. She encounters a Girl Scout troop, and
she immediately starts a local troop with her friends and a schoolteacher.
Throughout the film, Margaret moves through the ranks, earning badges
and helping those in need. Eventually she reaches the highest honor for a
Girl Scout, the Golden Eaglet. The film depicts Margaret and her fellow
Scouts as active, serious girls, who have a purpose in life. They are almost
constantly in motion throughout the film, and Girl Scouting looks
extremely attractive.[22]

In addition to developing these early film vehicles that found success,
the organizations distributed other films to Guide and Scout groups in
the years to come. Many of these movies featured fictional patrols in daring adventures that echoed the storylines in Guide fiction. Girls watched
these films, often with their companies; however, at least a few Guides did
not quite buy into what was being sold. A Guide living near Reading
(United Kingdom) noted in 1922 that "we witnessed some very thrilling
episodes in the life of a girl guide in a foreign country [but] (we all wondered if there ever had lived a girl who was such and [*sic*] ideal Guide)."[23]
Indeed, like the Guide novels and story papers, Guide films used stereotypes and "ideals" to great effect in making their points.

In addition to the occasional "official" film, Guide companies increasingly attended the popular cinema together, transforming an outing that
might draw girls away from Guide life into a communal Guide activity.
While this sometimes backfired as with Cicely Stewart-Smith's company
who used all their Guide funds to go to the cinema when the company disbanded, movies could usually serve as a nice addition to other group activities and outings.[24] The 6th Clapton (London) made movies a regular part
of their annual outings for tea and entertainment. Each January the whole
company went out to tea at a restaurant and to see a play or concert, but
in the late 1920s, they began including films in this rotation, attending
King of Kings in 1928.[25] Other companies mention cinema outings, especially by the 1930s and especially as part of combined activities between
older Rangers and their Scout counterparts, Rovers.

The rise of more activities that tapped into broader notions of teen and
mass culture helped usher in a new era of cooperation and joint events

between Scouts and Guides. Boys and girls who had formerly shared space for meetings (on different days), began joining together occasionally for rallies and public events, or for combined fundraising activities. Guides were, by the 1920s and 1930s, increasingly seeking more socializing opportunities with Boy Scouts as part of their regular weekly meetings and badge work. Although Guide policies began suggesting Scout/Guide cooperation as early as 1918, it took a few years for the idea to take root in the movements.[26] As can be easily imagined, the development of more coeducational activities and events reignited many of the debates of the early years about the harmful effects of coed interaction, both on the morals of the youth involved and on their gender identities. Leaders worried that the boys might see Scouting as "less manly" or that girls would become "too masculine" if too much cooperation took place. Robert Baden-Powell, when appealed to regarding the issue in 1931, took a predictably vague stance, saying that combined activities or camping for older Rovers and Rangers was "in accord with modern ideas now prevalent."[27] While not without its contentious aspects, such Scout/Guide cooperation and coeducational planning had established a firm foothold in the organizational culture by the late 1930s.

Yet the move toward mass culture and consumption was not the only pressure moving boys and girls to cooperate. Resources and space for meetings were continual struggles for some troops and companies, especially in poorer areas, so cooperation allowed the continuation of the movement itself. For instance, in a poor East London area in the interwar period, Guide Nellie Priest remembered that all Guide and Scout activities took place in the same church in her neighborhood, with shared rooms and supplies.[28] In such working-class communities, Guiding served as a form of escape, and as girls aged, it became an ideal place to meet "respectable" boys. Many memoirs mention this aspect of the Guide experience—that it widened horizons, provided safe entertainment, and allowed for friendships with both boys and girls that shaped subsequent lives.

Alice Linton had such a story about Guiding. Linton joined Guides at church when she was 13 (1921) and was an active Guide by the time she went to work at a laundry soon thereafter. Her company was "adopted" by a rich private school company, which meant that she received tea and a gift twice a year at their combined gatherings. Linton had ambitions to be a nurse, so she soaked up all the opportunities Guiding had to offer her in terms of first-aid classes and badges. When the captain announced that the company would start a savings fund for a summer camp, Linton obligingly gave her sixpence each week. The camp itself, in a farmer's field, exceeded her expectations for the first holiday she had ever experienced. She relished the tents, the open-air cooking, and the sense of freedom from obligation that camp offered. Linton also recounted the importance of her Guide company's interactions with the local Boy Scouts. The two groups first met in a combined church parade at which the girls "lined up beside them and tried to quietly sum them up and see which ones we would like." After this initial meeting, the Scouts came for a visit to their camp and as guests for their closing campfire concert. As Linton recorded years later, the Guides "had made friends with some of the scouts" and were reluctant to say goodbye, especially when it meant returning to "rows of dreary looking houses."[29]

As Linton's account reveals, much of the Boy Scout and Girl Guide cooperation was brief and well supervised by leaders, especially when it included girls aged under 16. Such cooperative activities provided a look into a different world for some girls, and it allowed for "practice" in coeducational socializing. Some of these encounters are almost comical in their "scoutiness"—Guides and Scouts competing in outdoor skills or giving each other gifts of Scout items. In Yorkshire, the 2nd Shipley Guides participated in the local Scouts' concert when the Scouts asked for their help. After the successful concert and its end-of-the-night campfire, the Scouts thanked the Guides with "a Morse buzzer to show their appreciation of our efforts."[30]

Of course not all Boy Scout and Girl Guide interaction was quite so innocuous, and many Guides found themselves dismissed from companies for inappropriate fraternization. Others faced punishment at home for meeting boys when they were supposed to be socializing with girls. May Rainer, a London Guide, felt particularly angry when the Guide captain tried to separate Scouts and Guides. She wrote in her later autobiography, "Having had so many restrictions at home the thought of constantly being told you must not talk to the young men in the Scout Hut by a prejudiced old maid" was something she could not accept, so she left Guiding. Rainer, however, continued to visit the Scout hut, and remembered fondly her dancing outings at age 15 with Scouts she met at the hut.[31]

Among older girls, however, Ranger and Rover socializing sometimes led to happy endings. British Guide Jeanne Holloway met her husband through combined Rover/Ranger activities, in this case service work singing in a hospital and playing in whist drives for charity. The two married in 1939 in their Ranger and Rover uniforms with a Boy Scout padre presiding. Jeanne and her husband, Edward, continued Scout and Guide work throughout their lifetimes, and indeed, Jeanne still volunteers at the local Guide archives and attends Trefoil Guild meetings, despite being in her nineties.[32] Holloway's experience was not unusual, and newspaper accounts in Britain in the 1930s were full of Ranger/Rover marriages and subsequent husband/wife teams in the organizations.[33]

The popularity of Boy Scout and Girl Guide cooperation, especially among the youth, reflected the broader leisure pursuits of teens in interwar Britain. In oral histories and surveys of young people, especially in working-class cities of northern England, dancing and cinema-going were the most frequent leisure activities, and both often included coed groups of teens.[34] Historian Paul Wild notes that this emphasis on dance halls and cinemas fit with new work and school patterns, allowing working-class youth to socialize with "limited commitment" and "casual usage," rather than committing to weekly meetings that required regular dues and activities as with Guiding.[35] Girls' clubs at community centers allowed for more intermittent participation as well, not requiring uniforms or regular attendance, providing flexibility for youth. Other forms of leisure pursuits such as church youth clubs and rambling or sport organizations often included both males and females, so Guiding had to contend not only with more flexible leisure pursuits but with coeducational competitors. Competing demands on girls' time in the 1930s led Guiding to try to articulate its difference, especially its adventure, service, and character-building components, even more. Also, by allowing for the possibility of combined Scout and Guide activities, especially for the older girls, Guiding may have managed to keep some girls active in the movement for a longer period of time. Baden-Powell recognized the pressures to compete with commercial leisure, and in a 1918 memo, pointed out how cooperation between Scouting and Guiding at all levels could only strengthen both: "Our respective aims and methods being practically identical, it would be suicidal now to ignore each other and not to profit by our own kinship. We have got to keep pace with [the] times to maintain our place."[36]

In fits and starts, but with local conditions determining the level of cooperation, Guiding and Scouting did draw closer together in the 1930s in Britain. Large, well-publicized cooperative events helped, such as the Boy Scout Coming-of-Age Jamboree in Liverpool in 1929. While largely a male gathering to celebrate Boy Scouting, the Cheshire Guides provided first aid and hospitality services at the jamboree at the invitation of the Scouts, and many Guide companies attended the event to meet Boy Scouts from around the world. The rise of female leaders in the Boy Scouts, especially in the Wolf Cubs, also increased visible cooperation, and the two movements even sponsored well-publicized joint trips, such as the Scout and Guide leader goodwill cruises in 1933 (Baltic), in 1934 (Mediterranean) and in 1938 (Arctic). These "floating camps" aimed ostensibly to bring British Scout and Guide leaders into contact with their counterparts in other parts of the world, but they also functioned as coeducational testing grounds for male and female leaders.[37] These cooperative leadership schemes became important after the outbreak of war in 1939, when in many places in Britain, Guiders and other adult women were asked to help the Boy Scouts with its leader shortage. Many women became Scoutmasters in the early 1940s.

Beyond Britain such Scout/Guide cooperation also occurred, although at different times in the organizations' histories. For most, the 1930s brought the issue to debate, if for no other reason than the depressed economies that made running units a challenge. In Sweden in 1932, for instance, Prince Gustaf Adolf, who was an active Scout, called on Guides and Scouts to work together to provide relief to the needy. With a joint special committee to administer the work, Guides and Scouts cooperatively collected and distributed food, clothing, and monetary assistance.[38] Also, female suffrage in many parts of the world in the 1910s and 1920s had opened up opportunities for women in government and business, providing an incentive for older girls to learn to hold their own in a mixed debate or gathering. Olga Malkowska, the Polish Guide leader, explicitly called for a combined Boy Scout and Girl Guide world conference to discuss joint roles in nation building and economic recovery. Her 1930 plea called for outreach: "Today we want the woman to cooperate with the man, to take her share in the work of building the world."[39] Malkowska and other Guide leaders recognized the value of single-sex organizations for building girls' independence and self-esteem, but they also understood that cooperative work would provide girls' with a broader stage and a wider experience. They sought a fusion of strategic cooperation with Boy Scouting while maintaining single-sex organizations.

Guiding in Canada successfully followed this model in the 1940s. Intermittent cooperation between Guides and Scouts had taken place prior to this time, both locally and nationally, but it was not until the post-World War II period that organized cooperative schemes developed. Beginning in 1945, a "Boy Scout-Girl Guide Week" was a featured part of the organizations' public relations as an annual reminder of the importance of the two youth groups. Planned and executed together by Scouts and Guides, the week featured joint community service projects, concerts, lectures, an advertising campaign, parties, dinners, rallies, and demonstrations. The planning for this annual event led to new connections between leaders and members, which in turn spawned additional cooperative events for males and females. In particular, sharing of resources increased, with joint headquarters office space, joint campsites or equipment, and combined trainings for leaders and older members. One visible sign of the new spirit of participation was in coed color parties of Scouts and Guides at "local ceremonies when 'New Canadians' [were] awarded full citizenship rights."[40] Such public cooperation did much to dispel fears about the dangers of mixing male and female youth and boosted the respectability of both organizations.

In the United States, where Girl Scouting and Boy Scouting seemed to be developing along different paths, cooperation between boys and girls was less evident despite a heavy reliance upon women leaders in the Cub branch of Scouting by the 1950s. Perhaps because each movement was successful in its own way, concerted cooperation seemed less necessary. While the United States did not really actively encourage cooperation, other areas of the world were alarmed at the whole idea. Particularly vociferous in their objections to Boy Scout and Girl Guide cooperation were associations in colonial zones, where white leaders' prejudicial racial attitudes affected their views of male-female mixing. Leaders worried that two things might undermine the movements in British, French, Dutch, and other European colonial settings: inappropriate sexual contact between "native" boys and girls, but even more worrisome, mixing of white and "native" youth. Olave Baden-Powell tried to explain her objections in a 1929 letter: "The reason for [these concerns] is that the feeling of insecurity where the natives are concerned and the very real dangers to white girls, lack of control, etc. make it quite definitely not safe for black and white girls to meet on equal footing."[41]

Many other British leaders felt that the "morals" of girls in colonial (especially tropical) settings would not allow them to be successful Guides, let alone Guides who could collaborate with Boy Scouts. In Belize, white Guide officials argued for several years about whether the movement could make any headway with girls in the country, given "loose" standards regarding illegitimacy. As one official wrote to Olave Baden-Powell, "The immoral loose characters of the class who would join the movement is a fact that we are all up against . . . . Little tots of seven talk of things our English children never know."[42] Even in areas where preconceptions about girls' ability to "safely" mix with boys were not evident, other constraints made joint Scout/Guide ventures difficult. Religious and cultural restrictions also played an important role in curbing interaction among Scouts and Guides, and at various times, clerics blocked moves to cooperate and mix girls with boys. In Malta, Roman Catholic leaders discouraged any joint activities between Guides and Scouts until the late 1960s, except for combined church services or rallies for national holidays.[43] Acceptance by Christian leaders in many countries, including parts of England, depended on single-sex segregation for much of Guiding's early history. Likewise, in some Muslim countries, for example, girls' parents allowed them to join Guiding because it promised single-sex socialization. Leaders in Malaya and Singapore noted in 1940s reports to headquarters that they "took great pains to avoid offending religious susceptibilities" given that parents had allowed girls to join Guiding only very reluctantly.[44]

Boy Scout and Girl Guide cooperation, while increasingly frequent in the 1940s, was still a local phenomenon in most areas. Individual districts or companies chose to cooperate or not, and national and world associations allowed these variations unless there were major complaints. This sporadic cooperation as well as major changes in the notion of youth socialization in the 1950s and 1960s led to a new impetus, which threatened not only to redefine the heart of Guiding, but in some cases to make it disappear. This thrust—for coeducational, combined Scouting on the male model—led to coeducational movements in many countries from the late 1960s until the end of the twentieth century. But for the Guides of the 1940s, Scout/Guide cooperation was a tentative venture at best that foreshadowed and echoed transformations taking place around the Guiding world between 1945 and 1960. In that period, most Guide programs revised their uniforms, handbooks, magazines, and "image" to address an emergent modern teen culture and to align themselves in response to the conservatism of the post-World War II world.

Guiding had recognized challenges with its program as early as the 1930s. In fact, the Girl Scouts of the USA even commissioned a study in 1934 to see why the organization had such turnover, especially in the teen years. The tenth world conference in 1938 also took up the question of "What Youth is Seeking—What Youth is Finding." The advent of the Second World War in 1939 postponed real change in most Guiding and Girl Scouting programs, but the lessons learned from the studies and conferences of the 1930s remained and were used to redesign the organizations in the late 1940s and 1950s. The 1936 U.S. study report, made available to Girl Scouts and Guides in other countries, and the conversations at the 1938 world conference confirmed what many local leaders had already suspected—some parts of the program were outdated, and girls felt it did not meet their needs. Particular problems identified included girls' new interest in vocational and professional training, their disinterest in "culture" unless it was "useful," and their longing for information about the "relationship of the sexes." Other parts of the reports noted that girls did seem to want physical activities and out-of-door adventures, something that gave Guiding an advantage. Also, many girls claimed to crave spiritual and moral development opportunities—something to provide meaning for their lives.[45]

With all these challenges in mind, national leaders sought with the reforms of the 1950s to make Guiding and Girl Scouting stand apart from their competition by emphasizing their strengths—character training and outdoor activity—and by modernizing some of their programmatic aspects, such as badges, uniforms, and tests. In the United States, for example, the extension of electricity to most of the nation by the beginning of World War II meant that Girl Scouts need no longer "learn to fill lamps" to be good housekeepers, so that test could be removed. Beyond such minor changes in tests and badges, another more subtle shift emerged from these reforms. While patrols and group work remained vital to the organizations, a new recognition of self was instilled. The U.S. Girl Scouts tried to articulate this shift in an article for the world magazine, *The Council Fire*:

> we want each Girl Scout to learn not only how to be a good member of a group, but also to realise that she cannot give herself to that group *unless there is a self to give* .... The steps from the formalized pattern of the Girl Scout of yesterday to the freedom—with responsibility—of the Girl Scout of tomorrow will be the most difficult to understand and to carry out of any of the changes suggested by the revised program .... To accomplish all this *the program must be flexible*.[46]

This new emphasis on more independence and freedom required flexibility as the Girl Scouts warned, but it also called into question the structural framework of the organization and its ability to "guide" girls appropriately. The challenge in the post-World War II world would be to balance the competing values of independence and discipline in an age of television, mass consumption, and educational change. Increasingly, the stakes were high for youth organizations, as the world saw a "baby boom" between 1946 and the 1960s that meant a much larger pool of young people would be available for membership in movements such as Guiding.

The war itself had complicated life for many girls, especially in war zones or countries severely affected by the conflict. In addition to the large numbers of displaced persons, war orphans, and war victims, during and just after World War II, rates of juvenile delinquency rose, leading Guide officials to consider ways they might address this problem. Guides had sponsored companies in juvenile correctional facilities and prisons since the 1910s, but postwar delinquency signaled a more serious systemic problem that Guides hoped to address. Leaders consulted a myriad of studies published in the 1950s and 1960s that looked at the root cause of delinquency, and Guides in Britain tried to target "at-risk" girls from broken homes who needed a social network.[47] In France, the Catholic Guides made work with delinquents a centerpiece of their postwar program, putting in place a reeducation program in juvenile institutions and reforms schools. They also worked with young women who had been drawn into petty crime and prostitution by the experience of war.[48]

As discussed earlier, the outbreak of World War II temporarily postponed program changes, reignited interest in war preparedness, and raised numbers of Guides worldwide. The 1940s also witnessed an important shift in leadership with the death of pioneers from the movement. Additionally, the war invigorated the World Association, which had continued to operate and coordinate Guide activities around the world during the conflict. WAGGGS, after 20 years of successful operations, underwent a major overhaul in 1948, reorganizing its executive bureau, and proposing the creation of a world badge and a new world song to unite all national organizations. Also, with a nod to the need for coordination with the media, the World Bureau created a public relations office.[49] Other national movements followed suit, with widespread reorganization and retooling taking place between 1946 and 1950. The Catholic Guides de France, for example, revised their regulations and published new programs for Guides and the younger "Jeannettes" in 1948.[50]

Some of the transformations in national movements were more or less cosmetic changes, with new uniforms or insignia or badges. Britain inaugurated one of the central awards in its Guiding program, the

Queen's Guide, in 1946.[51] The British had also announced a competition for a new uniform in 1945, which allowed Guides to vote on a few designs that appeared in *The Guide* and *The Guider* magazines. The winning uniform featured berets rather than hats, and Guides now wore light blue shirts and ties with navy skirts or light blue dresses.[52] Despite the new Queen's Guide award, the new uniforms, and other programmatic changes, Guiding faced challenges in the immediate postwar period as its membership began to slide from over 500,000 in 1943 to about 420,000 in 1949.[53] These membership losses as well as continued wartime controls and rising postwar financial constraints led the Guides to introduce annual membership fees, to reorganize their headquarters staff, and to set up an endowment fund.[54]

As in Britain, the United States also faced some postwar challenges and sought to reinvigorate its movement. U.S. Girl Scouts got a new uniform in 1948, with a distinctive woven bright green fabric produced especially for Girl Scouts and a design from the pen of Mainbocher, a major couturier. The long-sleeved uniform had a full skirt with big pockets, a beret, and a webbed belt with a special Girl Scout buckle. This uniform was used, largely in its original form, until the 1970s by the intermediate level Girl Scouts.[55] Like the British uniform, the American uniforms sought to keep up with changing fashions, while also retaining utilitarian features such as strong belts and skirts that allowed physical activity. Unlike in Britain, the U.S. Girl Scouts continued to enjoy growth in their membership, topping a million girls in 1944, 1.5 million by 1950, and two million by 1953.[56] Much of this success was due to the Executive Director, Constance Rittenhouse, who served from 1935 to 1950 in this position and who aggressively pursued ideas that made Girl Scouting distinctive. Under her watch, the Girl Scouts developed new branches for older girls and for "Wing Scouts," franchised its popular cookie fundraiser, developed new publicity and community relations outreach programs, and initiated an innovative "special area" program to target poor and underprivileged neighborhoods.[57] Much of this change accompanied Rittenhouse's last years in office, and reflected the other changes of the postwar period.

Another major shift in the postwar Guide movement came in the form of publication of new handbooks, especially in the United States and Britain. The British Guides had been using Robert Baden-Powell's *Girl Guiding* since its appearance in 1918, but with his 1941 death, headquarters staff thought a new book would at last be acceptable to membership. To help make it clear that Guide national leaders were not trying to ignore their own history, they asked Agnes "the Carpenter" Maynard, a pioneer of Girl Guiding in Britain, to author the new text. Maynard's book, *Be Prepared! Handbook for Guides*, first appeared in print in 1946 and continued to serve (with one major revision in 1960) as the official Guide handbook until 1968, when Guiding revamped its entire program based on a working party report.[58] It is important to note as well that many regions of the empire also used the British guidebook for their work, so the new edition either made its way to those areas or in some cases, prompted the creation of local handbooks.

Maynard's book included many of the same games and camp tips as Baden-Powell's earlier one, but its emphasis had shifted to include many more craft activities and a new prominent section on "Homecraft" that encouraged girls to envision their future lives:

> Nearly every girl has a home-making urge; perhaps she starts by making a little home under the trees in the garden and later decorates her own bedroom. One day you may have a chance to help to choose a new home or may be asked to report on a house for a friend; so BE PREPARED and start now observing other people's homes, and asking questions and learning what to look out for.[59]

Girls were not just to look for pretty houses, however. Maynard asked them to look at houses scientifically—how warm and energy efficient was it? Did it have sufficient sunlight? How was space used in the house? Maynard's approach to homecraft included cooking and cleaning, but it also encompassed architectural knowledge, energy awareness, and sanitary considerations. The updated Guide handbook echoed post-World War II scientific home management and home economics language, giving Guiding a fresh new look.

In the United States, Girl Scouts had seen major handbook revisions of the original 1913 book in 1920, 1929, and 1933, and in the postwar period, they continued to try to update their handbooks to meet changing times. Their first postwar attempt, *The Girl Scout Handbook*, was published in 1947 and sold almost 1.5 million copies before being replaced with the 1953 *Girl Scout Handbook*. This version, perhaps the best selling in Girl Scout history, made it into the hands of well over four million girls and women in its 10-year run. The next major handbook revision, in the 1960s, corresponded to a fundamental programmatic shift in the organization, which followed a commissioned research study.[60]

This pattern of studying girls and then adjusting the Guide/Scout program reflected a new societal emphasis on statistical and demographic analysis, polling, and surveys. Britain's Mass Observation project, which sought to gather massive amounts of data on ordinary people, was launched in 1937, while the U.S. Gallup Poll began in 1935. The rise of professional statistical associations and university research teams devoted to understanding social behavior led Guiding to turn to the experts to tell them what girls wanted. The Guides de France launched a major survey in 1955 to study all levels of its movement, while the U.S. Girl Scouts hired a University of Michigan team to survey its membership and adolescent girls in general in 1955. The Michigan study provides an interesting window into the kinds of things girls in the 1950s wanted, at least in one country. Given American presence in Europe, Asia and Latin America after the war and the preponderance of U.S. films and products in world markets, it seems reasonable to conclude that the U.S. study might provide a glimmer of insight into girls' desires in other places in the world as well.

The Michigan study first provided a picture of the current Girl Scout membership. Girl members hailed mostly from two-parent families, and the proportion in urban areas was much higher than among farm families. In terms of race, roughly 95 percent of the Scouts were white as opposed to about 92 percent white in the general adolescent population, but Girl Scouting did include at least some girls from every occupational category and racial group. Most of the girls who joined Scouts and stayed in for significant periods of time were from middle-class or wealthy families, and the researchers hypothesized that part of the problem might be lack of leaders in working-class communities, where working mothers could not volunteer as Scout leaders.[61] After providing a demographic snapshot of the Girl Scouts of the 1950s, the report went on to survey activities and interests. Many of the girls reported liking the Girl Scout emphasis on outdoor life and crafts, and most understood the promise and laws as important elements of the organization.

Perhaps one of the most fascinating findings of the study came from a hypothetical question asked first of Scouts and then of adolescent girls generally: "What do you think girls like to do best?" The Scouts (both intermediates and seniors) listed social activities first, followed by outdoor activities. In contrast, the general adolescent population who were surveyed answered the question with social activities first as well, but only half as many listed outdoor activities in their list of things girls like to do, and their second choices were sports and games followed closely by homemaking activities. Girl Scouts also reported more enjoyment of crafts and community service activities. Importantly, Girl Scouts also had higher expectations for their future life, with more than half reporting that they planned to go to college. Girl Scout leaders listened to what the girls said in the study, recognizing that many of the findings were positive for the organization. However, the lack of diversity in class and race seemed problematic, and Girl Scouting turned its energies in the 1950s and 1960s toward reversing this demographic. They also noted the interest in social activities and outings with boys, understanding that Scouting might have trouble competing in that arena, given the craze for rock and roll, fashion magazines, and "sock hops." Scouting used the study's findings to retool its program even further in the 1960s, paying particular attention to age divisions and age-appropriate activities in the hope of meeting girls' needs from childhood to young womanhood.[62] Like the U.S. Scouts, the French Guides also used their 1955 study to support a change in their staging of adolescence, moving to a four-level program (ages 8–11, 12–14, 15–16, and 17+) by the 1960s that reflected their research findings.[63]

While some Guide and Scout leaders adjusted their programs and appearances, other Guide associations faced more challenging postwar problems, given the political challenges that had arisen from wartime and postwar tensions. In Belgium, for instance, the Guides spent the immediate postwar years dealing with the hardening split between Flemish and French language communities in the small nation. Grey and Blue Guides, representing the two language communities, used much time and energy in the late 1940s and early 1950s negotiating these ideological and linguistic splits, sparring over the notion of unity.[64] While the Belgian controversies concerned language and identity, in Greece, the newly reformed Guides had to contend with the devastation of the Greek Civil War in the late 1940s, which hampered their ability to reformulate Guide troops. Many Greek Guides spent their time living and working in homeless hostels and refugee camps.[65] In other regions, revolutions and economic hardship raised challenges for postwar Guiding, which did not abate with the 1950s Cold War alignments and independence movements. If the United States struggled to attract teenagers more interested in Elvis and fashion, in much of the world, Guiding tried merely to maintain some semblance of normalcy in a world turned upside down by violence and political instability.

As Guiding aged and tried to change with the times, it looked for ways to demonstrate its fundamental difference from other youth movements and activities—for the most meaningful way to articulate its vision and to follow its own path. One of its most successful and unique aspects, that it increasingly relied upon to set it apart from other youth leisure forms, was its international focus. By the middle of the twentieth century, Guiding had a complex network of national, regional, and international gatherings, a world organization with its own headquarters, rules, officers and publications, a network of global pen pals, and a system for international exchange of personnel. This imaginative and actual connection between Guides and Girl Scouts around the world provided the stable and unique identity the organization needed to survive the local fluctuations in girls' interests and participation. It is not an exaggeration to say that Guiding's international focus from the 1920s until the twenty-first century helped sustain and nurture the movement, maintaining its status as the largest voluntary female youth movement in history.

NOTES

1. Robert Baden-Powell, "Look Wide!," *The Council Fire* 16:1 (January 1941), 4.

2. Agnes Baden-Powell and Robert Baden-Powell, *How Girls Can Help to Build the Empire: The Handbook for Girl Guides* (London: Thomas Nelson and Sons, 1912), vii.

3. Sally Mitchell, *The New Girl: Girls' Culture in England, 1880–1915* (New York: Columbia University Press, 1995), 126.

4. Mitchell, *The New Girl*, 126–138.

5. Mitchell, *The New Girl*, 173.

6. Mary Degenhardt and Judith Kirsch, *Girl Scout Collector's Guide: A History of Uniforms, Insignia, Publications, and Memorabilia*, 2nd Edition (Lubbock: Texas Tech University Press, 2005), 453–455.

7. Kirsten Drotner, "Schoolgirls, Madcaps, and Air Aces: English Girls and Their Magazine Reading Between the Wars," *Feminist Studies* 9:1 (Spring 1983), 35, 50.

8. Penny Tinkler, *Constructing Girlhood: Popular Magazines for Girls Growing up in England, 1920–1950* (London: Taylor & Francis, 1995), 183–185.

9. Drotner, "Schoolgirls, Madcaps, and Air Aces," 41.

10. Degenhardt and Kirsch, *Girl Scout Collector's Guide,* 443.

11. Nancy Beck Young, *Lou Henry Hoover: Activist First Lady* (Lawrence: University Press of Kansas, 2004), 114.

12. Cicely Stewart-Smith, "The Log of a Loafer in the Guides," 1923–1925, GGL.

13. Gill Frith, "'The Time of your Life': the Meaning of the School Story," in *Language, Gender and Childhood*, eds. Carolyn Steedman, Cathy Urwin and Valerie Walderdine (London: Routledge and Kegan Paul, 1985), 121.

14. Drotner, "Schoolgirls, Madcaps, and Air Aces," 40–41.

15. Annual Reports 1925, 1930, 1931, 1932, GGL.

16. Laurent Déom, "Où sont les femmes? À la recherche d'une hypothétique féminité dans les romans scouts," in *Guidisme, scoutisme et coéducation: Pour une histoire de la mixité dans les mouvements de jeunesse*, eds. Thierry Scaillet, Sophie Wittemans, and Françoise Rosart (Louvain-la-Neuve: Academia Bruylant, 2007), 159–160.

17. These storylines appeared in novels by F. O. H. Nash, Ethel Talbot, and Dorothea Moore, to name just a few.

18. F. O. H. Nash, *Rosie the Peddler* (London: Sheldon Press, 1925).

19. "The Girl Scouts Hope Chest," 1925, Pamphlet Collection, New York Public Library (NYPL).

20. *Highlights in Girl Scouting 1912–2001* (New York: Girl Scouts of the USA, 2002), 12.

21. TC/166 and TC/275, SAGP; Degenhardt and Kirsch, *Girl Scout Collector's Guide*, 506–507.

22. *The Golden Eaglet* (1919), VHS, distributed 1989.

23. 2nd Caversham Guide Company logbook, December 12, 1922, GGL.

24. Cicely Stewart-Smith, "The Log of a Loafer in the Guides," 1923–1925, GGL.

25. 6th Clapton (London) logbook, 1926–1928, GGL.

26. Mitchell, *The New Girl*, 187.

27. Scout and Guide Cooperation folder, TC/29 Founder's Files, SAGP.

28. "Nellie Priest" in *The Island: Life and Death of an East London Community, 1870–1970* (London: Centerprise Trust Ltd., 1979), 34–35. Interestingly, these shared spaces did not provide enough fraternization as she aged, and when she was 16 years old, she quit Guiding because she "got more interested in the boys then."

29. Alice Linton, *Not Expecting Miracles* (London: Centerprise Trust Ltd., 1982).

30. 2nd Shipley logbook, 1934, Ilkley archives/Sheila Marks.

31. May Rainer, *Emma's Daughter*, unpublished autobiography, Brunel University (1977), 56–58.

32. Author interview with Jeanne Holloway, January 27 and April 13, 1993.

33. For more information on this aspect of Guiding, see Tammy M. Proctor, *On My Honour: Guides and Scouts in Interwar Britain* (Philadelphia: American Philosophical Society, 2002), 115–120.

34. Claire Langhamer, *Women's Leisure in England 1920–60* (Manchester: Manchester University Press, 2002), 58–59.

35. Paul Wild, "Recreation in Rochdale, 1900–40," in *Working-Class Culture: Studies in Theory and History*, eds. John Clarke, Charles Critcher and Richard Johnson (Birmingham: Centre for Cultural Studies, 1979), 159.

36. Robert Baden-Powell Memo, "Our Attitude towards the Girl Guides Association," 1918, TC/29 Scout and Guide Cooperation, SAGP.

37. Rose Kerr, *The Cruise of the Calgaric* (London: Girl Guides Association, 1933); *The Cruise of the Adriatic* (London: GGA, 1934); *The Cruise of the Orduna* (London: GGA, 1938), 10.

38. "Sweden. The Girl Guides' and Boy Scouts' Relief Work," *The Council Fire* 8:2 (April 1933), 22.

39. Olga Malkowska, "Cooperation with Boy Scouts and Other Youth Movements," *The Council Fire* 5:4 (October 1930), 96.

40. Mary F. Bishop, "Scout-Guide Co-Operation in Canada," *The Council Fire* 23:3 (July 1948), 28–29.

41. Olave Baden-Powell to anonymous correspondent, December 9, 1929, Box 1229/South Africa: Native Affairs, Wayfarers/Pathfinders file, School of Oriental and African Studies (SOAS).

42. Katharine J. Burdon to Lady Baden-Powell, June 2, 1929, ST1/C15/Shelf 1 Box 2, Belize, GGL.

43. "Scouts and Guides Set Example in Positive Approach to Youth," Girl Guides Supplement, *Times* (Malta) (March 24, 1968), ST1/C15/Shelf 2 Box 10, Malta, GGL.

44. "Guiding in Malaya," 1943, ST1/C15/Shelf 2 Box 10, Malaysia, GGL.

45. "The Theme of the Conference," *The Council Fire* 13:4 (October 1938), 58–63.

46. Frances Lee, "Girl Scouting in the United States 1937 Model," *The Council Fire* 8:2 (April 1938), 20.

47. Pamela Cox, "Girls in Trouble: Defining Female Delinquency, Britain, 1900–1950," in *Secret Gardens: Placing Girls in European History, 1750–1960*, eds. Mary Jo Maynes, Birgitte Søland, and Christina Benninghaus (Bloomington: Indiana University Press, 2005), 192–205.

48. Marie-Thérèse Cheroutre, *Le scoutisme au féminin: Les guides de France, 1923–1998* (Paris: Les Éditions du Cerf, 2002), 261, 266.

49. Report of 1948 World Conference, *The Council Fire* 23:4 (October 1948), 46–49.

50. Cheroutre,*Le scoutisme au féminin*, 249, 253, 269.

51. *1910 . . . And Then? A Brief History of the Girl Guides Association* (London: GGA, 1990), 17.

52. Alix Liddell, *Story of the Girl Guides 1938–1975* (London: Girl Guides Association, 1976), 36–38.

53. Girlguiding UK census figures, GGL.

54. Liddell, *Story of the Girl Guides*, 39.

55. Degenhardt and Kirsch, *Girl Scout Collector's Guide*, 146, 173–178.

56. *Highlights in Girl Scouting*, 19–23.

57. Memo to Board Members, April 27, 1984, re: Constance Rittenhouse's death; Constance Rittenhouse to Eleanor Roosevelt, January 29, 1957, Personalities Box, Folder—Rittenhouse, Constance, GSUSA.

58. Major changes in the Guide Programme card, GGL.

59. Agnes Maynard, *Be Prepared!* (London: C. Arthur Pearson, 1946), 141–144.

60. Degenhardt and Kirsch, *Girl Scout Collector's Guide*, 384–390.

61. "A Highlight Summary of a Study: The Program of the Girl Scouts of the U.S.A.," by Survey Research Center, University of Michigan, Ann Arbor, MI, September 1958; Box Publications P, Program Objectives to Promenade All, Folder: Program of the Girl Scouts of the USA–Summary, GSUSA, 5–10.

62. "A Highlight Summary of a Study: The Program of the Girl Scouts of the U.S.A.," by Survey Research Center, University of Michigan, Ann Arbor, MI, September 1958; Box Publications P, Program Objectives to Promenade All, Folder: Program of the Girl Scouts of the USA–Summary, GSUSA.

63. Cheroutre, *Le scoutisme au féminin*, 324, 356–364.

64. Geneviève Iweins d'Eeckhoutte, "De l'oeuvre aux fédérations, le guidisme catholique en Belgique, 1915–1960, chronique d'un mouvement," in *Guidisme, scoutisme et coéducation*, 246–253.

65. Alix Liddell, "Greece," *The Council Fire* 24:3 (July 1949), 43.

6. International Friendship

When they began corresponding in July 1952 at the suggestion of the Guide Commissioner for the Transvaal, neither Myra Chilvers nor Maud Mbizela knew quite what to expect from the experimental "linking" by mail of their companies. Myra, a Guide captain from Nottingham in England, had volunteered to correspond with a South African Guide captain and to try to encourage the girls in her company to do so as well. There were complications, almost from the beginning, since Maud's mostly Xhosa-speaking company had limited English skills, and their lack of resources made the postage for letters to the United Kingdom a hardship. While some of the girls traded letters intermittently over the next couple of years, it was the captains that formed a pen friendship that endured for most of the 1950s.

Maud's and Myra's correspondence started as many new acquaintances do, with basic information about family, education, and background. Myra spoke of her young son, John, and of her pregnancy with a second child (Peter, born in late 1953). Maud explained that her native language was Xhosa, but that she had learned English at a mission school in Pietersburg. In 1952, Maud was working as a teacher at a private Christian school, where she had worked since 1936, but she also made time to care for her blind father and her son. Many of the women's early letters deal specifically with Guiding issues, and Myra tried hard to supply Maud's company with Guide literature and supplies, which were in short supply in Luipaardsvlei (a suburb of Johannesburg). Maud asked for advice on Guiding, as in May 1953, when she wrote to Myra to find out "how to prepare for the Coronation with the Guides we have not received the Bulletin yet so we don't know what to do. We have not even seen the badges yet. I wonder if the Guides will have to wear uniform on the Coronation Day?"[1]

While Guiding continued to be important to their letters and Maud always reported on how many Guides and Sunbeams (Brownies) she had at any given time, their letters subtly changed and became more personal as the years passed. As Myra told the Transvaal Guide Commissioner in 1955 in a letter, "We did not succeed in linking our two companies very well, but Maud and I became good friends. She wrote lovely long letters full of news, & in very good English. I sent her a

Commonwealth reply coupon in each letter so that she would not be short of a stamp for her reply." Their burgeoning friendship shines through the correspondence, with discussions of poor health and hardship, their families, and the political situation in South Africa. For Maud, the letters clearly provided her with a reason to keep up her Guiding work even as her job was threatened and the education system transformed before her eyes in apartheid South Africa. For Myra, she genuinely seemed to enjoy this glimpse into another family and lifestyle, and her worry for Maud was often present in her letters.

Myra and Maud's correspondence points to one of the sustaining features of Guiding in the last 100 years, its internationalist focus. A key part of Guiding and Scouting had been international friendship from early in their histories, but this became a central emphasis in the post-World War II period, as pen-pal schemes, international centers, and world conferences led to more connections. Not only were Guides encouraged to reach out to the world, but they were encouraged to see the world around them with new eyes. In the 1950 world magazine, *The Council Fire*, girls were encouraged to put the international perspective into their daily lives through "exploration of unknown territory whether close at hand or far away."[2] Above all, Guiding sought a shift in attitudes whereby girls "looked wide" at home and abroad.

This aspiration for international friendship really touched a nerve in the postwar world, as youth in many countries tried to reach beyond the bitterness of World War II. They rebuilt and regenerated their Guide movements on a platform of peace and international goodwill. However, the central insistence on international friendship became difficult to maintain in the face of rising Cold War divisions, and internationalist language became especially charged as national liberation movements led to independence of many former British and French colonies with strong Guide movements. With the elimination of Guiding in many communist countries by the 1950s and with the rapid decolonization of many parts of Africa, the Caribbean, and South/Southeast Asia from the 1940s to the 1970s, Guiding had to continually reassess the meaning of internationalism in a politically contentious world. International aspirations were present through most of the organization's 100-year history, but the 1930s through the 1970s served as particularly pivotal times in the articulation of the global vision of Guiding.

In the post-World War I and post-World War II periods, Guiding felt an acute need to reach out and create international bonds in the wake of the psychological and actual destruction of war. As Robert Baden-Powell told delegates at the world conference in 1928, "The ideal of Girl Guides is unity; to break down in the coming generation prevailing differences between classes, creeds and countries, and to bring about in their place peace and good-will in the world."[3] The organization wanted to use its program to chip away at walls of distrust and bitterness and to build peaceful coalitions among girls and women from a variety of backgrounds. This internationalist ethos began with the creation of the Guide international council and imperial council in 1919, advanced with the development of the World Association of Girl Guides and Girl Scouts in 1928, and expanded further with increased travel and international friendship opportunities in the 1950s and beyond.[4]

For leaders, effective international cooperation came mostly through the councils and world organizations, with adult Guiders striving to attend world conferences, meetings, or camps. World conferences, held every other year, were at first confined mostly to the United Kingdom, the United States, and Europe. However, as the international ethos became more important within Guiding, conferences rotated to different regions to allow for greater participation by groups around the world. This process of broadening world connections really accelerated by the late 1950s. Figure 6.1 demonstrates the variety of venues for world conferences and this broadening reach:

Not everyone could travel to a world conference, but many leaders and girls also read the WAGGGS magazine, *The Council Fire*, which provided news of Guides abroad and which kept them updated on changes in the Guide international organizations. Full reports of camps and conferences insured that leaders who never actually attended such a gathering could still vicariously experience the policy discussions, international campfires, and Guide festivities that marked these events. *The Council Fire* also reported on other changes in world policies, such as the new metal World badge, which was a blue and gold trefoil pin approved for use in 1948. The World Flag and World Song were available to Guide companies, and the World Association was featured prominently in national handbooks.

Other publications crossed national boundaries and helped forge connections between Guides and Girl Scouts around the world. The U.S. Girl Scout magazine, *The American Girl*, often included stories about Girl Scouts abroad in the 1940s and 1950s. In the early 1950s, for example, each issue included stories tying to the world movement, from articles

Figure 6.1   Guide World Conference Venues

1920	United Kingdom (England)
1922	United Kingdom (England)
1924	United Kingdom (England)
1926	United States
1928	Hungary
1930	United Kingdom (England)
1932	Poland
1934	Switzerland
1936	Sweden
1938	Switzerland
1946	France
1948	United States
1950	United Kingdom (England)
1952	Norway
1954	Netherlands
1957	Brazil[*]
1960	Greece
1963	Denmark
1966	Japan
1969	Finland
1972	Canada
1975	United Kingdom (England)
1978	Iran
1981	France
1984	United States
1987	Kenya
1990	Singapore
1993	Denmark
1996	Canada
1999	Ireland
2002	Philippines
2005	Jordan
2008	South Africa
2011	United Kingdom (Scotland)

on Thinking Day as it was celebrated around the world and continuing with features on international service and "worldmindedness." While the primary audience for *The American Girl* was U.S. Girl Scouts, its mailbag section included letters from girls in many countries who had obtained the magazine from pen pals, American military bases, or other sources. As one girl from Lancashire (United Kingdom) wrote, "Occasionally a friend of ours receives *The American Girl* from her pen pal and we borrow it from her. We think the magazine is super!"[5] This mixture of letters from girls abroad and stories about world activities was aimed to encourage girls to visualize their global association and act on its international friendship element locally.

Another way for leaders and Guides to connect to others around the world was more virtual than real, but it was through shared commemorations on a particular day. For example, upon Princess Elizabeth's wedding to Phillip in 1947 and her official coronation in 1953, Guides around the British Empire and Commonwealth celebrated simultaneously these joyous occasions. *The Council Fire* explicitly tried to draw in Guides around the world to the event, writing, "when a family wedding takes place absent members are entitled to expect a special and perhaps more intimate account of it from those of the family who were privileged to be there. So this account has been written by one member of the Guide family for others in the family, to describe the wedding of one of its own most loyal and enthusiastic members in the whole Empire."[6] As the writer noted, Princess Elizabeth went to her Sea Ranger muster as usual just before her wedding, invited close Guide friends to the palace, and used a Guide and Sea Ranger escort at the palace and at Westminster Abbey during the festivities. Her wedding cake even included Guide trefoils among its iced decorations. Such detailed accounts allowed Guides from all parts of the world to connect themselves to this international event even though they couldn't line the streets of London.

For Guide leaders and girls who were poor or who were struggling in countries with oppressive regimes, the vicarious psychological boost of being connected to Guiding outside their own local or national setting was important. In her letters to Myra, Maud spoke often of this prized connection. At one point she longed for a World Flag to display, while telling Myra how much she wished "I was one of those two girls who represented Africa" at a world conference.[7] Three years later when Maud lost her teaching job and had to take a job as a nanny for a white "madam" in Johannesburg, she wrote to Myra about how Guiding salvaged her pride and gave her hope in the face of political terror and personal misfortune:

> Oh. We are having hard times in South Africa. This month there are 140 people arrested of high treason, including ministers and attorneys and doctors . . . . Is it not terrible? What the Afrikaans official [*sic*] are doing is horrible . . . . I showed your letter to my madam, she was really speechless. She asked me how I happened to know you, and I said, through Guiding . . . . The Guides movement is very strong.[8]

As Maud struggled with the physical labor of housework and childcare, she held fast to the letters, snapshots, and Guide publications that Myra sent her, seeing Guiding as something important to the girls in her town, but also as a link to the world outside the violence and fear of apartheid South Africa.

Although such imaginative links between Guides and leaders could be fostered through letters and publications, there were other ways to experience the international linkages of Guiding, albeit in a smaller way. Leaders who could not attend a world camp, often could find the resources to take their Guides to a regional camp or conference, which were touted as miniature versions of the larger international gatherings. For example, the All-India Guiders' Training Camp in 1925 was designed to bring together leaders to coordinate their activities, while the Western Hemisphere encampment (1940) helped bring delegates from North, South, and Central America together, and the All-Africa conference of 1948 marked the first continental gathering of Guides in this region. These camps and meetings broke down barriers, even if only on a small scale. Whether world, continental, national, regional, or even divisional, conferences and gatherings that brought Guides into contact with difference, whether based on race, ethnicity, language, nationality, or social class, helped forge a "look wide" ethic in Guiding that emphasized finding common ground between women and girls of different backgrounds.

To take one example, the Girl Scouts of the USA published a report of its international activities in 1958, highlighting all the ways in which Girl Scouts had connected with the world in the course of the year. Its activities demonstrate the variety of experiences available to girls—travel to camps and conferences, hosting of international Guide visitors, participation in international service projects (such as collecting books or clothing for foreign countries), correspondence with pen pals abroad, and study of other cultures in Girl Scout meetings.[9] To further the 1957 connections, the United States also hosted a "Girl Scout Senior Roundup" in 1959, which brought together 10,000 girls and adults from 26 countries. Around the country, Girl Scouts were encouraged to brush up on their foreign languages in case they encountered some of these visitors; GSUSA published a brochure for troop use titled "Say It—In Another Language."[10]

Increasingly this Girl Scout and Guide internationalism also dovetailed with other organizations' work to connect the world or to help women and children, including the U.S. sponsored People-to-People Program, United Nations Children's Fund (UNICEF), and Cooperative for

Assistance and Relief Everywhere (CARE), all post-World War II projects.[11] Girl Scouts of the USA President Marjorie Culmer emphasized this point in an article for the YWCA magazine that aimed to suggest cooperation rather than competition would help both organizations. She pointed out that for Girl Scouts the "road to international friendship ha[d] been paved by 'interchange of persons projects,'" and that the YWCA had generously helped house traveling Guides and Girl Scouts. In pleading for more coordination and cooperation, Culmer reminded YWCA leaders that "our mutual desire to mold better citizens for tomorrow's world gives us a unity of purpose on which to continue developing our pattern of harmonious relationships."[12]

This outreach to other international organizations would become a hallmark of Guiding and Girl Scouting in its second 50 years of existence, leading to Guide presence on important world commissions on the status of women and children. Guiding began its institutional presence as consultants as early as the 1920s with the League of Nations, but it was after World War II that its world connections really blossomed. By the 1990s, WAGGGs had "consultative status" with the United Nations, the Food and Agriculture Organization (FAO), and the United Nations Educational, Scientific and Cultural Organization (UNESCO), and regularly cooperated with such groups as the International Labor Organization (ILO), the World Health Organization (WHO) and the United Nations Development Fund for Women (UNIFEM).[13] In the twenty-first century, WAGGGS has taken the lead in establishing places for its members on boards of world relief and humanitarian agencies, and at the present time, WAGGGS has teams working at six UN centers around the world. Guide and Girl Scout members and leaders are often invited to participate in international events of concern to women and children and to involve themselves in summits on global issues such as the environment and the HIV/AIDS crisis. While much of this activity draws in older girls and leaders, the international outreach for young girls is also a key ethos in the movement.

From Guiding's beginnings, girls pledged in the Fourth Guide Law to be "a friend to all, and a sister to every other Guide" so the emphasis on meeting people and making new friends was ingrained early in the organization's history.[14] Guides and Girl Scouts in interviews often pointed to this very principle as one of the most significant parts of the Guide experience. Making lifelong friends, but also meeting friends who they might not have met otherwise, were both key components of Guide interest in the organization. Those fortunate enough to have international experiences cite these as formative in their Guiding life, along with friendships, camping, and "usefulness." For example, Phyllis Lockyer, who joined Guiding in 1928 in Eltham (United Kingdom) said in a 1993 interview that she considered Guiding to be important because "it taught us to think of others not only here but all over the world."[15]

That emphasis on thinking of others, not just in a Guide's town or country, but in far-flung places, was institutionalized in Guiding and Girl Scouting with the worldwide holiday, Thinking Day, in 1926. First proposed at the world conference held in the United States, Thinking Day was set aside as a day where Guides and Girl Scouts all over the world "should remember each other, and send messages of friendship and goodwill flashing across the world by the wireless of thought."[16] Celebrated on February 22 every year, Thinking Day marked both Robert and Olave Baden-Powell's birthdays, and it commemorated George Washington's birthday in the United States, providing another linkage for that particular country. Each nation and many localities commemorated the day in ways peculiar to their national traditions. Large scale services were common and brought girls from different backgrounds within countries together; for instance, in the United Kingdom a big service is held every year at Westminster Abbey. Other nations used the occasion to bring together units who did not commingle within companies because of language, religious, or cultural barriers. In an account of the 1954 Egyptian Thinking Day open air service in Alexandria for its international Guide companies, one Guider celebrated the great diversity of girls who attended the service, which included a rabbi, a Roman Catholic priest, a Church of England vicar, a Scottish minister, and a Swiss pastor. The girls at the service came from more than two dozen nationalities, almost a dozen languages, and at least eight religious traditions.[17] All the girls belonged to the same association, but in segregated units.

In addition to religious services, girls in various countries celebrated Thinking Day with service projects and parades or rallies, as with the Hungarian Girl Scouts' 1939 celebration, which featured the simultaneous lighting of campfires all across the country.[18] Another feature of Thinking Day was the exchange of notes, cards, and postcards between Guides and Girl Scouts in different countries. I still receive the occasional Thinking Day card from women I interviewed in the early 1990s for my dissertation on Guiding! From its inception in 1932, the Thinking Day Fund has also asked girls in the organization to contribute funds to help

Guides worldwide. In 1933, Olave Baden-Powell suggested girls each send a "penny" on Thinking Day to support the international movement:

> Does thinking with us not usually lead to action, and wouldn't it be nice if this year we could perhaps give some *thing*—as well as our thoughts—to help develop the world friendship which is growing slowly each year and which we hope to see growing larger and larger all the time. Could we not each on Thinking Day send a tiny girl to our World Captain to help her with her work? . . . What a great help we should give to the World's Company Funds if—as I believe may happen—every Guide and Girl Scout will want to share in this Thinking Day offering this year. Then we should have to call it "Thanking Day" instead![19]

Today the Thinking Day Fund still collects money for the international growth of Guiding. During the past decade, the holiday was renamed to "World Thinking Day" and now features "global action themes." Guides are asked to focus on a particular world problem or issue for the year, often coinciding with the United Nations Millennium Development Goals. For instance, the theme for 2009's World Thinking Day activities was "stop the spread of AIDS, malaria and other diseases."[20] As Thinking Day funds and activities suggest, Guides did more than just "think" about others; they focused when possible on activities designed to inculcate worldmindedness.

Many girls without the means to travel were given the chance to attend world camps and conferences through the Juliette Low World Friendship Fund (JLWFF), established in honor of the Girl Scouts of the USA founder in 1927. This particular fund focused on international Girl Scouting, one of Low's passions. Over the years, the Fund has provided scholarships for U.S. Girl Scouts to travel abroad, and for Guides and Girl Scouts elsewhere to come to the United States. It helped pay for world gathering places and provided seed money for new troops and companies to start around the world.

One of the JLWFF's most significant contributions to world Guiding and Girl Scouting today is its financial support for the organization's world centers. These centers are at the heart of Guiding's international focus on friendship, exchange, travel, and outreach, and they are open to individual Guides or companies from around the world for camping and training. These world centers, like many of the camps and Guide training facilities around the globe, stand as testaments to the willingness of leaders and members to support Guiding financially. The first world center, Our Chalet, was the generous gift of U.S. Girl Scout enthusiast Helen Storrow, who was also responsible for donating one of Girl Scouting's first national training centers at Long Pond. Our Chalet, located in the mountains of Switzerland near Adelboden, officially opened in 1932 for skiing, camping, training, and workshops.[21]

When asked what the most memorable moments were in her long Guiding career, one British Guide who joined the movement in 1919 cited her company's trip to Our Chalet.[22] She was certainly not alone in enjoying the vigorous outdoor adventures in the mountains that Our Chalet offered. The chalet became a favorite meeting spot for Guides across Europe, yet it remained inaccessible to most of the world's Guides because of the cost and distance involved in traveling there. The World Association began to seek additional world centers to redress this geographical imbalance and to provide more and different adventures for Guides in the period before World War II. In 1939, WAGGGS opened a hostel and world center in London, paid for with pennies from Guides around the world. The World Bureau was also housed here, and initially the center was called "Our Ark." In 1959, Our Ark moved to another part of London, and the facility was renamed "Olave House" in honor of the Chief Guide in 1963.[23] The other two world centers, while more recently created, reached out to non-European parts of the world. Our Cabaña, in Cuernavaca, Mexico, was dedicated on Thinking Day 1956 and opened the following year, while Sangam in Pune, India, opened in 1966.[24]

Each center embraced a different vision for international outreach— Our Chalet focused on outdoor challenges, Our Ark on experiencing London and visiting Guide and WAGGGS headquarters, Our Cabaña emphasized service projects in nearby villages as well as traditional handicrafts, and Sangam provided a place for dialogue about and experience of cultural diversity. For all the world centers, the mission was to bring Guides together for interaction and conversation, to provide "special places" that belonged to the girls in Guiding and Girl Scouting. As a Girl Scout handbook from the 1970s advises, "Each of [the world centres] belongs to all Girl Guides and Girl Scouts. Perhaps you may visit one of them someday."[25] Most girls in the movement never would visit them, but each could dream of the possibility and contribute to the centers' upkeep on Thinking Day.

While dreaming of a visit to a world center or an international camp, Guides and Girl Scouts could reach out to others through correspondence. The International Post Box, a system for international linkages of Guides

and Girl Scouts for correspondence, began just after World War I and continues in many countries today. Individual Guides or whole companies
applied for a pen friend or pen pal in another country by submitting their
addresses to a central secretary. This scheme became very popular at points
in its history, and in fact, the Girl Scouts of the USA had to curtail their
pen-pal scheme and modify the Pen Pal badge in the 1950s, when the Post
Box secretary was unable to keep up with requests for pen pals abroad.[26]
Through schemes such as the pen pal program, Guides felt themselves part
of a diverse and international movement that was capable of bridging
differences.

As Guides sought to negotiate the diversity at hand, in some regions of
the world, international friendship took on a concrete and immediate
meaning. In the politically charged atmosphere of 1950s' Cyprus, for
instance, holding an "all-island" campfire and overnight camp, with services
in English, Greek, Turkish, and Armenian was a bold act. Just two years
later, all camping was suspended because of the "disturbed situation."[27]
In France, the Éclaireuses set up international friendship companies and
tried to sponsor international friendship camps in the immediate postwar
period. At one such camp in the French department of Indre-et-Loire (near
Tours), eight Muslim Guides spent a week camping with French Protestant
Guides from Paris. In reporting on this experiment, the French author
noted that "these young Muslim girls who, last year, camped across from
us, camped with us this year." Their week together led to frank discussions
about difference, about religious views of women's roles, about women's
emancipation, and about the cultural differences surrounding food, clothing, and ritual. In all, the girls felt the camp resulted in a desire among all
involved to "continue these fruitful exchanges."[28] Likewise, East and West
Pakistan sponsored an exchange of Guides in 1953 as a goodwill gesture
after the partition of the nation that followed Indian and Pakistani independence in 1947. Here too, Guides reported the visit to be a success and
asked for more exchanges to "break down prejudices and misconceptions
which may exist on both sides due to ignorance."[29] With such experiences,
the Guides hoped to repair the rifts that had developed within and between
societies.

In other areas of the world, fresh memories of World War II made
international friendship seem an impossibility, and rising Cold War tensions provided additional challenges. At a summer 1948 international
Guide camp on the beaches of the Baltic Sea, four national groups gathered
and initially, "what with language difficulties and the deep suspicion of

each other that is the legacy of the last war, the groups did not mix well together."[30] Yet by week's end, the camp was a success, proving to some that Guiding could make a difference in troubled times. While Guiding tried to build bridges in defeated countries with the creation of new units and companies, historically strong Guide associations were forced underground in countries such as Hungary, Poland, and Czechoslovakia with the banning of Scouting and Guiding by communist regimes in these states. As these associations resigned from WAGGGS around 1950, new or reformed associations in West Germany, Japan, Korea, Israel, Pakistan, and elsewhere resumed international Guide contact. One article from a Guide magazine in India captured the tense situation as Guides sought to leave bitterness and enmity behind. Its author urged Guides to practice "mental hospitality" or to "keep open house to all the strivings of your fellow beings struggling for a better world. Keep an open mind for the big questions of the day."[31] That would be the challenge for Guiding, especially in the 1950s and 1960s as the complications of Cold War bans on youth organizations and a broad range of independence movements brought major changes to its international linkages and conceptions.

One of the first intimations Guide world leaders had that the end of World War II would not bring peace and expansion for the movement in all countries was the distressing letters girls and adults were receiving from Guides in Europe. Some merely pleaded for help starting Guide companies in refugee and displaced persons' camps, while others wrote of their despair over political tensions. From Poland and Hungary, which had been founding members of WAGGGS, the announcement of the dissolution of their Guide organizations was a blow to the world of Guiding. Eventually with the banning of Guiding in China, Cuba, and the Baltic states, many Guides were in effect excommunicated from the world associations and their international connections. A few continued clandestine Guiding during the years of state ban, but for most, their reemergence did not occur until the 1990s. Interestingly enough, a movement of Scouts and Guides in Exile existed (especially from Hungary and Poland), but in 1961, the World Association required these members to join the movements of the nations where they lived if they wanted to keep world affiliation. Many chose to go their own way and continued as a separate "in exile" association with its own training camp into the 1980s.[32]

Offsetting the headaches of disappearing Guide organizations were the pleasures of new Guide members. The work of the Western Hemisphere committees, encampments, and visits had begun to pay off after the war with the founding of multiple new Guide companies in South and Central America. The Guide world leaders concentrated much of their efforts in the early 1950s in these nations, spending time and money in Costa Rica, Panama, Colombia, Ecuador, Venezuela, Argentina, Chile, Peru, Honduras, Bolivia, and Uruguay. In addition to these fledgling Guide regions, WAGGGS also had high hopes for the Muslim world, and they fostered movements in Lebanon, Jordan, Israel, Indonesia, Iran, Iraq, and Syria. Finally, the Guides reached out to girls' organizations in Italy, Spain, and Portugal as an extension of their work in other parts of Europe.[33] Their time, resources and efforts paid off, with almost 30 new WAGGGS member countries added to the roster between 1945 and 1960. An additional 32 more countries joined WAGGGS between 1961 and 1969.[34]

As Guiding watched their new organizations develop, of equal concern were the processes of decolonization that were shaking the remnants of European empires. From India and Pakistan's independence in 1947 to the latecomer, Zimbabwe, in 1980, the development of dozens of newly independent nations around the world, some with Guide movements already, presented major challenges. In 1954, Guiding changed its Imperial Headquarters (IHQ) to Commonwealth Headquarters (CHQ) to remove the imperial connotations from its title. Guide leaders worried that their organization would be considered "imperial" and be rejected by the youth in these new nations. This issue certainly factored into the decisions that newly independent associations made, but it was never as straightforward as an organization being pro- or anti-Guiding. In fact, the European connection, with its overtones of modernity, internationalism, and "civilization," often was a significant factor in attracting girls to the movement, even as others wanted nothing to do with what they saw as imperial apologia. The example of Syria in the 1940s is instructive in this regard. The girls of the Guides de France (in Syria) valued their association with French cultural forms as a sign of their modernity and status, while members of the competing Arab Scouts and Guides saw these "other" Guides as complicit with colonial occupation. As Keith Watenpaugh has argued, "Scouting was not a simple case of slavish derivation or unreflective collaboration," but instead a vehicle for youth to fashion their own identities in a complex and changing political and social environment.[35] Historian Timothy Parsons has made a related argument for Scouting in its African context, where boys and girls demonstrated their agency and self-definition by adapting the organization to fit their particular needs.[36]

Sometimes Scouting could boost status and other times it could be a dangerous affiliation.

The ambivalence about Guiding's European connections emerged in other places as well and featured changes in personnel to reflect newly independent nations and Guide associations. For example, in Yemen, Guiding began preparing for possible independence in 1965 by training more young Arabic-speaking leaders. As Lady Beatrice Turnbull explained to British headquarters, "There is no prejudice against the British connection, indeed it is greatly valued, but [it] is the language question that is the key to the situation and the only person who will make an impression upon the young up-and-coming Guiders is someone who can speak to them in their language." As part of this transition to independence, then, the English commissioner resigned and was replaced in 1966 by Ferida Haider Ali (Mrs. Anis Jaffer).[37] When Yemen's formal independence occurred in 1970, Guiding already had structural changes in place to anticipate the shift.

In other areas, governments felt that in establishing their authority they should sever ties with organizations that appeared colonial to the populace. In Malawi, the independent government denounced Scouts and Guides as:

> foreign organisations brought here by colonialism under Colonial rule. They are not African organisations . . . these organisations contribute nothing to the development of Malawi. The young people in these organisations are made to do nothing but marching and parading. They were not taught any skills such as farming and carpentry . . . . African youths of this country must not waste their time by just marching, parading and drinking tea . . . there is nothing of value that any of these three organisations can teach.[38]

Guiding in Malawi withered under this criticism, and the Guide movement did not revive until the 1990s.

Another concern for Guiding was the violence and disruption that accompanied many independence movements. Guides were often forced to take sides or to curtail severely their activities in order to remain safe. In Anguilla, for instance, a British crown colony in the Caribbean, Guiding weathered a political storm in 1967 when street demonstrations led to violence, and the Government House was burnt to the ground. As Guide leaders reported to British headquarters, "We had no celebrations [for Thinking Day]; owing to the dissatisfaction of the majority of the people."[39] Anguilla remained under British control, today as an overseas territory, and Guiding recovered. Other areas of the world witnessed a much more difficult struggle.

Two illustrative cases of the difficulty Guides and Scouts had in negotiating colonial independence movements are Kenya and Algeria. In Kenya, Kikuyu youth experienced pressure to join the nationalist movement after World War II with increasing unrest over land inequities, joblessness, and high taxes. With the development of the Mau Mau Emergency in the early 1950s, Kikuyu youth found themselves in the midst of a guerilla war and in a double bind. Guiding and Scouting, which were tied very heavily to the mission schools in central Kenya, found themselves under suspicion by the government for subversive activities. Yet as colonial government-sponsored associations, Guides and Scouts also became targets of anti-government rhetoric and physical violence. As Timothy Parsons has argued, for many students and teachers in these schools, they faced a choice between arrest for siding with Mau Mau fighters or attack for being pro-government.[40] Like Kenya, Algeria also experienced prolonged violence between white settlers and "indigenous" Algerians during its war for independence from the 1950s to 1962. Here too, Scouts and Guides sometimes had to choose sides in the conflict, embracing the nationalist agenda and tactics, or serving the colonial regime in "maintaining" the peace.[41] Unsurprisingly, youth split on these questions based on their individual political beliefs, but Scouts and Guides were among those arrested for nationalist activities in the late 1950s.[42]

Whether Guides had to survive violence or easy transition on the road to independence, in all cases of newly independent associations, reorganization was the order of the day. Guides had to face up to a past of discriminatory practices in some areas in order to move ahead. In the Bahamas, where 1930s debates about including "colored" companies had shut the entire movement down, Guide leaders tried to start anew with an integrated association in the 1940s.[43] In South Africa, the challenge was not to combat popular prejudice as much as it was to battle government apartheid. The Guides faced down the government, holding interracial rallies without permission, awarding a Guide Friendship badge that required meeting a person from another racial group, and refusing state funding because it might compromise their ability to function in accordance with the Guide laws.[44] Here, their connection to an international association with members who frequently visited, helped the South African Guides defy the authorities.

Guide internationalism also played an important role in policing questions of discrimination as well by the 1970s and 1980s. At international camps and large regional gatherings, the Guides insisted upon multiracial camping and interaction, but more importantly, members of the world Girl Scout and Guide associations brought pressure to bear on member nations that were not acting in accordance with Scout and Guide principles. This was particularly true in the case of apartheid South Africa, which faced expulsion from the World Association for its continued segregationist policies.[45] In fact, the frequent conferences of WAGGGS officials created a space for conversations about the direction of world Guiding. WAGGGS officials used their control of association membership rules to police actions by nations that seemed antithetical to Guiding's mission.

For most newly independent nations, a Guiding priority was replacing European leaders with local women. This could be difficult in areas with poorly developed secondary school systems for girls that had developed few indigenous teachers as Guide leaders. In the Congo, for example, this lack of female leaders arose from the structure of the school system but also from the practice of early marriage, multiple languages in the country, and communication difficulties. In a country where African higher education had been systematically neglected in the years prior to independence, Congolese Guides had to improvise when independence came in 1960, and they had to build their movement with deliberation. With approximately 6,000 members in 1960 and under new leader Beatrice Nimy, the Guides began to adapt their program to be "Congolese," and "Africanized," but their efforts were in vain.[46] Guiding was banned by the government in Zaire in the 1960s, and it did not revive again until the 1990s.

Zaire was not alone in trying to develop an "adapted" program to fit newly independent nations. Kenya also "Africanized" its leadership after independence in 1963, choosing a newly elected Kenyan Member of Parliament as chair and appointing its first African national trainer and its first African national executive all in the early months of Kenya's existence as a nation. To enhance its connection to the new government, Kenyan Guiding also named President Kenyatta's wife, H. E. Mama Ngina Kenyatta, as patron of the movement in 1965. The changes worked, and by 1973, there were more than 43,000 Guides in Kenya.[47] For women in Kenya and other newly independent nations, Guiding represented an opportunity for leadership training and advancement, but also for international travel and connections. Many of the women who embraced Guiding in the 1960s and 1970s realized its potential for helping them with education, employment, and social networking.

Anne Barangi, who joined Guiding in Kenya as a Ranger in 1962, worked her way up in the movement to become a national trainer. When asked what Guiding had done for her, she replied: "Friendship with people of all ages, locally and internationally, gained a sense of belonging to a world-wide family, fun and stimulations of mind; responsibility." Another Kenya Guide, Mrs. Maggie Gona, joined in 1947 when she was a schoolgirl. As she moved from Guide to patrol leader to Guide leader, Gona said that the movement gave her "international friends who I never forget and still communicate with. How else could I love working for people if this is not what I learned as a young Guide. Guiding leaves a mark on one that one never forgets even at old age."[48]

As these testimonials from Kenyan Guiding suggest, the organization's appeal by the 1960s depended very heavily on its image of world connections. The international friendships and the sense of belonging to something bigger than one's company, town, region, or even nation, helped Guiding survive the rocky political transformations of the 1950s and 1960s. Guiding argued successfully in the 1960s that it was not merely a colonial movement, but something that could be adapted. From its inception, the Scout movement had adapted and changed to face the inclusion of females, the challenge of two world wars, and the creation of "teenagers"—by espousing a willingness to transform itself to meet local needs of youth, it survived the decolonization process. Importantly, however, the national movements emerged within a world context that was vital to Guiding's success. The notion of international friendship was a bond that transcended both colonial pasts and nationalist presents, and it proved to be an important glue for holding Guiding together as a concept.

In a 1952 issue of *The American Girl*, an article on "worldmindedness" summarized for girls the way they should be approaching the Fourth Girl Scout Law, "A Girl Scout is a friend to all and a sister to every other Girl Scout."[49]:

> Here are a few questions we can ask ourselves on this subject of international friendship: . . . Do I believe the people of the United States of America can learn helpful things from citizens from other nations . . . do I wear my World Pin as well as my Girl Scout pin and understand what

they both mean? Do I contribute regularly to the Juliette Low World Friendship Fund? An open mind and an open heart can lead to understanding of others on a world scale! ... It's a good time to begin the important task of training ourselves to be world-minded. We have to start with ourselves and work out. We have to defend our country not only from the atomic bomb, but from the evil ignorance that sets person against person, family against family, creed against creed, and race against race.[50]

The notion of national defense through international friendship fit well with the postwar ethos of nuclear preparedness, but it also echoed the broader humanitarian programs of the 1940s such as the Marshall Plan. In fact, the worldmindedness article followed closely articles on Girl Scout involvement in American Friends Service Committee projects, such as the Clothes for Friendship initiative. With this project, Girl Scouts made clothing kits for girls in countries in need; by 1948, they had sent well over a million garments.[51] All this world activity was highlighted by two films released by the Girl Scouts of the USA in 1948 (*World Friendship*) and 1954 (*Hands Across the Sea*, later renamed *The Wider World*) that showed Guides and Girl Scouts from around the world interacting in a friendly and constructive manner.[52]

In Britain as well, internationalism became the focus of projects, badges, and rhetoric. Perhaps the best example comes from the theme for the 1950 WAGGGS world conference held in Oxford. The theme, "Scrolls of Friendship," reflected a massive effort among British Guide units to create hand-painted scrolls, which were passed "hand to hand" until they reached Oxford, where they were presented to Guides and Girl Scouts from other countries. As the Guide official historian enthused, "Mounted on ponies or penny-farthing bicycles ... riding in hay wagons or hansom cabs or fire engines ... the messengers converged on Oxford. It was meant to be fun—and it was fun—and as a Public Relations exercise it could hardly have been bettered. People from all over the country came out to watch the scrolls being hand over, and sent on their way."[53] The scrolls took on a new life in the hands of the recipients as well. For instance, the scroll presented to the Canadians went on a national tour, and at each stop Canadian Guides signed a logbook, which was then sent back to Britain as a gift.

The worldmindedness such experiences fostered helped boost Guide and Scout membership after the Second World War. In Britain, membership figures rose from around 450,000 in 1946 to more than 600,000 by

1961.[54] By 1957, Girl Scouts of the USA had seen a spike in its membership of more than a million girls in four years, bringing the total to more than three million.[55] Yet these increases in numbers masked several shifts that were transforming Guiding worldwide by the late 1950s and early 1960s, including the loss of older girls in the movement and a rise in competing youth activities. Guide movements sought to reverse this trend using several strategies, such as reorganizing age levels, instituting programmatic and uniform changes, and exploring coeducational work with the Boy Scouts. Countries took different routes toward addressing the challenges of changing demographics and interests among their girl members, but all had to face hard truths by the 1960s and make choices about what kind of girls' organization each would be. The worldmindedness that Guide leaders had in mind had to meet the challenge of the worldliness the girls themselves seemed to crave.

NOTES

1. All material taken from the Maud Mbizela-Myra Chilvers correspondence (1952–1958), ST1/C15/Shelf 3, Box 16, South Africa, GGL.

2. Alix Liddell, "The Heart of the Matter," *The Council Fire* 25:3 (July 1950), 49.

3. Notes from Robert Baden-Powells' speech in the "Historical Report of the Conference 1928," *The Council Fire* 3:10 (July 1928), 52.

4. Tammy Proctor, "Scouts, Guides and the Fashioning of Empire," in *Fashioning the Body Politic: Dress, Gender, Citizenship*, ed. Wendy Parkins (Oxford: Berg, 2002), 128–129.

5. "A Penny for your Thoughts," *The American Girl* 30:9 (September 1947), 38; Browne Popular Culture Library, Bowling Green State University (BPCL).

6. "Great Britain. Wedding of the Chief Ranger of the Empire," *The Council Fire* 32:1 (January 1948), 5–6.

7. Maud Mbizela to Myra Chilvers (May 11, 1953), ST1/C15/Shelf 3, Box 16, South Africa, GGL.

8. Maud Mbizela to Myra Chilvers (December 15, 1956), ST1/C15/Shelf 3, Box 16, South Africa, GGL.

9. "Highlights of 1957 International Program of GSUSA," 1958; Folder: International, WAGGGS, General; Box: International WAGGGS, GSUSA.

10. *Highlights in Girl Scouting, 1912–2001* (New York: GSUSA, 2002), 25.

11. CARE originally was founded in 1945 as the Cooperative for American Remittances to Europe, but its name was changed to reflect its broader mission. The United Nations Charter was signed and ratified in 1945, and UNICEF was created in 1946.

12. Marjorie M. Culmer, "The Goals We Share," *YWCA Magazine* (October 1958); Folder: International, WAGGGS, General; Box: International WAGGGS, GSUSA.

13. *Girl Guiding/Girl Scouting: A Challenging Movement* (London: WAGGGS, 1992), 37.

14. Agnes Baden-Powell and Robert Baden-Powell, *The Handbook for Girl Guides or How Girls Can Help Build the Empire* (London: Thomas Nelson and Sons, 1912), 39.

15. Author interview/questionnaire with Phyllis Lockyer, April 1993.

16. Rose Kerr, "A Thinking Day," *The Council Fire* 2:4 (February 1927), 3.

17. "International Girl Guides in Egpyt, 1913–1956," ST1/C15/Shelf 1 Box 5, Egypt, GGL.

18. Antonia Lindemeyer, "Thinking Day Programme of the Hungarian Girl Scouts," *The Council Fire* 14:1 (January 1939), 10.

19. Olave Baden-Powell, "A Letter from the Chief Guide," *The Council Fire* 8:1 (January 1933), 1.

20. http://www.worldthinkingday.org/en/about; WAGGGS.

21. *The Story of Our Chalet, Our Ark, Our Cabana: Three World Centres for Girl Guides and Girl Scouts* (London: WAGGGS, 1961), 5–7, 15, 18.

22. Interview/questionnaire with Sidney Brock, April 1993.

23. Alix Liddell, *Story of the Girl Guides 1938–1975* (London: Girl Guides Association, 1976), 104. Later, Olave House became Olave Centre, and eventually, in 1991, it was renamed Pax Lodge World Centre.

24. *The Story of Our Chalet, Olave House, Our Cabaña, Sangam: Four World Centres for Girl Guides and Girl Scouts* (London: WAGGGs, 1967), 39–49.

25. *Junior Girl Scout Handbook* (New York: GSUSA, 1963), 229.

26. Mary Degenhardt and Judith Kirsch, *Girl Scout Collector's Guide: A History of Uniforms, Insignia, Publications, and Memorabilia* (Lubbock: Texas Tech University Press, 2005), 158.

27. "Memo on Situation in Cyprus, ca. 1960," ST1/C15/Shelf 1 Box 5, Cyprus, GGL.

28. "Camp Franco-Musulman," [reprint from *Le Tréfle*], *The Council Fire* 24:1 (January 1949), 15.

29. C. Bilqees Taseer, "East to West in Pakistan," *The Council Fire* 28:4 (October 1953), 116–118.

30. Elizabeth Hartley, "Rebirth of German Guiding," *The Council Fire* 24:1 (January 1949), 6–7.

31. "Mental Hospitality," [reprinted from *The Indian Guide*], *The Council Fire* 24:1 (January 1949), 12.

32. "The Forgotten Movements. Hungary," ST1/C15/Shelf 1, Box 7 Hungary, GGL.

33. Alix de Saint Victor, "Tenderfoot and Other Countries," *The Council Fire* 29:4 (October 1954), 121–125.

34. http://www.wagggs.org.

35. Keith Watenpaugh, *Being Modern in the Middle East: Revolution, Nationalism, Colonialism, and the Arab Middle Class* (Princeton: Princeton University Press, 2006), 291–294.

36. Timothy Parsons, *Race, Resistance, and the Boy Scout Movement in British Colonial Africa* (Athens: Ohio University Press, 2004), 17, 148–149.

37. Beatrice Turnbull to Mrs. P Moffett, November 24, 1965; correspondence re: Ferida Haider Ali; report on the position of the British Guides in Aden 'B' Division, July 14, 1966; ST1/C15/Shelf 1 Box 1: Aden, GGL.

38. Clipping "Malawi Does Not Recognise Girl Guides Says Muwalo," August 9, 1968, ST1/C15/Shelf 2 Box 9: Malawi, GGL.

39. Wilma Lake to Miss Mitchell, March 10 and March 21, 1967, ST1/C15/Shelf1 Box 1: Anguilla, GGL. From a massive British imperial Guide movement in the 1940s, Girlguiding UK in 2009 has only nine branch associations among its overseas territories: Anguilla, Bermuda, British Virgin Islands, Cayman Islands, Falkland Islands, Gibraltar, Montserrat, St. Helena, and Turks & Caicos Islands.

40. Parsons, *Race, Resistance, and the Boy Scout Movement*, 164–167.

41. Jean-Jacques Gauthé, "Quand le scoutisme prépare à la guerre . . . Les Scouts musulmans algériens vus par l'armée française (septembre 1945)," in *Le scoutisme entre guerre et paix au XXe siècle* (Paris: Harmattan, 2006), 217.

42. Marie-Thérèse Cheroutre, *Le scoutisme au féminin: Les guides de France, 1923–1998* (Paris: Les Éditions du Cerf, 2002), 331.

43. Betty Murphy to Olave Baden-Powell, September 8, 1949, ST1/C15/Shelf 1 Box 2: Bahamas, GGL.

44. Parsons, *Race, Resistance, and the Boy Scout Movement*, 219.

45. Parsons, *Race, Resistance, and the Boy Scout Movement*, 253–255.

46. Sophie Wittemans, *Le Guidisme catholique au Congo belge et au Ruanda-Urundi 1923–1960* (Bruxelles: Centre Historique Belge du Scoutisme, 2008), 20–22.

47. Mary M. Khimulu, *The Girl Guide Movement in Kenya* (Nairobi: Kenya Girl Guides, 1987), 4–5.

48. "The Girl Guide Movement in Kenya," 1973, 44–46, ST1/C15/Shelf 2 Box 8: Kenya, GGL.

49. *Girl Scout Handbook* (New York: GSUSA, 1943), 7.

50. Marie E. Gaudette, "World-mindedness," *The American Girl* 35:2 (February 1952), 16.

51. "All over the map," *The American Girl* 32:3 (March 1949), 39; BPCL.

52. "The Wider World," *The Council Fire* 31:4 (October 1956), 136–138.

53. Alix Liddell, *Story of the Girl Guides 1938–1975* (London: GGA, 1976), 41–42.

54. Girlguiding UK census figures.

55. *Highlights in Girl Scouting 1912–2001* (New York: GSUSA, 2002), 24.

7. Challenges

In a 1975 letter to the national headquarters of the Girl Scouts of the USA, a longtime Girl Scout volunteer from Milwaukee, Wisconsin, expressed her disgust with the latest appointment to the national board, writing: "To say that I am upset over the invitation extended to Betty Friedan to join the National Girl Scouts of America Board is an understatement . . . how can I in good conscience represent an organization that is leaning more and more towards the Women's Lib movement . . . and further away from basic Judeo-Christian moral principles?"[1] This letter, one of many filling a fat file in the New York headquarters archive, represents the heart of the battle Guiding and Girl Scouting found themselves in by the 1960s and 1970s. While many issues regarding the "modernness" of the Guide program had been brewing for several years, the appointment of Friedan, author of *The Feminine Mystique* and founding member of the National Organization for Women, to the U.S. Girl Scout board in 1974 provided an important flashpoint.

Most of the letter writers were active Girl Scout leaders or parents whose children were enthusiastic Girl Scouts. Almost to a person, the complaints centered around competing notions of womanhood. As one mother from Fort Wayne, Indiana, wrote, "Betty Friedan's stand on American womanhood is directly opposed to the American Christian family life." Another woman from Florida echoed this concern, "The ideals of womanhood for which Ms. Friedan and NOW stand are not in line with what I believe to be the ideals of scouting." Other letters and petitions appeared at headquarters with many of the same complaints about the appointment. Some leaders also questioned the impact women's liberation might have on the movement's ability to get leaders. As one frustrated volunteer wrote from North Carolina, "I could just cry . . . . Where in the name of the Lord do you all think we are going to get these beautiful, selfless women who aren't working at becoming liberated? . . . We can't even find mothers who will come to encampments because they are too busy being liberated."[2]

Friedan, a middle-class Jewish girl from the Midwest, had been a Girl Scout herself as a child in the 1930s, in Peoria, Illinois, a town in which she remembered feeling the sense that she was a cultural outsider. Later, as a student at Smith and through her role as a writer, she explored her personal independence and voice at a time, in the 1940s, when momentous world changes were occurring. This early activism and activity set the stage for her disillusionment with life as a suburban wife and mother in 1950s America.[3] It was not until the publication of her bestseller, *The Feminine Mystique*, in 1963, that Friedan argued persuasively that women needed to develop their own interests apart from home and family alone, echoing some of the same ideas that Girl Scouts and Guides had been promulgating for decades.[4] In the book and her later writing, Friedan spoke frequently about the need to liberate women from housework and to reorganize family life, which many adults involved in Girl Scouting saw as a betrayal of "proper" womanly roles despite its connection to some Scouting ambitions. Especially by the mid-1970s when Friedan joined the Girl Scout board, a backlash had developed against feminism, and Friedan increasingly was labeled as a dangerous "radical." Many people feared that feminists sought to abolish difference between the sexes, and Friedan, as an outspoken proponent of equality for women, came to symbolize much of the power of the 1970s feminist movement.

As the Friedan controversy in Girl Scouting illustrates, the 1960s and 1970s constituted a sea change for Girl Scouts and Guides around the world, as women's work and home lives changed while their leisure activities expanded. In many countries, the movements for women's liberation combined with new attention by many international organizations on women's lives. Together these trends led Guiding and Girl Scouting to grapple with questions about their stances on women's emancipation and equality. Additionally, the development of competing activities for girls, particularly with the rise in girls' organized sports, multiple clubs, and media (such as television), forced the Guide and Girl Scout movements to strive to innovate. This changing program, along with the opening of Boy Scouting to girls in some countries and with the decline of adult volunteers, led to significant challenges for the organizations. Guiding and Girl Scouting walked a fine line between feminist forces of change that attracted many girls and a reliance on the organizations' traditional strengths, which had kept Guiding strong for decades.

As Girl Scouts around the United States absorbed the news of the appointment of one of the best known feminists in the country to their national board, other news in 1975 seemed to confirm rumors that the Girl Scouts were becoming radically feminist. Among those marching in New York City for International Women's Day that year were Friedan, feminists Gloria Steinem and Bella Abzug, organizations such as Catholics for a Free Choice and the National Gay Task Force—and the Girl Scouts of the USA. Inevitably, more letters rolled in from Girl Scout leaders, most denouncing such actions. A letter from Scarsdale, New York, sums up the complaints:

> By association with NOW, National Gay Task Force, Catholics for a Free Choice, Grey Panthers . . . you put Girl Scouts into a category I doubt the grassroots leaders would tolerate . . . . Your grassroots leaders in this area are family and church-oriented people with a deep respect for life and for others in the community . . . . Your [organization] liberated women in 1912, remember.[5]

The notion raised in this letter, that women had already been liberated, but in a more acceptable way, by Girl Scouting was not an isolated opinion. Others also wrote about their concern that Friedan's brand of liberation, especially with its emphasis on sexual liberation, was too radical for Girl Scouting. A Girl Scout leader from West Virginia expressed this sentiment best, writing: "We are not opposed to some aspects of equal rights for women, and we do feel that women are individuals who should reach their fullest capacities. At the same time, we working at the 'grassroots' level of Girl Scouting feel that Ms. Friedan could possibly be detrimental to the image and purposes of Girl Scouting."[6] This question of the image and purpose of Girl Scouting was at the heart of the dilemma; women involved in the movement wanted to empower girls but they also recognized the dangers to the wide success of the movement should it be painted as an organization aiming to destroy homes or women's traditional roles in them.

While parents and leaders struggled over the national image of the Girl Scouts in the United States, the girls themselves had their own discussion in the pages of *American Girl*. By the 1960s, the magazine had dropped the initial "The" from its title and changed its image. Gone were the serial romance stories and fresh-faced models; now the magazine included serious articles on women's occupations, money management, and world issues. As the editors noted in a 1971 statement, "So we're going to start calling attention—at various spots in every issue—to the connection between *features of general interest* (such as a career article) and *things that girls do in Girl Scouting* (such as vocational exploration . . .)."[7] In short, the editors hoped to make Girl Scouting relevant to the life issues girls were facing.

Girls themselves had already embraced this principle, and from the late 1960s into the 1970s, they carried on a vigorous debate in the letter to the editor section about such topics as women's liberation, "hippies," and careers. These overtly political debates coexisted with letters regarding fashion and other teen cultural issues in a strange blend of topics that expressed well the changing face of girls' movements. A sampling of the 1971 mailbag from *American Girl* illustrates the variety of issues and positions (Figure 7.1).

The variety of letters represented here in this small sample from only one month of the magazine shows that Girl Scouts were interested in the world around them, the political situation, and their own place in the nation, but they still wanted to compare notes on high school student councils and the latest fashion trends. Particularly significant, however, is the fact that Girl Scouting provided them with the forum to debate all these issues.

Figure 7.1 Letters in "A Penny for your Thoughts" Section of *American Girl*, January 1971

Author's age and location	Topic of Letter	Position on Topic
Age 14, Ohio	Student council	Asking for opinions and ideas
Age 15, New York	Women's liberation	"It's time for woman to be recognized as man's equal."
Age 16, Texas	Women's liberation	"Femininity has always meant playing up to the male . . . it means subservience to the male ego, even if he flunked his courses while you made Honor Roll."
Age 13, Washington	Women's liberation	"Woman was made to be man's helper, not his competitor."
Age 12, Guatemala	Midis (dress/skirt)	"I hated midis, but the more I saw the more I liked them."
Age 11, Mississippi	Midis	"When the line was first put out, I wanted one. Now I am sort of glad my mother would not let me get one."
Age 14, California	Flag-burning	"it symbolizes this nation's hypocrisy. We are financing a war never officially declared by Congress."
Age 13, Michigan	Flag-burning	"If you dislike something about our country, flag-burning is the wrong way to show it. You only alienate people."
Age 17, Tennessee	Population crisis	"if we continue to allow the population to increase at its present rate, these resources [open land] will cease to exist."

The United States was not alone in facing pressures to react to questions of women's equality and girls' education in a modern world. Particularly fraught topics included sex education and abortion, women's place in the workplace, and equal pay for equal work legislation. As clubs that worked with female youth, Guiding and Girl Scouting were particularly sensitive to issues of girls' sexuality, and they tried to protect their image as "appropriate" places for girls' socialization while also embracing modern discussions of dating, sex education, and other politicized issues. In 1969, the Girl Scouts of the USA filed a lawsuit against a company for producing a poster of a heavily pregnant teen girl in a Girl Scout uniform, with the caption "Be Prepared." While the poster promoted something Girl Scouting was beginning to see as an important issue facing teen girls, safe sex, its mockery of the Girl Scout uniform and its explicit connection between pregnancy and Girl Scouting was too much for the organization to ignore. While the lawsuit was thrown out of court and the poster was upheld as a satirical object, the judge in the case admonished the Girl Scouts to relax, noting that he doubted the Girl Scouts' good name could be "sullied" by such a poster and explaining that "the reputation of the plaintiff is so secure against the wry assault of the defendant that no such damage has been demonstrated."[8]

With the International Year of Woman in 1975, women's and girls' organizations fell under additional scrutiny as media outlets tried to assess where women stood in societies. As legislation regarding equal rights, family and parental leave, and sexual harassment changed the face of societies, Guiding had to absorb these transformations and determine to what extent it would react. Changes in religious policy affected some Guide movements as well, especially in Catholic countries where Vatican II in the 1960s led to wide-ranging discussions about Catholic social action and family life. Finally, the world population explosion that followed the Second World War expanded the pool of possible girl members, but also stretched the financial and human resources of the movement as Guiding tried to recruit enough leaders to meet demand.

Guiding's foray into a "modern" youth movement was not merely reactive, however, and much of the transformation in program and outlook occurred prior to the 1970s with its proactive assessments of girls' lives and interests. Alix Liddell, official Guide historian, captured the spirit of change that was sweeping youth movements, noting that, "With the dawn of the 1960s a murmuring that had been heard for some time grew to a crescendo. The question was being asked loud and clear 'Is the Movement out-of-date?' "[9] Although not a new query for Guiding, the question did attract attention among national leaders in Britain and other countries in the 1960s as adults sought to keep Guiding fresh and modern. While numbers remained strong, what concerned leaders were the shifting currents of youth culture, magnified in media reports of the time. Not only did girls enjoy greater freedoms than in the past, but they had many more options for spending their time as organized sport, youth clubs, and vocational training claimed their interests.

Part of the reason Guiding was looking to its members for guidance was that the social foundation of women's leisure was shifting, and the organizations needed help knowing how many of these activities could be or should be incorporated into the Guides and Girl Scouts. For instance, the advent of television and popular radio in the 1950s had opened up new opportunities for women and girls, leading to interest in fan magazines, dance and fashion crazes, and record collecting. By the late 1960s, for instance, "there was one television set for every five people in western Europe," making it possible for most young people to spend time in front the television on a daily basis.[10] The expansion of education, especially higher educational opportunities, for more young women also created new competition for their time. Student political movements, such as feminism and the peace movement, also began to draw older girls, who often saw the Guides as old-fashioned compared to their aspirations for sexual and political liberation. In the United States, the visible representation of women in the civil rights movement and antiwar protests also "challenged women's so-called traditional domestic role in society," bringing them and their voices into the public sphere of politics.[11]

The 1970s also marked the explosion of other areas of competition for Guiding and Scouting, including expanded opportunities for education, work, and sport. Examples include the 1972 Title IX rules in the United States that prohibited sexual discrimination in educational (and cocurricular) activities and the British 1975 Sex Discrimination Act, which also aimed to put women on an equal footing with men in education and workplace.[12] These acts and other gender-oriented legislation provided for equal access to secondary school and higher education classes, in some cases opening up funding for girls to embrace the life of the mind. Other workplace changes protected women's jobs further, leading to a rise in the number of women employed by the 1970s and 1980s, despite continued problems with pay that lagged behind their male counterparts.

The legislation that opened up education and restructured work for women also had consequences for women's physical fitness and access to sport. Although women had been playing sports since the advent of Guiding, new legislation opened up increased funding and opportunities for organized female sports in schools and universities. Sports also offered adventure and activity for girls, sometimes in a coeducational setting, providing an alternative to the hiking that Guiding and Scouting featured. Girls who might have spent their time Guiding now juggled practice times for sporting pursuits with their weekly Guide or Girl Scout meetings. From the 1970s on, participation of girls in organized sports expanded as did their interest in fitness; by 1998, a French study found that more than 60 percent of teen girls said that they participated in sports.[13] Likewise in the United States, an estimated one in twenty-seven girls participated in organized sport at high schools in 1972; by 2008, that number was one in three girls.[14]

This expansion of organized sports echoed changes in notions of the body by the 1980s as well. As Ina Zweiniger-Bargielowska has argued, the ideal bodies of women and girls in 1910 Britain (and elsewhere) looked very different from the model bodies celebrated by the 1990s. By this point, the notion of a muscled female body that was trim and fit became celebrated in popular magazines and other media. Studios focusing on aerobics, gyms with expensive fitness equipment, and a whole range of products aimed at toning women's bodies and changing their eating habits flooded the market in the 1980s and 1990s. Zweiniger-Bargielowska cites a figure that captures this expansion—in 1977 in Britain only about 2 percent of women reported "working out" regularly, typically through yoga and "keep fit" classes. However, by the 1990s that figure had risen to one-third of women under 30.[15]

Beyond changes in education, political consciousness, work and body culture, the 1970s and 1980s also ushered in a new world of media access for girls. Expansions in television and the advent of premium programming such as MTV and HBO by the 1980s certainly broadened the scope of issues girls could absorb from the privacy of their homes. Guiding and Scouting battled not just the concerns about feminism and changing roles for women in society, but the insidious attraction of televisions, and later, computers. Adults, too, found reasons to stay at home rather than volunteering their time in service organizations such as the Guides, making it difficult to attract and retain qualified leaders. With such challenges in mind, Guide organizations around the world began redoubling their efforts to change with the times.

One of the first areas for focused change in the movements in the 1960s came in the form of redistributed age groups. Several nations, such as the United States, United Kingdom, and France, paid for professional studies of their membership, compiling statistics on background, interests, and competing activities. What virtually all the studies showed was that Guiding was losing girls at the older age levels, and that their strength increasingly came from younger girls. Added to this demographic reality, educational reform in the 1960s had led to new staging within many school systems, so Guiding hoped to change its age levels to reflect these transformations. In France, for example, the Guides de France initiated a new four-stage program in the late 1960s: *Jeannettes* (ages 8–11) with a focus on the forest world and nature; *Guides* (ages 12–14) with a focus on adventure; *Caravelles* (ages 15–16) with a focus on enterprise and world knowledge; and *Jeunes en marche* [Jem] (ages 17+) with a focus on cooperation with Boy Scouts. The changes never really succeeded, however, and the Guides de France were faced with falling numbers in the late 1960s and early 1970s. They reacted quickly with a new study in 1975–1976, which found that 75 percent of their members were aged 9–14. It was clear from the study that Guiding was not able to keep older teen girls in the movement and that it would need to change its program if it hoped to attract the late teen cohort.[16]

British Guiding found itself in a similar predicament by the 1960s. A 1960 local study of youth in Essex paved the way for research into children's lives and interests, when its results showed that children "belonged to many more organizations outside their homes," that they were less interested in organized games, and they wanted to be treated like grown-ups. The study, a repeat of a 1946–1947 survey, found marked differences in activities, number of clubs, and stated interests. The Guides, along with other youth clubs took note of these results, published as *The Leisure Activities of School Children*, and made plans to survey their own members.[17] Guiding convened a series of study groups to determine the movement's current status and future directions. The groups met multiple times over a period of two years, from 1964–1966, before drafting a report.

Like the French, British leaders saw a shift in age groupings. As the report noted, "We consider that the basic principles are still valid . . . [at] the same time, we have been aware that the present day girl is 'older' at each stage than her 1908 contemporary, and also that she is living in an entirely different world."[18] One of the more interesting parts of the study, which was gleaned from questioning Guides and their leaders, was its survey of what Guides liked most. Of the various activities girls listed, camp overwhelmingly led the responses, followed by games, outdoor work, hiking, and badge work. When adults were asked what they did not like about the program, most cited problems such as excessive rules and red tape, but they also thought some original aspects of Guiding should be abolished, such as semaphore and drill.[19] In the end, the study confirmed what many Guide officials had suspected—that they attracted young girls who liked outdoor life and adventure, but who were receptive to other educational and world friendship aspects of the organization's program. However, they were not always keeping these girls in the movement, and there was a significant drop in membership at or around age 14.[20] As in France, the strength of the movement appeared to be from ages 8 to 14 years old. In an attempt to reverse this trend, the British even tried to attract older girls with modern "airline-stewardess" style uniforms in 1966 and a new handbook in 1968 that featured lots of artwork and less text.[21]

Like British and French Guides, U.S. Girl Scouts also got a facelift in the 1960s, based in part on the results of their national survey from the 1950s. They adopted "mix and match" uniforms that allowed girls to express their style and that might be more affordable as a nod to girls' lifestyles by the late 1960s and 1970s. One news article wryly described the shift in perspective:

> It seems that even Girl Scouts aren't safe from the research lads and lassies who go around asking questions, acquiring surveys, punching cards for computers and all that razzle-dazzle . . . so now they've sold this idea to the Girl Scout organization: that these days girls from seven to 17 are different from the Scouts of Mom's day, *being more mature in interests, needs and problems.*[22] [emphasis added]

The Girl Scouts, as the author implied, were transforming their age categories to bring them in line with emerging research on adolescent development and to address concerns raised by their national study. Girl Scouts now occupied four age categories, much like the French Guides de France structure. The new program encouraged Brownies (aged 7–8) to learn a simpler promise and to focus on group activities and feelings of belonging, while Junior Girl Scouts (aged 9–11) moved from "Brownie fancy to [the] real, concrete world." The third stage, Cadette Girl Scouts (aged 12–14), organized itself around a "greater emphasis on thinking, problem-solving, decision making and evaluation" and focused on developing "increasing independence from adults." Finally, the Senior Girl Scouts (aged 15–17) worked toward widening their "circle of opportunities . . . beyond the troop."[23] In addition, Girl Scouts invited older girls in the movement, aged 15 to 17, to participate as advisors to adult leaders at the annual conference.[24] Officials hoped that the girls would offer advice on how to appeal to more young people in a changing world.

This retooling of the Girl Scout program heavily relied on developmental adolescent models, and many of the program resources distributed to leaders emphasized psychological and sociological factors in girls' developing selves as much as they did games, activities, and camping. The shift in age groupings, but more importantly, the move toward surveying and responding to members of the organizations, represented a fundamental shift in the operation of Guide and Girl Scout movements around the globe. Increasingly sophisticated research on girls and their sexual, psychological, and educational development helped shape decisions about the programs offered, but also the reliance on feedback as an essential factor in changing the organizational structure marked Guiding from this point forward. Prior to any planned major change today, most Guide movements engage in some kind of study or survey of membership before proceeding.

As the century proceeded, more sophisticated studies of Guide membership and interests pointed to a need to retool age categories yet again by the 1980s. With Guide and Girl Scout movements around the world seeking ways to compete and to bolster their flagging memberships, the question of just how young or how old Guides should be became a focus for conversation. A new round of studies in the 1970s showed that membership was continuing to trend toward younger girls. For instance, in the French study of Catholic Guides in the 1970s, officials found out that more than half of French Catholic Guides were 13 or under.[25] Other countries experienced similar trends as the leisure and educational changes of the 1970s and 1980s pulled more older youth away from Guiding. Although Guiding meant to fight for older youth through revitalized activities, coeducational experiments, and other transformations, the organization also decided on a major shift in program in many countries by the 1980s. Guiding, a youth movement aimed for years at teens and preteens, now expanded to include younger girls, aged as young as five and six. Boy Scouting followed suit, developing younger branches as well. In the United States, Daisy Scouts (named after Juliette Low's nickname) were created in the 1980s, while Britain's Rainbow Guides were launched in 1987. The names for these young branches vary widely by country, from Nutons among French Catholic Guides in Belgium, to Blossoms in Barbados, to Beavers in the Netherlands, to Sparks in Canada.

Despite variety in naming, many Guide associations around the world have embraced this concept and made it central to their plans for growth in the future. In fact, some national Guide associations are inviting girls as young as three to join these younger branches, as with the "Pepes" in the Cook Islands. While some have criticized associations for bringing in children who are too young to absorb their character-building messages, Guide and Girl Scout officials defend the changes. In 1984 when the Girl Scouts of the USA launched Daisy Scouts, National Executive Director Frances Hesselbein pointed out that Girl Scouting was reflecting societal shifts: "It seemed a logical step for us and of critical importance for the American family .... When you look at all the single-parent households, the Girl Scouts can be almost indispensable."[26] This argument, that Girl Scouting was being sensitive to shifts in labor and household patterns, was echoed in other countries that instituted younger branches.

In most nations that instituted young branches for five-year-old children, the program has been a success. Little girls jumped at the chance to join Guiding and Girl Scouting, seeing an opportunity to join in the activities that they witnessed their older siblings and friends enjoying. Also, for girls who might have spent time in after-school or daycare settings while their parents worked, being able to go to a Girl Scout or Guide meeting, even if only once per week, was a significant draw for girls and their parents. In countries where movements were also coeducational, girls often met or surpassed boys in joining early in their lives—by 2007 in Britain at least half of Beaver Scouts (Scouting's youngest branch) were girls.[27] Clearly the younger child found Guiding and Girl Scouting attractive. The question was how to keep those same girls interested from age five to eighteen, and in the twenty-first century, this is the key question facing Guiding and Girl Scouting as they move forward into the future.

Another initiative that became important in international Guiding and Girl Scouting in the 1960s was the question of coeducation, which emerged as a major issue at local, national, and international levels. Coeducation, a debate within Scout communities since their foundation in the early twentieth century, was also a concept at the heart of broader discussions of education for children. In Europe the widespread introduction of coeducation into schools in the period after World War II transformed educational policy and ignited debates about whether single-sex or coeducational schooling served the needs of children best.[28] The sides in the battle over coeducation in schools echoed the long-time tension in Guiding and Scouting between the notions of complementary roles for the sexes and absolute equality between boys and girls.

Complementarity versus equality came to dominate debates in Guiding among members and in policy disputes at the international level of the organization. Each of the proposed coeducational "solutions" faced challenges and problems, particularly regarding the thorny issues of gender role socialization. The difficulties with resolving disputes about gender led the World Organization of the Scout Movement (WOSM) to embrace a somewhat contradictory statement in 1977, when girls were first admitted officially at the international level. The 1977 stance proposed that "the relationship between males and females is one of equality and complementarity."[29] Here the international leadership allowed national movements to bring girls into their organizations either as Scouts equal to the boys or as "girl" Scouts, which in practice could be very different things. Neither fish nor fowl, this open-ended statement regarding boys and girls remained WOSM policy until it revised its statement in 1999 to reflect a shift toward egalitarian language in Scouting.

Diversity of perspective regarding the meaning of coeducation has meant diversity of experience within the movements. Even today as the world movement has changed its stance to emphasize ideas of gender equality much more specifically, Scouting coeducational policies tend to be multitudinous and creative. Coeducation encompassed different models from the 1960s until the present, but the three major proposals for coeducation were 1) amalgamation between Boy Scouts and Girl Scouts; 2) admission of girls into Boy Scouting; 3) admission of boys into Girl Guiding. All three of these strategies emerged in national movements in the period between the 1960s and the 1990s, and all three possibilities still exist today in international Guiding. These differing models reflected cultural and local conditions in various countries, but they also echoed and extended the larger disagreement about whether coeducation was supposed to aim for gender equality or complementarity.

Perhaps the most successful amalgamation of boys and girls movements occurred in Sweden in 1960, when the Swedish Boy Scouts and Girls Scouts combined their organizations and held parallel camps.[30]

By the 1970s, the Swedish Guide and Scout Association had a joint com-mittee and integrated units of boys and girls. Swedish Girl Scouts now had access to resources from the Guide international organization (WAGGGS) as well as the boys' executive, the World Organization of the Scout Movement (WOSM). Also, financially the amalgamation made sense for the struggling Guides. Yet as Bodil Formark has argued in her work, the amalgamation was a gendered and colonizing process, which forced females in the movement to stake a claim for themselves as Scouts or lose their identity entirely. When the groups merged the boys had nearly double the membership of the girls (45,000 to 28,000), and they had already experimented with opening their organization to girls, putting Boy Scout officials in a position of power in negotiations.[31] Amalgamation was never an entirely equal or complete process, and Formark argues that Girl Scout officials accepted the merger in order to avoid the creation of a two-tiered Girl Scouting system, with Girl Scouts (under their control) and Boy-Girl Scouts (under the Boy Scout executive's control). In the Swedish case, all the debates about gender roles and single-sex versus coeducational training emerged anew as the organizations negotiated their merger.

Other countries, particularly in Scandinavia, also merged their Boy Scout and Girl Guide movements in the period from the 1960s to the 1990s, often responding to falling numbers or financial difficulties. With changing work patterns, finding qualified leaders could be a problem, and merging girls and boys could help alleviate pressure for extra leaders. It is important to note that within these merged associations, various approaches were taken. Sometimes girls and boys met in merged troops, other times the merger was more of an organizational convenience and gender-segregated troops were maintained. For example, in Turkey, which merged its boys' and girls' sections into a federation in 1991, "there are girl only units and some mixed units . . . depending on the interests and needs of the young people."[32] Some of the other states that today have combined male and female movements include Austria, Chile, Costa Rica, Czech Republic, Finland, France (although the Catholic Guides remain single sex), Iceland, Israel, Jordan, Latvia, Liechtenstein, Mauritania, Monaco, Netherlands, Poland, Slovak Republic, and Switzerland.

The second form of coeducational development within the Scout world came with the admittance of girls into national Boy Scout move-ments, often against the wishes of the Guide Associations in those coun-tries. In some cases, the admittance of girls was conditional, as with

Canada. In the early 1970s the Rover section for young adults experimented with coeducation, finding the program to be a success, then in the 1980s the Venture Scout section (aged 14 to 17) followed the Rovers by opening their ranks to girls. Several years of discussion and experimentation ensued, with some rural groups integrating boys and girls in the younger sections to keep their troops alive in sparsely populated areas. Finally in 1998, the whole Canadian Scout Association became officially coed after a series of surveys regarding interest. The last stage in the process came with a name change in 2007 from Boy Scouts to Scouts.[33]

Boy Scouting in the United States seemed headed down a path of incremental change similar to Canada's when in 1969 girls were allowed into the units for older youth, today in the U.S. called Venture Scouts.[34] Despite the inclusion of girls in the senior sections, however, American Scouting has not moved to apply the policy to younger children, perhaps partly because of resistance from its own membership and from the Girl Scouts of the USA. With the move by the Boy Scouts of America to make sections for youth aged 14 to 20 coed in the late 1960s and 1970s, the all-female U.S. Girl Scout association reiterated its single-sex nature, declared itself a "feminist organization" and supported the Equal Rights Amendment, seeking to distinguish their program and goals from what the Boy Scouts had to offer.[35] At their national convention in 1975, delegates "voted overwhelmingly" to remain a single-sex organization, while allowing male Girl Scout leaders. As one 17-year-old Girl Scout told reporters, "If we need boys to sell Girl Scouts, we need to re-evaluate our program."[36]

While Guide and Scout organizations negotiated coeducational membership for youth, they also debated the makeup of their adult leadership pool. In the United States, for example, women had served as Cubmistresses from the younger branch's creation, but females had been barred from actively serving as troop leaders for the older boys (even though many in practice had been leading troops). However, with the rise of single-parent families and with shortages in leaders in the Boy Scouts of America, the organization reversed its ban on female troop leaders in 1988.[37] The Girl Scouts of the USA, like its male counterpart, also welcomed male leaders, despite the ban on boy members.[38] For both groups, the needs of modern families, the difficulties in recruiting leaders, and the popular demands for diversity of leadership helped make these policies possible.

Other countries faced similar decisions in regard to adult leaders. In Singapore, for instance, despite a long ban on women serving as Boy

Scout unit leaders, the association moved to open its warranted ranks to women for the first time, allowing them to run Scout troops for older boys, not just Cub groups. In the discussion that ensued about the new policy, one of the realities that kept surfacing was that increasingly women served as the teachers in grammar and secondary schools in Singapore. With "the majority of Scouting based in the schools" in Singapore, the association argued that it made sense to encourage women, especially female teachers, to run Scout troops as well as their traditional Guide units. As training for such roles, Singapore's older branch, the Rovers, also opened its ranks to girls.[39]

While the United States and Singapore represent those countries with Boy Scout associations that opened their older ranks to women, both as leaders and as "senior" level Scouts, other nations' Boy Scout organizations threw open their tents to all girls. The best example of such policies is Great Britain, where in 1993 Scouting publicly invited girls to join its organization in a new move toward "Gender-free Scouting."[40] Despite the objections of the Girl Guides, who saw themselves as the appropriate Scout organization for girls in Britain, the Scouts moved ahead with acceptance of girls, setting up a head-to-head competition with Guiding for the allegiance of British girls. Guides reiterated their single-sex policy in 1990 and continued to maintain that single-sex movements better met girls' needs:

> At a time when more and more equal opportunities and especially opportunities for leadership are being offered to women, we believe that the provision of specialized help for girls is more important than ever. We wouldn't begin to know how to help boys but, after 80 years, we do think we know something about helping girls.[41]

Even with the Guides' protestations, Scouting charged forward with its intention of admitting girls throughout the 1990s. Since the advent of this policy, Scout membership figures in Britain have dropped from more than 600,000 in the early 1990s to fewer than 450,000 in 2005. This may be attributed to other factors beyond the inclusion of girls into Boy Scouting, however, since Girl Guide membership has also dropped—from more than 730,000 in 1995 to just over 540,000 in 2005.[42] As they seek to boost membership and keep alive "the spirit of Scouting," both associations have called into question the boundaries of gender in Scouting and Guiding, as established a century ago.

With the opening of Boy Scout doors to girls in some countries, Guiding also faced the question of making their organizations coeducational, the third option for changing the gender makeup of the movements in this period. In the 1980s, several Guide associations in nations such as Greece, Belgium, France, and Brazil, experimented with admitting boys into their Guide memberships. As boys began joining the movement and advancing through its ranks, the World Association of Girl Guides and Girl Scouts felt the need to make policy about the presence of boys in its midst. While it was one thing for countries to utilize male leaders, the active participation of boys in Guiding meant careful consideration of Guiding's ideological and practical aims. At the 1992 WAGGGS gathering, leaders from countries with boy members presented their positions and discussed how the experiment was working. However, despite reported success in some countries with the inclusion of boy members, WAGGGS made a decision to "keep" the boys already in the organization as "male members" but not to allow any further expansion of the movement to boys in other nations. In its official stance, WAGGGS continued as a movement for "girls and young women" with male members in its ranks. This ambiguous and slightly deceptive position has led to continued conversations at the international level and a call by some members of the Guiding world for a change.[43] In nations that admitted boys, such as Belgium, the program has proved successful in attracting male youth. The Guides Catholiques de Belgique, for instance, counted among its members about 20 percent boys in 2008.[44]

Other countries' Guide movements also studied opportunities for coeducation and cooperation, sometimes setting up pilot or experimental schemes. The problem, as several officials and scholars have noted, however, was that it was hard to avoid a "false egalitarianism" inherit in notions of universality.[45] Typically as the Scouts or Guides opened doors to the other sex, their expectations barely changed for the youth; boys were often expected to embrace the Guide culture and girls to make themselves fit into Scout programs. Also, often times the "minority" sex in the movements became dependents within the larger framework of their movements, expected to play certain, sometimes gender-specific roles.

In a study by a Norwegian scholar commissioned by WOSM, four national Scout organizations with coeducational programs (Russia, Slovakia, Portugal, and Denmark) provided a blueprint for addressing some of the continuing problems associated with mixing boys and girls into one program. As the author noted in her conclusions, the cultures and hierarchies within the organizations and their societies must be addressed in order for true coeducation to work:

> [T]he girls we have met in this study joined Scouting for the same reasons as the boys: freedom, friends, fun and adventure .... Thus, with the present recruitment, making Scouting more girl-friendly does not seem to imply that the main concept of activities should be changed. What should be worked on, however, is the symbolic gender and the gender culture surrounding these basic activities .... As long as these aspects are not addressed, the girls will remain "the second sex" in Scouting, left to negotiate their gender on unequal terms with the boys.[46]

This underlying, unspoken gender hierarchy makes any notion of coeducation difficult as long as girls in Scouting and boys in Guiding must prove themselves "in spite of their gender."[47] As the Guide movement continues into its second century, the question of coeducation is one that must be addressed.

Guiding's growing pains, expressed with monumental drops in membership, shifts in age categories, and experiments with coeducation, came to a decisive point in the 1990s. Faced with funding and membership problems, Guide organizations around the world made hard decisions about their futures, in some cases entirely reorganizing their programs. A bright spot in the world Guiding picture in this period was the creation or recreation of Guide and Girl Scout associations in countries where the movement had been banned for decades. With the fall of the Berlin Wall and the waves of political reform in Eastern Europe in the 1990s, Guiding emerged after 40 or more years of hiatus in several nations. WAGGGS had its hands full, in fact, with trying to keep up with applications for training and assistance. Throughout the area that had been "behind the Iron Curtain," fledgling Guide movements began organizing or reorganizing themselves, often with help from established associations around the world.

Belarus, for instance, had not had a viable Guide movement since it was banned under the Soviet Union in the 1920s. With the Chernobyl nuclear disaster in 1986, communities in other parts of Europe began opening their homes up to Belarusian children under humanitarian schemes that provided summer holidays for children in areas affected by radiation. One of those projects was sponsored by WAGGGS, and Belarusian children were "invited to summer camps by European

National Scout and Guide Associations, [which] enabled the children and adults accompanying them, to get to know the activities" of Scouting and Guiding. With this introduction as a basis and with connections already established with international Guiding, Belarus began its first Guide companies in Minsk in 1992. A decade later the movement had more than 1,600 members aged 7 to 18.[48]

Other nations that also rejoined the Guide world in the mid-1990s include Poland, Hungary, Romania, and the Baltic nations. Because these nations had been strong proponents of Guiding prior to the 1950s, they were able to develop their movements relatively quickly, but with mixed success. Many older people who had been Guides prior to the ban or who had been Guides in exile helped to reorganize the structures of Guiding in these countries. Of all these newly integrated Guide nations, Poland has been the most successful in recruiting youth. From the reintroduction of Guiding in 1990 to 2001, the movement recruited more than 106,000 female youth in just over a decade.[49]

As nations such as Poland rebuilt movements after decades of drought, other countries struggled to reinvigorate their memberships in the face of falling numbers. With the end of the twentieth century came increased competition from technology and other leisure activities for teens, but also the swirling debates regarding feminism, coeducation, and age groups shaped what associations felt they could or should do in their countries. The shifting sands of family life, work patterns, and young people's ambitions made it difficult for any established youth movement to find a place to stand amid such transformations. For Guiding, one key to the future was to talk with youth. Over the course of the last 50 years, Guiding and Girl Scouting made it a policy to include youth in decision-making and leadership roles in the organizations, and officials have continued to survey members about their interests, complaints, and dreams for Guiding. The opening of communication channels between adults and youth has helped usher in changes that youth can embrace.

However, the challenge amidst the changes continued to focus around the mission of Guiding and Girl Scouting in relationship to other youth clubs and activities. Were Guides aiming only to include girls? What age best absorbed the character training and service work of Girl Scouting? How could the movements remain true to their origins while still embracing the future? Perhaps Guiding's response to these challenges was summed up best in a comment by Patience, Lady Baden-Powell (a Guide official who is married to Robert Baden-Powell's grandson) in

1982: "We are in the people business . . . [and] young people want to do good."[50] This central concept has been at the heart of Guiding and Girl Scouting since their inceptions, and the more the organizations can keep this sentiment in mind while continuing to modernize programs and respond to youth needs, the better they will be able to sustain the mission and vision of the original movements.

NOTES

1. Letter to Mrs. William M. Ittman (President, GSA), January 11, 1975, Personalities Box, Folder—Betty Friedan, Correspondence 1974–1978, GSUSA.

2. Chronology of events, articles, and correspondence concerning Ms. Betty Friedan in central or public relations files as of April 10, 1975, Personalities Box, Folder—Betty Friedan, Correspondence 1974–1978, GSUSA.

3. Daniel Horowitz, *Betty Friedan and the Making of the Feminine Mystique: The American Left, the Cold War, and Modern Feminism* (Amherst: University of Massachusetts Press, 1998), 22–23, 50, 153–155.

4. William H. Chafe, *The Paradox of Change: American Women in the 20th Century* (New York: Oxford University Press, 1991), 195–197.

5. Chronology of events, articles, and correspondence concerning Ms. Betty Friedan in central or public relations files as of April 10, 1975, Personalities Box, Folder—Betty Friedan, Correspondence 1974–1978, GSUSA.

6. Chronology of events, articles and correspondence concerning Ms. Betty Friedan in central or public relations files as of April 10, 1975, Personalities Box, Folder—Betty Friedan, Correspondence 1974–1978, GSUSA.

7. The Editors, "1971," *American Girl* 54:1 (January 1971), 11.

8. "Girl Scouts Sue A Poster Concern; Cite 'Defamation'," *New York Times* (August 5, 1969); "Girl Scouts Lose Court Bid to Halt a Satirical Poster," *New York Times* (October 10, 1969).

9. Alix Liddell, *Story of the Girl Guides 1938–1975* (London: GGA, 1976), 64.

10. Cited in Lynn Abrams, "Women at Home in the Family," in *The Routledge History of Women in Europe since 1700*, ed. Deborah Simonton (London: Routledge, 2006), 43.

11. Anne McLeer, "Practical Perfection: The Nanny Negotiates Gender, Class, and Family Contradictions in 1960s Popular Culture," *NWSA Journal* 14:2 (Summer 2002), 81.

12. Chafe, *The Paradox of Change*, 215; Harold L. Smith, "The Women's Movement, Politics and Citizenship, 1960s–2000," in *Women in Twentieth-Century Britain*, ed. Ina Zweiniger-Bargielowska (Harlow, Essex: Pearson Education, 2001), 282.

13. Alain Chenu and Nicolas Herpin, "Une pause dans la marche vers la civilization des loisirs?" [1998 Emploi du Temps], *Economie et statistique* No. 352–353, 2002; available from http://www.insee.fr/.

14. Jeffrey Thomas, "U.S. Gender Equity Law Led to Boom in Female Sports Participation," (April 1, 2008), U.S. Department of State's Bureau of International Information Programs; available from http://www.america.gov.

15. Ina Zweiniger-Bargielowska, "The Body and Consumer Culture," in *Women in Twentieth-Century Britain*, 183, 192.

16. Marie-Thérèse Cheroutre, *Le scoutisme au féminin: Les guides de France, 1923–1998* (Paris: Les Éditions du Cerf, 2002), 356–363, 450–452. Belgium (Catholic Guides) followed France with the shift in age categories in the 1960s as well.

17. "'Changes' in Children: New Pursuits since Survey of 1947," *The Times* (May 11, 1960).

18. Girl Guides Association, *Tomorrow's Guide: Report of the Working Party Appointed by the Executive Committee of the Council in May 1964* (London: GGA, 1966), 8.

19. *Tomorrow's Guide*, 167–170.

20. *Tomorrow's Guide*, 155.

21. Girlguiding UK program and uniform cards.

22. Roy P. Stewart, "Girl Scouts Start Modern Program," *Daily Oklahoman*, September 9, 1963; Folder: Program—General—1960s/1963 Program Change—Fliers, Articles, Fact Sheet; Box: Program, General 1963 Program Change, GSUSA.

23. Program Resource Training packets, Folder: Program—General—1960s/1963 Program Change—Training Guide Packet; Box: Program, General 1963 Program Change, GSUSA.

24. *New York Times* (October 26, 1969).

25. Cheroutre, *Le scoutisme au feminin*, 452.

26. James Barron, "Girl Scouts Lower Membership Age," *The New York Times* (October 28, 1984).

27. *An Official History of Scouting* (London: Hamlyn, 2006), 165.

28. Rebecca Rogers, "Learning to be Good Girls and Women," in *The Routledge History of Women Since 1700*, 123–125.

29. Harriet Bjerrum Nielsen, *One of the Boys? Doing Gender in Scouting* (Geneva: WOSM, 2003), 3; available from http://www.euroscout.org, accessed January 23, 2009.

30. WAGGGS, *Trefoil Round the World* (London: WAGGGS, 2003), 303–304.

31. Bodil Formark is completing a dissertation on Swedish Guiding, but she has already written on the topic in her master's work: Bodil Formark, "Reaktionärer i takt med tiden. En analys av samgåendet mellan Sveriges Flickors

Scoutförbund och Sveriges Scoutförbund med anledning av ett framtida avhand-lingsprojekt," Master's thesis, Department of History, Lund University, 2005. The material here is taken from her conference presentation, "Scouting for Gender Equality? The Amalgamation of the Swedish Boy and Girl Scout Association and the Construction of Swedish Identity," at the Centennial Scout Symposium at Johns Hopkins University in February 2008.

32. WAGGGS, *Trefoil Round the World* (London: WAGGGS, 2003), 324–325.

33. Steve Bobrowicz, "Here Come the Girls," *Scouting Life* (November/ December 2008), 6–11. Canada today has two older branches, the Venture Scouts and the Rovers, both of which allow girls.

34. In the United States, the Boy Scouts' section for older youth was called the Explorers until 1998, but it is now known as Venturing.

35. M. Rothschild, "Girl Scouts," in *Encyclopedia of Children and Childhood in History and Society*, ed. Paula Fass (New York: Macmillan Reference, 2004), volume 2.

36. *New York Times* (October 29, 1975).

37. *The Guardian* (February 15, 1988).

38. *New York Times* (March 12, 1982).

39. Kevin Y. L. Tan and Wan Men Hao, *Scouting in Singapore 1910–2000* (Singapore: Singapore Scout Association, 2002), 180, 256–257.

40. "Three Cheers Postponed," and "Gender Free Scouting," *Scouting* 87:11 (November 1993), 9–13.

41. Alan Hamilton, "Boredom and Boys Cut Girl Guide Rolls," *The Times* (May 31, 1990).

42. The UK Scout Association 2004–05 Annual Report and Girlguiding UK census figures, 1910–2007.

43. Heather Brandon and Garth Morrison working paper, "WAGGGS/WOSM Relationships," prepared for January 14, 2001 meeting of the WAGGGS/WOSM Consultative Committee; available from http://www.euroscout.org/satw/wosm_wagggs/missions_e.pdf, accessed January 26, 2009.

44. Thanks to Sophie Wittemans for providing background information and statistics on boys in Belgian Guiding.

45. This phrase and an excellent discussion of the problem comes from Cheroutre, *Le scoutisme au féminin*, 541.

46. Nielsen, *One of the Boys?*, 161.

47. Nielsen, *One of the Boys?*, 163. For more on the philosophical difficulties with combining boys' and girls' notions of Scouting, see Sophie Wittemans, "The Double Concept of Citizen and Subject at the Heart of Guiding and Scouting," in *Scouting Frontiers: Youth and the Scout Movement's First Century*, eds. Nelson R. Block and Tammy M. Proctor (Newcastle upon Tyne: Cambridge Scholars Press, 2009), 56–71.

Conclusion

What do Queen Elizabeth II, supermodel Kate Moss, comedian Lucille Ball, Britain's first astronaut Helen Sherman, U.S. Secretary of State Hillary Clinton, and U.S. Supreme Court Justice Sandra Day O'Connor have in common?[1] All, of course, were Girl Guides or Girl Scouts in their youth. Over its 100-year existence, Guiding has touched the lives of millions of women, teaching them self-reliance and adventure. It has also struggled mightily to define women's roles in society, through the changes of war, social upheaval, and political change. For a youth organization to survive and thrive, as Guiding has, it must embrace a certain measure of change and adaptability. This short conclusion examines the compromises and transformations Guiding has made in order to survive, while suggesting some of the challenges it will continue to face as it enters its second century.

One of the ways Guiding has tried to remain modern is to embrace the ideas of girls themselves. In the twenty-first century, Guide and Girl Scout organizations around the world have altered their programs to meet girls' needs and to combat perceptions that they are old-fashioned or out of touch. A 12-year-old Guide in Scotland addressed this adaptation directly in a 2007 newspaper interview:

> People don't realise how exciting it is in the Guides now. There are so many good badges and activities. We've learned about team building and we visited Switzerland and got to go husky sledging. We do science experiments, where we make popcorn or slime, and we do outdoor pursuits like climbing, surfing and kayaking. We also learn about issues in the world. I feel confident about discussing things at the Guides.[2]

This Scottish Guide, in her short response, captures all the possibilities for Guiding's future and its continuing challenges as it moves forward into the future. The mix she describes of travel, outdoor activities, learning, world citizenship, and career exploration marks Guiding today.

Surveys of Guides and Girl Scouts continually point to girls' interest in outdoor activities, always a staple of Guide programming, but now they want more adventure: bungee-jumping, climbing, and wind-surfing; like the Scottish Guide, they love the sense of freedom that comes from leaving the everyday behind. World issues and connections remain central to Guiding's mission, and girls respond to this feature, often citing their interest in even more programming regarding environmental issues, HIV/AIDS in the world, and the world economy. Active learning, something Robert Baden-Powell emphasized heavily in Scout and Guide development, has also continued to be a defining part of the movement, with hands-on science experiments, handicrafts, nature exploration, and badge work. In fact, much of the core of Guiding has remained true to the founder's vision.

Yet, in terms of actual Guide activities, the organization has adapted frequently to the tremendous changes in society over the past 100 years. With more diversity in membership, girls have learned to deal with cultural difference in their own troops, not just in the world movement. Swedish Girl Scouting has launched a focused program to deal more effectively with an influx of immigrants in the past 30 years, while Girl Guiding in Britain has incorporated Hindu, Muslim, and Sikh youth into its troops, especially in the past two decades. Given highly publicized incidents of race-motivated crime in Europe and rising numbers of poor in societies around the world, Guiding has chosen to define itself as a progressive movement, hoping to combat such prejudices. Diversity training, for leaders and girls, has become central to most Guide organizations.

Another feature of Guiding today, which probably would have surprised its founders, is its emphasis on sex education. With the advent of AIDS and concern about rates of teen pregnancy, Girl Scouting and Guiding began addressing sex education in a more concerted way to help girls negotiate the shoals of an ever more sex-oriented society. In Scotland Guides set up a peer education program called "Get Wise" to help girls deal with pressures about sex. Scottish Guide officials hoped to address Scotland's teen pregnancy rate, among the highest in Europe.[3] Many Guide associations have introduced sex education programs that correspond to their branches—from rudimentary lessons on strangers for young girls to information on contraception for the oldest girls in the movement.

In the United States, Girl Scouting commissioned a 2003 study titled, "Feeling Safe: What Girls Say," in order to ascertain what made girls feel afraid or unsafe. Predictably, girls feared unwanted sexual activity, but many also feared physical violence, kidnapping, and emotional harm.[4] Girl Scouting used this research to help establish parameters for creating "safe" atmospheres for girls in their Girl Scout meetings and activities that allowed for both physical and emotional safety. This was important in making it possible to tackle sensitive issues regarding sexual activity, drugs, alcohol, and other stresses girls faced in their daily lives.

One area that Guiding sees as critical to its future mission is the fight against AIDS and other sexually transmitted diseases, hence the need for frank conversation about sex education. In Uganda, which has been fighting against AIDS infection rates with governmental programs for two decades, First Lady Janet Museveni appealed to Guiding in 2008 to be "role models" and to "promote abstinence" among young girls.[5] In other African communities, such as Congo, Tanzania, Kenya, and Rwanda, Girl Guides have also taken a lead in the fight against AIDS with education and advocacy programs. In more than 100 countries around the world, including Trinidad and Tobago, Malaysia, and Taiwan, Guides have earned an AIDS badge, which works toward prevention, care and support, and education.[6]

Beyond a new emphasis on girls' sexual health and the worldwide fight against AIDS, Guiding has also made compromises with the consumer culture of the twenty-first century. In Anguilla, Guides opened an Internet cafe at Guide headquarters to provide a place for girls to connect with Girl Guiding worldwide and to allow for a safe social environment for Internet access.[7] Canadian Guides have broadened their activities to include spa nights, laser tag events, and self-defense courses.[8] British Guides in a 2007 poll reported wanting to learn to manage their money, assemble furniture, and learn computer software programs, in addition to their "traditional" activities of pitching tents and cooking meals.[9] In the United States, Girl Scouts now have a whole line of "Groovy Girl" dolls to promote the Girl Scout laws; each doll is named for a feature of the laws, such as Caring Caitlin, Respectful Roxi, Courageous Camara, and Honest Hala. Such commercial ventures help promote Girl Scouting and its values outside of the traditional troop setting.

The World Association, while recognizing local adaptation of the movement to meet girls' interests, has tried to provide a coherent mission for the future of the organization with its Millennium Development Goals, enacted in 2008. These ambitious goals touch on many of the concerns girls at the local level expressed, while also laying out broad humanitarian principles to which Guides could aspire. The goals are as follows: Eradicate poverty, achieve universal primary education, promote gender equality, reduce child mortality, improve maternal health, combat HIV/AIDs and malaria, ensure environmental sustainability, and create peace through partnerships. As WAGGGS notes in its announcement of the initiatives, this "theme encourages girls, young women and members of all ages to make a personal commitment to change the world around them."[10]

Throughout the world, Guide and Girl Scout associations *have* embraced change over the past 100 years, and if they hope to compete in the future, they will continue to transform themselves to meet girls' new interests and needs. Despite the flexibility they have shown in all activities, Guide and Girl Scout organizations have remained true to their original goals and character. The movement remains a uniformed organization, although the uniforms are now much more casual and often mix-and-match. Guides and Girl Scouts still learn a promise and law, they still pursue badge work, and they still aim to be good local, national, and international citizens. Gender socialization and the question of single-sex education remains a central debate in Guiding, as it has since its earliest days.

In fact, while much has changed since 1910, the core values of Guiding are still recognizable in today's programs, namely, the empowerment of girls through adventure, character building, home skills, outdoor pursuits, and active learning. As Guides and Girl Scouts move into their second century, their challenge will be to remain true to their founding values while remaking themselves on a regular basis. Given the changing nature of today's societies and the serious problems girls face on a daily basis, Girl Guides and Girl Scouts will need to take their motto, "Be Prepared," seriously if they hope to march forward successfully into the future.

NOTES

1. Both Girlguiding UK and the Girl Scouts of the USA compile information on women of note who were Girl Guides or Girl Scouts.

2. Samantha Booth, "Be Prepared: For Lessons on Sex, Stress, Abuse, Boozing, Gluttony and Bullying as Girl Guides Enter the 21st Century," *Daily Record* (January 4, 2007).

3. Booth, "Be Prepared."

4. Judy Schoenberg, Toija Riggins, Kimberlee Salmond, *Feeling Safe: What Girls Say* (New York: Girl Scouts of the USA, 2003).

5. "Uganda: We Need More Girl Guides," *Africa News* (December 18, 2008).

6. AIDS Badge Curriculum, http://www.wagggsworld.org/en/projects/GAT/aids_badge, accessed January 23, 2009.

7. "Guides to Have Internet Cafe," *The Anguillan* (February 11, 2008).

8. Tralee Pearce, "Guiding the Modern Girl: How Does a Canadian Institution Stay Current without Shedding Its Good-Girl Aura?" *The Globe and Mail* (January 8, 2008).

9. "Today's Guides Want a Badge in Safe Sex," *Daily Mail* (July 25, 2007).

10. Global Action Theme, http://www.wagggsworld.org/en/projects/GAT, accessed February 13, 2009.

Bibliography

ARCHIVES

Browne Popular Culture Library, Bowling Green State University, Ohio (USA)
  Popular magazine collection
Brunel University Library (UK)
  May Rainer. *Emma's Daughter*. Unpublished autobiography. 1977.
Girlguiding UK Archives [GGL], London (UK)
  Annual Reports
  Census
  Changi Prison
  Country boxes
  Early Days of Guiding box
  Foxlease box
  Headquarters Record Book (1919–1924)
  Headquarters Record Book (1925–1930)
  History—Girl Guides (Organisation)
  Logbooks and journals
  Miscellaneous history
  Press Cuttings 1910–1922
Girl Scouts of the USA National Heritage Center [GSUSA], New York, NY (USA)
  Defense, General—Japanese Relocation Camps
  Girl Guiding
  International WAGGGS
  Personalities
  Program, General 1963 Program Change
  Publications
  WAGGGS, General

New York Public Library [NYPL], New York, NY (USA)
>   *Pamphlet Collection*
School of Oriental and African Studies [SOAS], London (UK)
>   *Box 1229/South Africa: Native Affairs, Wayfarers/Pathfinders file*
Scout Association Archives, Gilwell Park [SAGP], Chingford, Essex (UK)
>   *TC/26*
>   *TC/29*
>   *TC/39*
>   *TC/42*
>   *TC/166*
>   *TC/219*
>   *TC/275*
>   *TC/296*

NEWSPAPERS AND PERIODICALS

Africa News (Uganda)
American Girl (USA)
The Anguillan (Anguilla)
The Council Fire (UK)
Daily Gleaner (Jamaica)
Daily Mail (UK)
Daily Mirror (UK)
Daily Oklahoman (USA)
Daily Record (UK)
The Girl Guides Gazette (UK)
The Globe and Mail (Canada)
The Guider (UK)
Home Chat (UK)
Jewish Chronicle (UK)
Le Figaro (France)
Manchester Guardian (UK)
Memphis Magazine (USA)
Monmouth Post (UK)
Newbury Weekly News (UK)
New York Times (USA)
Scouting (UK)
Scouting Life (Canada)
The Spectator (UK)
This England (UK)

Times (Malta)
The Times (UK)
The Warsaw Voice (Poland)
Yorkshire Observer (UK)

PUBLISHED SOURCES

Allan, Sheila.*Diary of a Girl in Changi, 1941–1945*. Kenthurst, Australia: Kangaroo Press, 1994.

Avery, Gillian. *Childhood's Pattern*. London: Hodder & Stoughton, 1975.

Baden-Powell, Agnes, and Robert Baden-Powell. *The Handbook for Girl Guides, or How Girls Can Help to Build the Empire*. London: Thomas Nelson and Sons, 1912.

Baden-Powell, Olave. *Training Girls as Guides*. London: C. Arthur Pearson, 1917.

Baden-Powell, Olave, [as told to Mary Drewery], *Window on my Heart*. London: Hodder & Stoughton, 1973.

Baden-Powell, Robert. *Girl Guiding*. London: C. Arthur Pearson, 1921.

———. *Pamphlet A: Girl Guides*. London: Girl Guides Association, 1910.

———. *Scouting for Boys: The Original 1908 Edition*. Mineola, NY: Dover Publications, 2007.

Block, Nelson R., and Tammy M. Proctor, eds. *Scouting Frontiers: Youth and the Scout Movement's First Century*. Newcastle upon Tyne: Cambridge Scholars Press, 2009.

Brown, Phyllis Stewart. *All Things Uncertain: The Story of the GIS*. London: Girl Guides Association, 1967.

Chafe, William H. *The Paradox of Change: American Women in the 20th Century*. New York: Oxford University Press, 1991.

Chenu, Alain, and Nicolas Herpin, "Une pause dans la marche vers la civilization des loisirs?" [1998 Emploi du Temps], *Economie et statistique* No. 352-353, 2002; available from http://www.insee.fr/.

Cheroutre, Marie-Thérèse. *Le scoutisme au féminin: Les guides de France, 1923–1998*. Paris: Les Éditions du Cerf, 2002.

Choate, Anne, and Helen Ferris, eds., *Juliette Low and the Girl Scouts*. New York: Girl Scouts, 1928.

Clarke, John, Charles Critcher, and Richard Johnson, eds. *Working-Class Culture: Studies in Theory and History*. Birmingham: Centre for Cultural Studies, 1979.

Crocker, Dorothy. *All About Us: A Story of the Girl Guides in Canada, 1910–1989*. Kitchener, Ontario: Girl Guides of Canada-Guides du Canada, 1990.

De Ras, Marion E. P. *Body, Femininity and Nationalism: Girls in the German Youth Movement 1900–1934*. London: Routledge, 2008.

Dedman, Martin. "Baden-Powell, Militarism, and the 'Invisible Contributors' to the Boy Scout Scheme, 1904–1920." *Twentieth-Century British History* 4:3 (1993), 201–223.

Degenhardt, Mary, and Judith Kirsch. *Girl Scout Collector's Guide: A History of Uniforms, Insignia, Publications, and Memorabilia*, 2nd Edition. Lubbock: Texas Tech University Press, 2005.

Drotner, Kirsten. "Schoolgirls, Madcaps, and Air Aces: English Girls and Their Magazine Reading Between the Wars." *Feminist Studies* 9:1 (Spring 1983), 33–52.

Dyhouse, Carol. *Girls Growing Up in Late Victorian and Edwardian England*. London: Routledge, 1981.

Girl Guides Association. *1910 . . . And Then? A Brief History of the Girl Guides Association*. London: Girl Guides Association, 1990.

———. *Religion and the Girl Guides*. London: Girl Guides Association, 1927.

———. *Tomorrow's Guide: Report of the Working Party Appointed by the Executive Committee of the Council in May 1964*. London: Girl Guides Association, 1966.

Girl Guides Association of New Zealand. *Thirty Years of Guiding in New Zealand, 1923–1953*. Auckland: GGANZ, 1953.

Girl Guides Association of Trinidad and Tobago. *Diamond Jubilee 1914–1974*. n.p.: GGATT, 1974.

Girl Guiding/Girl Scouting: A Challenging Movement. London: WAGGGS, 1992.

Girl Scout Handbook. New York: Girl Scouts of the USA, 1943.

Gloin, Anne. *Like Measles, It's Catching!* Toronto: Girl Guides of Canada, 1974.

The Golden Eaglet (1919), VHS, distributed 1989.

Hahner, Leslie. "Practical Patriotism: Camp Fire Girls, Girl Scouts, and Americanization," *Communication and Critical/Cultural Studies* 5:2 (June 2008), 113–134.

Hargreaves, Jennifer. *Sporting Females: Critical Issues in the History and Sociology of Women's Sports*. London: Routledge, 1994.

Highlights in Girl Scouting, 1912–2001. New York: Girl Scouts of the USA, 2002.

Hillcourt, William. *Baden-Powell: The Two Lives of A Hero*. New York: G. Putnam's Sons, 1964.

Holmes, G. V. *The Likes of Us*. London: Frederick Muller Ltd., 1948.

Horowitz, Daniel. *Betty Friedan and the Making of the Feminine Mystique: The American Left, the Cold War, and Modern Feminism*. Amherst: University of Massachusetts Press, 1998.

Hoxie, W. J. *How Girls Can Help Their Country: The 1913 Handbook for Girl Scouts*. Bedford, MA: Applewood Books, 2001.

Inness, Sherrie A., ed. *Delinquents and Debutantes: Twentieth-Century American Girls' Cultures*. New York: New York University Press, 1998.

The Island: Life and Death of an East London Community, 1870–1970. London: Centerprise Trust Ltd., 1979.

Jeal, Tim. *The Boy Man: The Life of Lord Baden-Powell*. London: Century Hutchinson Ltd., 1989.

Junior Girl Scout Handbook. New York: Girl Scouts of the USA, 1963.

Kelley, Mary, ed. *Woman's Being, Woman's Place: Female Identity and Vocation in American History*. Boston: G. K. Hall & Co., 1979.

Kerr, Rose. *The Cruise of the Adriatic*. London: Girl Guides Association, 1934.

———. *The Cruise of the Calgaric*. London: Girl Guides Association, 1933.

———. *The Cruise of the Orduna*. London: Girl Guides Association, 1938.

———. *The Story of a Million Girls: Guiding and Girl Scouting Round the World*. London: Girl Guides Association, 1937.

———. *The Story of the Girl Guides*. London: Girl Guides Association, 1940.

Khimulu, Mary M. *The Girl Guide Movement in Kenya*. Nairobi: Kenya Girl Guides, 1987.

Langhamer, Claire. *Women's Leisure in England 1920–60*. Manchester: Manchester University Press, 2002.

Lees, Muriel. *A Job in a Lifetime*. London: Girl Guides Association, 1976.

Le scoutisme entre guerre et paix au XXe siècle. Paris: Harmattan, 2006.

Liddell, Alix. *Story of the Girl Guides, 1938–1975*. London: Girl Guides Association, 1976.

Linton, Alice. *Not Expecting Miracles*. London: Centerprise Trust Ltd., 1982.

Low, Juliette. "Girl Scouts as an Educational Force." *Department of the Interior Bureau of Education Bulletin* 33 (1919), 3–8.

Mangan, J. A., ed. *Making Imperial Mentalities: Socialisation and British Imperialism*. Manchester: Manchester University Press, 1990.

Matthews, Jill Julius. "They had Such a Lot of Fun: The Women's League of Health and Beauty Between the Wars." *History Workshop Journal* 30 (Autumn 1990), 22–54.

Maynard, Agnes. *Be Prepared!* London: C. Arthur Pearson, 1946.

Maynes, Mary Jo, Birgitte Søland, and Christina Benninghaus, eds. *Secret Gardens, Satanic Mills: Placing Girls in European History, 1750–1960*. Bloomington: Indiana University Press, 2005.

McLeer, Anne. "Practical Perfection: The Nanny Negotiates Gender, Class, and Family Contradictions in 1960s Popular Culture." *NWSA Journal* 14:2 (Summer 2002), 80–101.

McRobbie, Angela, and Mica Nava, eds. *Gender and Generation*. London: Macmillan, 1984.

Miller, Susan. *Growing Girls: The Natural Origins of Girls' Organizations in America*. New Brunswick: Rutgers University Press, 2007.

Mitchell, Sally. *The New Girl: Girls' Culture in England, 1880–1915*. New York: Columbia University Press, 1995.

Nash, F. O. H. *Rosie the Peddler*. London: Sheldon Press, 1925.

Newman, Sally. "The Archival Traces of Desire: Vernon Lee's Failed Sexuality and the Interpretation of Letters in Lesbian History." *Journal of the History of Sexuality* 14:1/2 (January/April 2005), 51–75.

Nielsen, Harriet Bjerrum. *One of the Boys? Doing Gender in Scouting*. Geneva: WOSM, 2003. Available from http://www.euroscout.org, accessed January 23, 2009.

An Official History of Scouting. London: Hamlyn, 2006.

Pages for Patrol Leaders. London: Girl Guides Association, 1930.

Parkins, Wendy, ed. *Fashioning the Body Politic: Dress, Gender, Citizenship*. Oxford: Berg, 2002.

Parsons, Timothy. *Race, Resistance and the Boy Scout Movement in British Colonial Africa*. Athens, OH: Ohio University Press, 2004.

Perry, Elisabeth Israels. "From Achievement to Happiness: Girl Scouting in Middle Tennessee, 1910s–1960s." *Journal of Women's History* 5:2 (Fall 1993), 75–94.

———. " 'The Very Best Influence': Josephine Holloway and Girl Scouting in Nashville's African-American Community." *Tennessee Historical Quarterly* LII:2 (Summer 1993), 73–85.

Philipps, Roland E. *The Patrol System for Girl Guides*. London: C. Arthur Pearson, 1920.

Pickles, Katie. "Edith Cavell—Heroine, No Hatred or Bitterness for Anyone?" *History Now* 3:2 (1997), 1–8.

Policy, Rules and Organisation. London: Girl Guides Association, 1919.

Proctor, Tammy M. *Female Intelligence: Women and Espionage in the First World War*. New York: New York University Press, 2003.

———. *On My Honour: Guides and Scouts in Interwar Britain*. Philadelphia: American Philosophical Society, 2002.

———. " 'A Separate Path': Scouting and Guiding in Interwar South Africa." *Comparative Studies of Society and History* 42:3 (July 2000), 605–631.

———. "(Uni)Forming Youth: Girl Guides and Boy Scouts in Britain, 1908–1939." *History Workshop Journal* 45 (Spring 1998), 103–134.

Renshaw, Winifred. *An Ordinary Life: Memories of a Balby Childhood*. Doncaster: Doncaster Library Services, 1984.

Reynolds, E. E. *Baden-Powell: A Biography of Lord Baden-Powell of Gilwell.* London: Oxford University Press, 1943.

Rothschild, Mary Aickin. "To Scout or To Guide? The Girl Scout–Boy Scout Controversy, 1912–1941." *Frontiers: A Journal of Women Studies* 6:3 (Autumn 1981), 115–121.

Sarafis, Marion. "Review." *History Workshop Journal* 13:1 (1982), 157–158.

Scaillet, Thierry, Sophie Wittemans, and Françoise Rosart, eds. *Guidisme, scoutisme, et coéducation: Pour une histoire de la mixité dans les mouvements de jeunesse.* Louvain-la-Neuve: Bruylant-Academia, 2007.

Scannell, Dorothy. *Mother Knew Best: Memoir of a London Girlhood.* USA: Pantheon, 1974.

Schoenberg, Judy, Toija Riggins, and Kimberlee Salmond. *Feeling Safe: What Girls Say.* New York: Girl Scouts of the USA, 2003.

Shultz, Gladys Denny, and Daisy Gordon Lawrence. *Lady from Savannah: The Life of Juliette Low.* Philadelphia and New York: J. B. Lippincott Company, 1958.

Simonton, Deborah, ed. *The Routledge History of Women in Europe since 1700.* London: Routledge, 2006.

Smith, Michelle. "Be(ing) Prepared: Girl Guides, Colonial Life, and National Strength." *Limina: A Journal of Historical and Cultural Studies* 12 (2006), 52–63.

Soulsby, Lucy H. M. *The Use of Leisure.* London: Longman, 1900.

Steedman, Carolyn, Cathy Urwin, and Valerie Walderdine, eds. *Language, Gender and Childhood.* London: Routledge and Kegan Paul, 1985.

The Story of Our Chalet, Our Ark, Our Cabana: Three World Centres for Girl Guides and Girl Scouts. London: WAGGGS, 1961.

Suchcitz, Andrzej. "The Grey Ranks (1939–1945)." London: Polish Home Army Association, n.d. http://www.polishresistance-ak.org, accessed July 29, 2008.

Tan, Kevin Y. L., and Wan Men Hao. *Scouting in Singapore 1910–2000.* Singapore: Singapore Scout Association, 2002.

Tedesco, Laureen Ann. "A Nostalgia for Home: Daring and Domesticity in Girl Scouting and Girls' Fiction, 1913–1933." PhD diss., Texas A&M University, 1999.

Thomas, Jeffrey. "U.S. Gender Equity Law Led to Boom in Female Sports Participation." (April 1, 2008), U.S. Department of State's Bureau of International Information Programs, available from http://www.america.gov.

Tinkler, Penny. *Constructing Girlhood: Popular Magazines for Girls Growing up in England, 1920–1950.* London: Taylor & Francis, 1995.

Voeltz, Richard. "The Antidote to 'Khaki Fever'? The Expansion of the British Girl Guides during the First World War." *Journal of Contemporary History* 27 (1992), 627–638.

WAGGGS. *Biennial Reports 1928–1930*. London: WAGGGS, 1931.

———. *Constitution and Bye-Laws*. London: WAGGGS, 1936.

———. *Ninth Biennial Report*. London: WAGGGS, 1946.

———. *Trefoil Round the World*. London: WAGGGS, 2003.

———. *WAGGGS Information*. London: WAGGGS, 1938.

Watenpaugh, Keith. *Being Modern in the Middle East: Revolution, Nationalism, Colonialism, and the Arab Middle Class.* Princeton: Princeton University Press, 2006.

White, Margaret C. *A History of The Girl Guide Movement in Sheffield*. Sheffield: County of Sheffield Girl Guides Association, n.d.

Wittemans, Sophie. *Le Guidisme catholique au Congo belge et au Ruanda-Urundi 1923–1960*. Bruxelles: Centre Historique Belge du Scoutisme, 2008.

Woodford, Doreen E. *Seventy-Five Remarkable Years: A Record of Deaf People and the Girl Guide Movement 1910–1985.* Feltham, UK: British Deaf Society Publications, 2005.

Young, Nancy Beck. *Lou Henry Hoover: Activist First Lady*. Lawrence: University Press of Kansas, 2004.

Zweiniger-Bargielowska, Ina, ed. *Women in Twentieth-Century Britain*. Harlow, Essex: Pearson Education, 2001.

Index

ABOUT THE AUTHOR

Tammy M. Proctor is Professor of History at Wittenberg University in Springfield, Ohio. She is the author of *On My Honour: Guiding and Scouting in Interwar Britain* (2002), *Female Intelligence: Women and Espionage in the First World War* (2003), and co-editor of *Scouting Frontiers: Youth and the Scout Movement's First Century* (2009).